Publisher
Jim Scheikofer
The Family Handyman®

Director, Publication Services
Sue Baalman-Pohlman
Home Design Alternatives, Inc.

Editor
Kim Karsanbhai
Home Design Alternatives, Inc.

Newsstand Sales
David Algire
Reader's Digest Association, Inc.

John Crouse
Reader's Digest Association, Inc.

Marketing Manager
Andrea Vecchio
The Family Handyman

Production Manager
Judy Rodriguez
The Family Handyman

Plans Administrator
Curtis Cadenhead
Home Design Alternatives, Inc.

Copyright 2004 by
Home Service Publications, Inc.,
publishers of
The Family Handyman Magazine,
2915 Commers Drive, Suite 700,
Eagan, MN 55121.
Plan copyrights held by home
designer/architect.

The Family Handyman Contents

Vol. 18, No. 2

P9-EJJ-283

Featured Homes

Plan #705-0113 is featured on page 71.
Photo courtesy of HDA, Inc.

Plan #705-DBI-3019 is featured on page 178.
Photo courtesy of Design Basics

Sections

The Family Handyman magazine and Home Design Alternatives (HDA, Inc.) are pleased to join together to bring you this collection of affordable and easy to build home plans from some of the nation's leading designers and architects.

Technical Specifications - At the time the construction drawings were prepared, every effort was made to ensure that these plan and specifications meet nationally recognized building codes (BOCA, Southern Building Code Congress and others). Because national building codes change or vary from area to area some drawing modifications and/or the assistance of a professional designer or architect may be necessary to comply with your local codes or to accommodate specific building conditions. We advise you to consult with your local building official for information regarding codes governing your area.

On The Cover . . .

Plan #705-AX-93305 is featured on page 182.
Photo courtesy of Axelrod Designs - Mark Englund, pho...

Tranquility Of An Atrium Cottage

1,384 total square feet of living area

Price Code A

Rear View

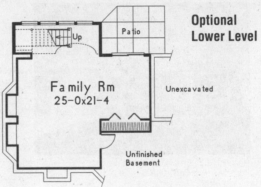

Optional Lower Level

Patio

Up

Family Rm
25-0x21-4

Unexcavated

Unfinished Basement

Special features

- Wrap-around country porch for peaceful evenings

- Vaulted great room enjoys a large bay window, stone fireplace, pass-through kitchen and awesome rear views through atrium window wall

- Master suite features double entry doors, walk-in closet and a fabulous bath

- Atrium open to 611 square feet of optional living area below

- 2 bedrooms, 2 baths, 1-car side entry garage

- Walk-out basement foundation

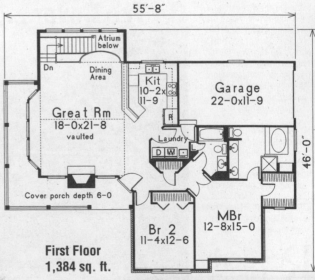

55'-8"

46'-0"

Atrium below

Dn

Dining Area

Kit
10-2x11-9

Garage
22-0x11-9

Great Rm
18-0x21-8
vaulted

Laundry

D W

Cover porch depth 6-0

Br 2
11-4x12-6

MBr
12-8x15-0

First Floor
1,384 sq. ft.

Two surprisingly small speakers.
One remarkable surround sound experience.

Presenting the *newest* member of the 3·2·1 system family: the 3·2·1*GS* system.

Introducing another step toward our goal: Good sound that's heard, not seen. We've made our award-winning 3·2·1 DVD system even smaller and better. Our new 3·2·1*GS* DVD home entertainment system produces an enhanced surround sound experience from just two incredibly small speakers. With Bose® patented speaker technology and our latest signal processing, the two speakers deliver many of the benefits of a surround sound experience without running wires to the back of your room. A hideaway Acoustimass® module (not shown) produces low notes that give impact to movies and music. The 3·2·1*GS* system delivers the unique combination of simplicity and performance that won our original 3·2·1 system "Product of the Year" from *Electronic House*. Experience the power of two speakers with the 3·2·1 systems from Bose. They're just one of the reasons Bose is the most respected name in sound.

The 3·2·1 DVD home entertainment system.

The *new* 3·2·1*GS* DVD home entertainment system.

For Bose stores and dealers near you, call 1-888-321-BOSE, Ext. N66
Learn more at 321.bose.com/wn66

BOSE®
Better sound through research®

©2003 Bose Corporation. Quote is reprinted with permission: *Electronic House*, 9/02. JN31262

Distinguished Styling For A Small Lot

1,268 total square feet of living area

Price Code A

Special features

- Multiple gables, large porch and arched windows create classy exterior

- Innovative design provides openness in great room, kitchen and breakfast room

- Secondary bedrooms have private hall with bath

- 3 bedrooms, 2 baths, 2-car garage

- Basement foundation

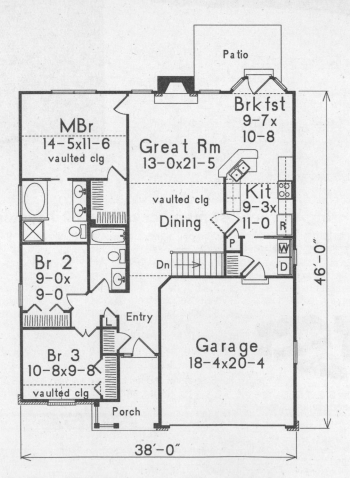

TO ORDER BLUEPRINTS USE THE FORM ON PAGE 15 OR CALL TOLL-FREE 1-877-671-6036

View thousands more home plans online at www.familyhandyman.com/homeplans

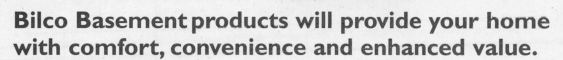

Floridian Architecture With Mother-In-Law Suite

2,408 total square feet of living area

Price Code D

Special features

- Large vaulted great room overlooks atrium and window wall, adjoins dining room, spacious breakfast room with bay and pass-through kitchen

- A special private bedroom with bath, separate from other bedrooms, is perfect for mother-in-law suite or children home from college

- Atrium open to 1,100 square feet of optional living area below

- 4 bedrooms, 3 baths, 3-car side entry garage

- Walk-out basement foundation

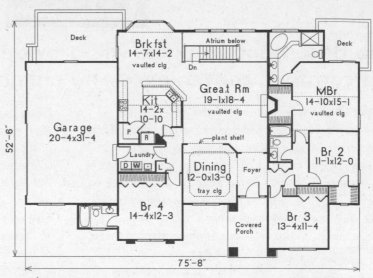

**First Floor
2,408 sq. ft.**

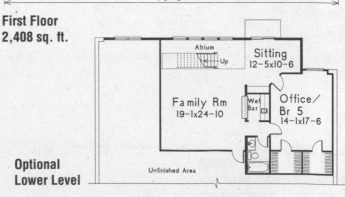

**Optional
Lower Level**

TO ORDER BLUEPRINTS USE THE FORM ON PAGE 15 OR CALL TOLL-FREE 1-877-671-6036
View thousands more home plans online at familyhandyman.com/homeplans

Ranch Of Enchantment

1,559 total square feet of living area

Price Code B

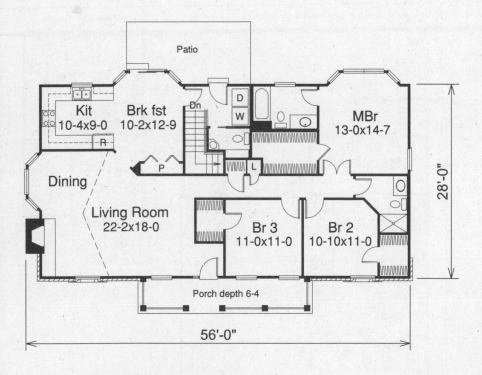

Patio

Kit
10-4x9-0

Brk fst
10-2x12-9

Dn

D
W

MBr
13-0x14-7

R

Dining

P
L

Living Room
22-2x18-0

Br 3
11-0x11-0

Br 2
10-10x11-0

28'-0"

Porch depth 6-4

56'-0"

Special features

- A cozy country appeal is provided by a spacious porch, masonry fireplace, roof dormers and a perfect balance of stonework and siding

- Large living room enjoys a fireplace, bayed dining area and separate entry

- A U-shaped kitchen is adjoined by a breakfast room with bay window and large pantry

- 3 bedrooms, 2 1/2 baths, 2-car side entry drive under garage

- Basement foundation

Dining With A View

1,524 total square feet of living area

Price Code B

Special features

- Delightful balcony overlooks two-story entry illuminated by oval window
- Roomy first floor master suite offers quiet privacy
- All bedrooms feature one or more walk-in closets
- 3 bedrooms, 2 1/2 baths, 2-car garage
- Basement foundation

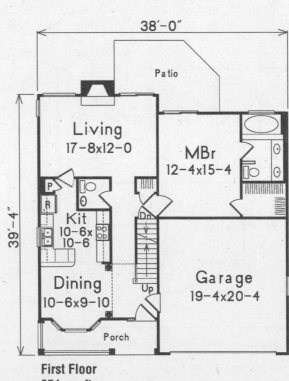

38'-0"

Patio

Living
17-8x12-0

MBr
12-4x15-4

Kit
10-6x
10-6

Dining
10-6x9-10

Garage
19-4x20-4

Porch

39'-4"

First Floor
951 sq. ft.

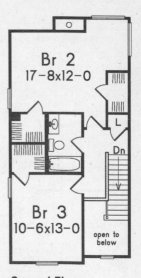

Br 2
17-8x12-0

L

Dn

Br 3
10-6x13-0

open to below

Second Floor
573 sq. ft.

Country-Style With Wrap-Around Porch

1,597 total square feet of living area

Price Code C

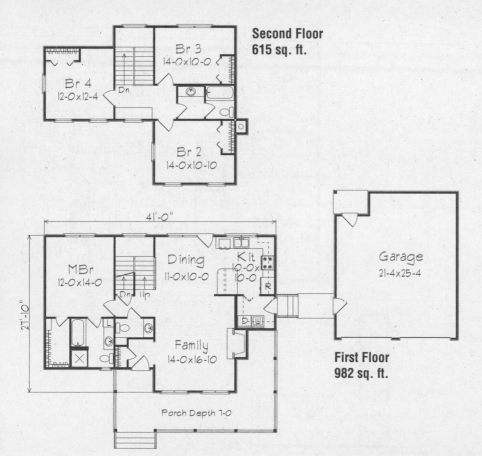

Second Floor
615 sq. ft.

Br 3
14-0x10-0

Br 4
12-0x12-4

Dn

Br 2
14-0x10-10

41'-0"

21'-10"

MBr
12-0x14-0

Dining
11-0x10-0

Kit
10-0x
10-0

Garage
21-4x25-4

Dn Up

Family
14-0x16-10

Porch Depth 7-0

First Floor
982 sq. ft.

Special features

- Spacious family room includes fireplace and coat closet
- Open kitchen and dining room provides breakfast bar and access to the outdoors
- Convenient laundry area located near kitchen
- Secluded master suite with walk-in closet and private bath
- 4 bedrooms, 2 1/2 baths, 2-car detached garage
- Basement foundation

TO ORDER BLUEPRINTS USE THE FORM ON PAGE 15 OR CALL TOLL-FREE 1-877-671-6036
View thousands more home plans online at www.familyhandyman.com/homeplans

9

Small Home Is Remarkably Spacious

914 total square feet of living area

Price Code AA

Special features

- Large porch for leisure evenings
- Dining area with bay window, open stair and pass-through kitchen creates openness
- Basement includes generous garage space, storage area, finished laundry and mechanical room
- 2 bedrooms, 1 bath, 2-car drive under garage
- Basement foundation

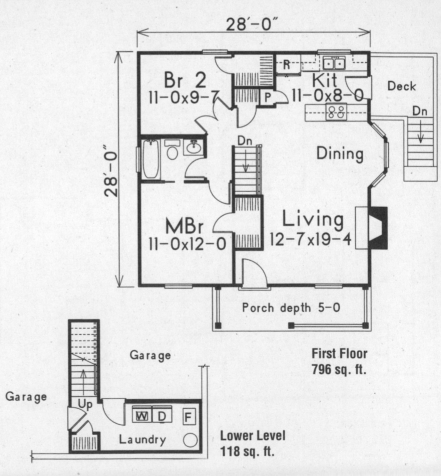

28'-0"

28'-0"

Br 2
11-0x9-7

Kit
11-0x8-0

Deck

Dn

R

P

Dn

Dining

MBr
11-0x12-0

Living
12-7x19-4

Dn

Porch depth 5-0

**First Floor
796 sq. ft.**

Garage

Garage

Up

W D F

Laundry

**Lower Level
118 sq. ft.**

TO ORDER BLUEPRINTS USE THE FORM ON PAGE 15 OR CALL TOLL-FREE 1-877-671-6036
View thousands more home plans online at www.familyhandyman.com/homeplans

Chalet Cottage

1,073 total square feet of living area

Price Code AA

Width: 24'-0"
Depth: 36'-0"

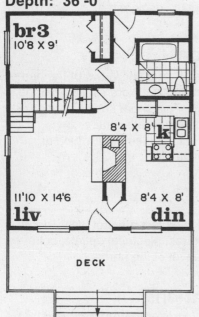

Second Floor
401 sq. ft.

First Floor
672 sq. ft.

Special features

- The front-facing deck and covered balcony add to outdoor living areas
- The fireplace is the main focus in the living room, separating the living room from the dining room
- Three large storage areas are found on the second floor
- 3 bedrooms, 1 1/2 baths
- Basement or crawl space foundation, please specify when ordering

TO ORDER BLUEPRINTS USE THE FORM ON PAGE 15 OR CALL TOLL-FREE 1-877-671-6036
View thousands more home plans online at www.familyhandyman.com/homeplans

11

Our Blueprint Packages Offer...

Quality plans for building your future, with extras that provide unsurpassed value, ensure good construction and long-term enjoyment.

A quality home - one that looks good, functions well, and provides years of enjoyment - is a product of many things - design, materials, craftsmanship.

But it's also the result of outstanding blueprints - the actual plans and specifications that tell the builder exactly how to build your home.

And with our BLUEPRINT PACKAGES you get the absolute best. A complete set of blueprints is available for every design in this book. These "working drawings," are highly detailed, resulting in two key benefits:

- Better understanding by the contractor of how to build your home and...
- More accurate construction estimates.

When you purchase one of our designs, you'll receive all of the BLUEPRINT components shown here - elevations, foundation plan, floor plans, sections, and/or details. Other helpful building aids are also available to help make your dream home a reality.

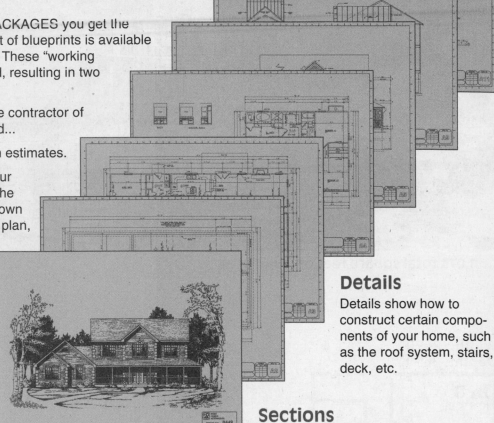

Cover Sheet

The cover sheet is the artist's rendering of the exterior of the home. It will give you an idea of how your home will look when completed and landscaped.

Interior Elevations

Interior elevations provide views of special interior elements such as fireplaces, kitchen cabinets, built-in units and other features of the home.

Foundation Plan

The foundation plan shows the layout of the basement, crawl space, slab or pier foundation. All necessary notations and dimensions are included. See plan page for the foundation types included. If the home plan you choose does not have your desired foundation type, our Customer Service Representatives can advise you on how to customize your foundation to suit your specific needs or site conditions.

Details

Details show how to construct certain components of your home, such as the roof system, stairs, deck, etc.

Sections

Sections show detail views of the home or portions of the home as if it were sliced from the roof to the foundation. This sheet shows important areas such as load-bearing walls, stairs, joists, trusses and other structural elements, which are critical for proper construction.

Floor Plans

The floor plans show the placement of walls, doors, closets, plumbing fixtures, electrical outlets, columns, and beams for each level of the home.

Exterior Elevations

Exterior elevations illustrate the front, rear and both sides of the house, with all details of exterior materials and the required dimensions.

What Kind Of Plan Package Do You Need?

Now that you've found the home you've been looking for, here are some suggestions on how to make your Dream Home a reality. To get started, order the type of plans that fit your particular situation.

YOUR CHOICES

- **THE 1-SET STUDY PACKAGE -** We offer a 1-set plan package so you can study your home in detail. This one set is considered a study set and is marked "not for construction". It is a copyright violation to reproduce blueprints.

- **THE MINIMUM 5-SET PACKAGE -** If you're ready to start the construction process, this 5-set package is the minimum number of blueprint sets you will need. It will require keeping close track of each set so they can be used by multiple subcontractors and tradespeople.

- **THE STANDARD 8-SET PACKAGE -** For best results in terms of cost, schedule and quality of construction, we recommend you order eight (or more) sets of blueprints. Besides one set for yourself, additional sets of blueprints will be required by your mortgage lender, local building department, general contractor and all subcontractors working on foundation, electrical, plumbing, heating/air conditioning, carpentry work, etc.

- **REPRODUCIBLE MASTERS -** If you wish to make some minor design changes, you'll want to order reproducible masters. These drawings contain the same information as the blueprints but are printed on erasable and reproducible paper which clearly indicates your right to copy or reproduce. This will allow your builder or a local design professional to make the necessary drawing changes without the major expense of redrawing the plans. This package also allows you to print copies of the modified plans as needed. The right of building only one structure from these plans is licensed exclusively to the buyer. You may not use this design to build a second or multiple dwelling(s) without purchasing another blueprint. Each violation of the Copyright Law is punishable in a fine.

- **MIRROR REVERSE SETS -** Plans can be printed in mirror reverse. These plans are useful when the house would fit your site better if all the rooms were on the opposite side than shown. They are simply a mirror image of the original drawings causing the lettering and dimensions to read backwards. Therefore, when ordering mirror reverse drawings, you must purchase at least one set of right reading plans.

Other Helpful Building Aids...

Your Blueprint Package will contain the necessary construction information to build your home. We also offer the following products and services to save you time and money in the building process.

- **MATERIAL LIST -** Material lists are available for many of the plans in this book. Each list gives you the quantity, dimensions and description of the building materials necessary to construct your home. You'll get faster and more accurate bids from your contractor while saving money by paying for only the materials you need. See the Home Plans Index on page 14 for availability. Refer to the order form on page 15 for pricing.

- **DETAIL PLAN PACKAGES:** Framing, Plumbing & Electrical Plan Packages - Three separate packages offer homebuilders details for constructing various foundations; numerous floor, wall and roof framing techniques; simple to complex residential wiring; sump and water softener hookups; plumbing connection methods; installation of septic systems and more. Each package includes three-dimensional illustrations and a glossary of terms. Purchase one or all three. Cost: $20.00 each or all three for $40.00. Note: These drawings do not pertain to a specific home plan.

- **THE LEGAL KIT™ -** Our Legal Kit provides contracts and legal forms to help protect you from the potential pitfalls inherent in the building process. The Kit supplies commonly used forms and contracts suitable for homeowners and builders. It can save you a considerable amount of time and help protect you and your assets during and after construction. Cost: $35.00

- **EXPRESS DELIVERY -** Most orders are processed within 24 hours of receipt. Please allow 7-10 business days for delivery. If you need to place a rush order, please call us by 11:00 a.m. CST and ask for express service (allow 1-2 business days).

- **TECHNICAL ASSISTANCE-** If you have questions, call our technical support line at 1-314-770-2228 between 8:00 a.m. and 5:00 p.m. CST. Whether it involves design modifications or field assistance, our designers are extremely familiar with all of our designs and will be happy to help you. We want your home to be everything you expect it to be.

HOME DESIGN ALTERNATIVES, INC.

Home Plans Index

Plan Number	Sq. Ft.	Price Code	Page	Mat. List
705-0105	1,360	A	83	X
705-0106	1,443	A	87	X
705-0112	1,668	C	99	X
705-0113	1,992	C	71	X
705-0119	1,833	C	274	X
705-0138	2,286	E	303	X
705-0151	2,874	E	215	X
705-0152	2,935	E	312	X
705-0161	1,630	B	145	X
705-0162	1,882	D	162	X
705-0171	2,058	C	246	X
705-0172	1,643	B	72	X
705-0173	1,220	A	43	X
705-0174	1,657	B	194	X
705-0176	1,404	A	93	X
705-0181	1,408	A	78	X
705-0183	2,847	E	126	X
705-0184	2,411	D	66	X
705-0185	2,396	D	181	X
705-0188	1,800	C	167	X
705-0189	2,177	C	223	X
705-0190	1,600	C	292	X
705-0191	1,868	D	38	X
705-0192	1,266	A	249	X
705-0193	2,252	D	261	X
705-0195	988	AA	135	X
705-0198	1,416	A	218	X
705-0200	1,343	A	94	X
705-0201	1,814	D	60	X
705-0203	1,475	B	196	X
705-0212	1,707	C	317	X
705-0214	1,770	B	168	X
705-0218	1,998	D	280	X
705-0222	2,358	D	268	X
705-0223	2,328	D	91	X
705-0224	2,461	D	101	X
705-0225	1,260	A	168	X
705-0226	1,416	A	259	X
705-0227	1,674	B	42	X
705-0229	1,676	B	301	X
705-0237	1,631	B	274	X
705-0239	1,496	A	229	X
705-0241	829	AAA	157	X
705-0244	1,994	D	307	X
705-0246	1,539	B	227	X
705-0249	1,501	B	57	X
705-0252	1,364	A	76	X
705-0253	1,458	A	121	X
705-0255	1,340	A	267	X
705-0256	1,698	B	128	X
705-0257	1,862	C	160	X
705-0264	1,689	B	224	X
705-0265	1,314	A	127	X
705-0267	1,453	A	80	X
705-0268	1,135	AA	272	X
705-0273	988	AA	63	X
705-0276	950	AA	48	X
705-0277	1,127	AA	271	X
705-0279	1,993	D	76	X
705-0280	1,847	C	121	X
705-0281	1,624	B	226	X
705-0282	1,642	B	86	X
705-0284	1,672	C	191	X
705-0286	1,856	C	254	X
705-0291	1,600	B	118	X
705-0292	1,304	A	257	X
705-0295	1,609	B	125	X
705-0296	1,396	A	169	X
705-0297	1,320	A	115	X
705-0298	3,216	F	90	X
705-0310	2,363	D	190	X
705-0312	1,921	D	62	X
705-0316	1,824	C	269	X
705-0318	2,147	C	258	X
705-0319	3,796	F	137	X
705-0320	2,228	D	81	X
705-0322	2,135	D	225	X
705-0335	1,865	D	95	X
705-0342	2,089	C	68	X
705-0348	2,003	D	85	X
705-0352	3,144	E	56	X
705-0357	1,550	B	119	X
705-0360	2,327	D	132	X
705-0364	2,531	D	65	X
705-0365	2,336	D	106	X
705-0368	2,452	D	174	X
705-0370	1,721	C	29	X
705-0379	1,711	B	152	X
705-0382	1,546	B	172	X
705-0384	2,013	C	179	X
705-0385	1,814	C	209	X
705-0393	1,684	B	231	X
705-0410	1,742	B	156	X
705-0412	2,109	C	67	X
705-0415	1,492	A	129	X
705-0416	1,985	C	234	X
705-0417	2,828	E	299	X
705-0418	3,850	F	295	X
705-0419	1,882	C	148	X
705-0425	2,076	C	219	X
705-0434	2,357	D	205	X
705-0438	2,558	D	273	X
705-0441	1,747	B	79	X
705-0442	1,950	C	270	X
705-0443	2,255	D	316	X
705-0447	1,393	B	52	X
705-0448	1,597	C	9	X
705-0449	2,505	D	103	X
705-0450	1,708	B	291	X
705-0461	828	AAA	210	X
705-0462	1,028	AA	157	X
705-0476	576	AAA	82	X
705-0477	1,140	AA	130	X
705-0478	1,092	AA	185	X
705-0479	1,294	A	306	X
705-0485	1,195	AA	313	X
705-0486	1,239	A	255	X
705-0487	1,189	AA	264	X
705-0493	976	AA	243	X
705-0494	1,085	AA	243	X
705-0495	987	AA	130	X
705-0498	954	AA	185	X
705-0502	864	AAA	39	X
705-0503	1,000	AA	161	X
705-0505	1,104	AA	265	X
705-0507	1,197	AA	281	X
705-0510	1,400	A	151	X
705-0515	1,344	A	148	X
705-0518	1,705	B	188	X
705-0529	1,285	B	31	X
705-0534	1,288	A	183	X
705-0536	1,664	B	247	X
705-0582	800	AAA	211	X
705-0650	1,020	AA	210	X
705-0652	1,524	B	8	X
705-0655	632	AAA	82	X
705-0656	1,700	B	195	X
705-0657	914	AA	10	X
705-0669	1,358	A	277	X
705-0670	1,170	AA	97	X
705-0671	1,427	A	17	X
705-0676	1,367	A	149	X
705-0677	3,006	E	45	X
705-0678	1,567	B	61	X
705-0679	1,466	A	310	X
705-0685	1,844	C	163	X
705-0686	1,609	B	240	X
705-0690	1,400	A	199	X
705-0692	1,339	A	96	X
705-0702	1,558	B	53	X
705-0703	2,412	D	192	X
705-0705	2,758	E	193	X
705-0706	1,791	B	21	X
705-0711	1,575	B	297	X
705-0712	2,029	C	23	X
705-0717	1,268	A	4	X
705-0718	1,340	A	239	X
705-0719	2,483	D	54	X
705-0721	2,437	D	59	X
705-0728	2,967	E	293	X
705-0729	2,218	D	170	X
705-0730	2,408	D	6	X
705-0731	1,761	B	216	X
705-0732	1,384	A	[illegible]	X
705-0734	929	AA	236	X
705-0739	1,684	B	41	X
705-0741	1,578	B	238	X
705-0747	1,977	C	73	X
705-0749	2,727	E	150	X
705-0755	1,787	B	24	X
705-0769	1,440	A	256	X
705-0770	2,400	D	241	X
705-0773	2,179	C	189	X
705-0774	1,680	B	49	X
705-0775	2,240	D	311	X
705-0776	2,200	D	134	X
705-0777	2,458	D	276	X
705-0779	1,277	A	159	X
705-0783	3,035	E	175	X
705-0794	1,433	A	250	X
705-0799	1,849	C	155	X
705-0803	3,366	F	25	X
705-0806	1,452	A	88	X
705-0807	1,231	A	123	X
705-0808	969	AA	213	X
705-0809	1,084	AA	202	X
705-0811	1,161	AA	110	X
705-0825	1,559	B	7	X
705-0830	1,365	A	232	X
705-AMD-1135	1,467	C	22	X
705-AMD-1213	2,197	C	104	X
705-AMD-2175	1,464	C	251	X
705-AMD-2189	1,994	D	177	
705-AP-1002	1,050	AA	98	
705-AP-1205	1,296	B	207	
705-AP-1812	1,886	C	164	
705-AP-1908	1,998	C	320	
705-AP-2117	2,187	C	304	
705-AX-301	1,783	D	108	
705-AX-2301	2,282	E	28	
705-AX-5376	2,092	D	290	
705-AX-5380	1,480	A	245	X
705-AX-93305	2,567	F	182	
705-AX-94341	1,040	B	197	
705-BF-1314	1,375	A	176	
705-BF-1901	1,925	C	154	
705-BF-DR1109	1,191	AA	20	
705-BF-DR1819	2,424	D	318	
705-CHD-11-27	1,123	AA	116	
705-CHD-13-2	1,397	A	296	
705-CHD-13-61	1,379	A	18	
705-CHD-20-54	2,036	C	105	
705-CHD-23-10	2,350	D	122	
705-CHP-1332A	1,363	A	44	
705-CHP-1532-A-141	1,500	B	107	
705-CHP-1732-A-101	1,704	B	198	
705-CHP-2233-B-21	2,697	E	315	
705-CHP-2443-A-38	2,481	D	298	
705-DBI-1748-19	1,911	C	26	X
705-DBI-24035-9P	1,395	A	117	
705-DBI-24045-9P	1,263	A	220	
705-DBI-2619	1,998	C	308	X
705-DBI-3019	1,479	A	178	X
705-DDI-92103	960	AA	30	
705-DDI-95-114	1,018	AA	158	
705-DDI-95-234	1,649	B	286	
705-DDI-98-106	1,588	B	180	
705-DDI-100-215	1,757	B	74	
705-DH-1377	1,377	A	230	
705-DH-1716	1,716	B	102	
705-DH-1786	1,785	B	120	
705-DH-2005	1,700	B	32	
705-DH-2214	2,214	D	206	
705-DL-16653L1	1,665	B	319	
705-DL-17104L1	1,710	B	34	
705-DL-17353L1	1,735	B	131	
705-DL-19603L2	1,960	C	214	
705-DR-1051	1,092	AA	201	X
705-DR-1738	1,245	A	300	X
705-DR-2772	1,494	A	111	X
705-DR-3812	2,129	C	58	X
705-FB-282	1,425	A	230	
705-FB-327	1,281	A	55	
705-FB-347	1,671	B	19	
705-FB-582	1,497	A	113	
[illegible]	1,373	A	187	
705-FB-1158	2,072	C	141	
705-FD8103	1,225	A	287	
705-FD8166-L	2,061	C	242	
705-FDG-7913	1,702	B	27	
705-FDG-7963-L	1,830	C	166	X
705-GH-10839	1,738	B	70	
705-GH-20083	1,575	B	302	X
705-GH-20198	1,792	B	143	
705-GH-24326	1,505	B	288	X
705-GH-24700	1,312	A	200	
705-GM-1253	1,253	A	144	X
705-GM-1333	1,333	A	33	
705-GM-1842	1,842	C	222	
705-GM-2158	2,158	C	142	X
705-GM-2361	2,361	D	262	
705-GSD-1023-C	1,890	C	37	
705-GSD-1123	1,734	B	138	
705-GSD-1748	1,496	A	221	
705-GSD-2004	1,751	B	212	
705-HDG-97001	1,872	C	55	X
705-HDG-97006	1,042	AA	278	
705-HDG-99004	1,231	A	217	
705-HDS-1167	1,167	AA	77	
705-HDS-1442-2	1,442	A	40	
705-HDS-1558-2	1,885	C	140	
705-HDS-1571	1,571	B	165	
705-HDS-2173-2	2,173	D	100	
705-HP-B810	1,536	B	235	
705-HP-C460	1,389	A	64	X
705-HP-C659	1,118	AA	89	
705-HP-C689	1,295	A	124	X
705-JA-50294	1,430	A	284	
705-JA-51394	1,508	B	260	
705-JA-60595	1,472	A	153	
705-JA-65996	1,962	C	84	
705-JA-77798	1,461	A	248	
705-JFD-10-1436-1	1,436	A	147	
705-JFD-10-1456-2	1,456	A	69	
705-JFD-10-2096-2	2,096	C	173	
705-JFD-20-1887-1	1,887	C	244	
705-JFD-20-2050-1	2,050	C	309	
705-LBD-13-1A	1,310	A	279	
705-LBD-15-4A	1,575	B	186	
705-LBD-18-5A	1,862	C	305	
705-LBD-19-16A	1,993	C	50	
705-MG-01240	2,272	G	112	
705-MG-02245	1,821	E	289	
705-MG-9305	1,606	B	314	
705-MG-97086	1,277	E	203	
705-MG-97099	1,093	AA	252	
705-NDG-102	1,381	A	109	
705-NDG-113-1	1,525	B	46	
705-NDG-145-2	1,680	B	294	
705-NDG-148	1,538	B	171	
705-NDG-150	1,353	A	208	
705-RDD-1374-9	1,374	A	35	
705-RDD-1429-9	1,429	A	253	
705-RDD-1815-8	1,815	C	285	
705-RDD-1895-9	1,895	C	47	
705-RJ-A1079	1,021	AA	266	
705-RJ-A1387	1,382	A	283	
705-RJ-A1485	1,436	A	51	
705-RJ-A1684	1,656	B	275	
705-RJ-A14106	1,497	A	133	
705-SH-SEA-008	1,073	AA	11	
705-SH-SEA-023	1,358	A	114	
705-SH-SEA-100	2,582	D	204	
705-SH-SEA-225	1,230	A	263	
705-SH-SEA-242	1,408	A	136	
705-SRD-123	1,782	B	36	
705-SRD-150	1,508	B	75	
705-SRD-244	1,593	B	139	
705-SRD-279	1,611	B	184	
705-SRD-335	1,544	B	233	
705-UDG-92007	1,753	B	237	X
705-UDG-97008	2,086	C	146	X
705-UDG-99003	1,425	A	278	X
705-VL947	947	AA	266	X
705-VL-1233	1,233	A	92	
705-VL-1372	1,372	A	217	
705-VL-1458	1,458	A	[illegible]	
705-VL-1594	1,594	B	228	

◆ **Exchange Policies** - Since blueprints are printed in response to your order, we cannot honor requests for refunds. However, if for some reason you find that the plan you have purchased does not meet your requirements, you may exchange that plan for another plan in our collection. At the time of the exchange, you will be charged a processing fee of 25% of your original plan package price, plus the difference in price between the plan packages (if applicable) and the cost to ship the new plans to you.

◆ **Building Codes & Requirements** - At the time the construction drawings were prepared, every effort was made to ensure that these plans and specifications meet nationally recognized codes. Our plans conform to most national building codes. Because building codes vary from area to area, some drawing modifications and/or the assistance of a professional designer or architect may be necessary to comply with your local codes or to accommodate specific building site conditions. We advise you to consult with your local building official for information regarding codes governing your area.

Please note: Reproducible drawings can only be exchanged if the package is unopened, and exchanges are allowed only within 90 days of purchase.

Questions? Call Our Customer Service Number
1-877-671-6036

BLUEPRINT PRICE SCHEDULE
BEST VALUE

Price Code	1-Set*	SAVE $110 5-Sets	SAVE $200 8-Sets	Material List**	Reproducible Masters
AAA	$225	$295	$340	$50	$440
AA	$275	$345	$390	$55	$490
A	$325	$395	$440	$60	$540
B	$375	$445	$490	$60	$590
C	$425	$495	$540	$65	$640
D	$475	$545	$590	$65	$690
E	$525	$595	$640	$70	$740
F	$575	$645	$690	$70	$790
G	$650	$720	$765	$75	$865
H	$755	$825	$870	$80	$970

Plan prices guaranteed through August 31, 2004.
Please note that plans are not refundable.

◆ **Additional Sets** - Additional sets of the plan ordered are available for $45.00 each. Five-set, eight-set, and reproducible packages offer considerable savings.

◆ **Mirror Reverse Plans** - Available for an additional $5.00 per set, these plans are simply a mirror image of the original drawings causing the dimensions and lettering to read backwards. Therefore, when ordering mirror reverse plans, you must purchase at least one set of right reading plans.

◆ **One-Set Study Package** - We offer a one-set plan package so you can study your home in detail. This one set is considered a study set and is marked "not for construction". It is a copyright violation to reproduce blueprints.

*1-Set Study Packages are not available for all plans.
**Available only within 90 days after purchase of plan package or reproducible masters of same plan.

SHIPPING & HANDLING CHARGES

U.S. SHIPPING

	1-4 Sets	5-7 Sets	8 Sets or Reproducibles
Regular *(allow 7-10 business days)*	$15.00	$17.50	$25.00
Priority *(allow 3-5 business days)*	$25.00	$30.00	$35.00
Express* *(allow 1-2 business days)*	$35.00	$40.00	$45.00

CANADA SHIPPING (to/from) - Plans with suffix DR & SH

	1-4 Sets	5-7 Sets	8 Sets or Reproducibles
Standard *(allow 8-12 business days)*	$25.00	$30.00	$35.00
Express* *(allow 3-5 business days)*	$40.00	$40.00	$45.00

Overseas Shipping/International - Call, fax, or e-mail (plans@hdainc.com) for shipping costs.

* For express delivery please call us by 11:00 a.m. CST

How To Order

For fastest service, Call Toll-Free
1-877-671-6036
24 HOURS A DAY

Three Easy Ways To Order

1. CALL toll-free 1-877-671-6036 for credit card orders. MasterCard, Visa, Discover and American Express are accepted.

2. FAX your order to 1-314-770-2226.

3. MAIL the Order Form to:

   HDA, Inc.
   4390 Green Ash Drive
   St. Louis, MO 63045

ORDER FORM

Please send me -
PLAN NUMBER   705BT - _____

PRICE CODE _____ (see Plan Index)

Specify Foundation Type - **see** plan page for availability
☐ Slab   ☐ Crawl space   ☐ Pier
☐ Basement   ☐ Walk-out basement

☐ Reproducible Masters $ _____
☐ Eight-Set Plan Package $ _____
☐ Five-Set Plan Package $ _____
☐ One-Set Study Package (no mirror reverse)$ _____
☐ Additional Plan Sets
   _____ (Qty.) at $45.00 each $ _____
☐ Print in Mirror Reverse
   _____ (Qty.) add $5.00 per set $ _____
☐ Material List $ _____
☐ Legal Kit (see page 13) $ _____
Detail Plan Packages: (see page 13)
   ☐ Framing ☐ Electrical ☐ Plumbing $ _____
                           SUBTOTAL $ _____
SALES TAX (MO residents add 6%) $ _____
☐ Shipping / Handling (see chart at left) $ _____
   TOTAL ENCLOSED (US funds only) $ _____
   (Sorry no CODs)

I hereby authorize HDA, Inc. to charge this purchase to my credit card account (check one):

☐ MasterCard   ☐ VISA   ☐ DISCOVER NOVUS   ☐ AMERICAN EXPRESS Cards

Credit Card number _____

Expiration date _____

Signature _____

Name _____
(Please print or type)

Street Address _____
(Please **do not** use PO Box)

City _____

State _____ Zip _____

Daytime phone number (_____) - _____

I'm a ☐ Builder/Contractor   I ☐ have
      ☐ Homeowner   ☐ have not
      ☐ Renter   selected my
                                 general contractor

Thank you for your order!

QUICK AND EASY CUSTOMIZING
MAKE CHANGES TO YOUR HOME PLAN IN 4 STEPS

HERE'S AN AFFORDABLE AND EFFICIENT WAY TO MAKE CHANGES TO YOUR PLAN.

1 Select the house plan that most closely meets your needs. Purchase of a reproducible master is necessary in order to make changes to a plan.

2 Call 1-877-671-6036 to place your order. Tell the sales representative you're interested in customizing a plan. A $50 refundable consultation fee will be charged. You will then be instructed to complete a customization checklist indicating all the changes you wish to make to your plan. You may attach sketches if necessary. If you proceed with the custom changes the $50 will be credited to the total amount charged.

3 FAX the completed customization checklist to our design consultant at 1-866-477-5173 or e-mail custom@drummonddesigns.com. Within *24-48 business hours you will be provided with a written cost estimate to modify your plan. Our design consultant will contact you by phone if you wish to discuss any of your changes in greater detail.

4 Once you approve the estimate, a 75% retainer fee is collected and customization work gets underway. Preliminary drawings can usually be completed within *5-10 business days. Following approval of the preliminary drawings your design changes are completed within *5-10 business days. Your remaining 25% balance due is collected prior to shipment of your completed drawings. You will be shipped five sets of revised blueprints or a reproducible master, plus a customized materials list if required.

*Terms are subject to change without notice.

BEFORE
Plan 2829

Customized Version
of Plan 2829

AFTER

MODIFICATION PRICING GUIDE

CATEGORIES	Average Cost from... to
Adding or removing living space (square footage)	Quote required
Adding or removing a garage	$400 $680
Garage: Front entry to side load or vice versa	Starting at $300
Adding a screened porch	$280 $600
Adding a bonus room in the attic	$450 $780
Changing full basement to crawl space or vice versa	Starting at $220
Changing full basement to slab or vice versa	Starting at $260
Changing exterior building material	Starting at $200
Changing roof lines	$360 $630
Adjusting ceiling height	$280 $500
Adding, moving or removing an exterior opening	$55 per opening
Adding or removing a fireplace	$90 $200
Modifying a non-bearing wall or room	$55 per room
Changing exterior walls from 2"x4" to 2"x6"	Starting at $200
Redesigning a bathroom or a kitchen	$120 $280
Reverse plan right reading	Quote required
Adapting plans for local building code requirements	Quote required
Engineering stamping only	Quote required
Any other engineering services	Quote required
Adjust plan for handicapped accessibility	Quote required
Interactive illustrations (choices of exterior materials)	Quote required
Metric conversion of home plan	$400

Note: Any home plan can be customized to accommodate your desired changes. The average prices specified above are provided only as examples for the most commonly requested changes, and are subject to change without notice. Prices for changes will vary according to the number of modifications requested, plan size, style, and method of design used by the original designer. To obtain a detailed cost estimate, please contact us

Large Windows Grace This Split-Level Home

1,427 total square feet of living area

Price Code A

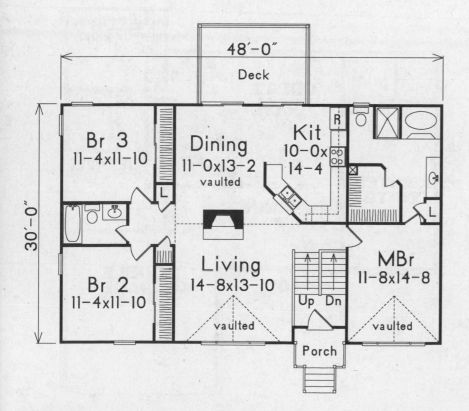

Special features

- Practical storage space situated in the garage
- Convenient laundry closet located on lower level
- Kitchen and dining area both have sliding doors that access the deck
- Large expansive space created by vaulted living and dining rooms
- 3 bedrooms, 2 baths, 2-car drive under garage
- Basement foundation

Comfortable Living In This Ranch

1,379 total square feet of living area

Price Code A

Special features

- Vaulted great room makes a lasting impression with corner fireplace and windows

- Formal dining room easily connects to kitchen making entertaining easy

- Master bath includes all the luxuries such as a spacious walk-in closet, oversized tub and separate shower

- 3 bedrooms, 2 baths, 2-car garage

- Slab foundation

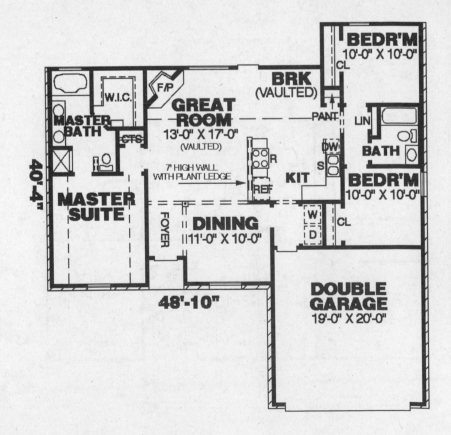

Luxurious Master Suite

1,671 total square feet of living area

Price Code B

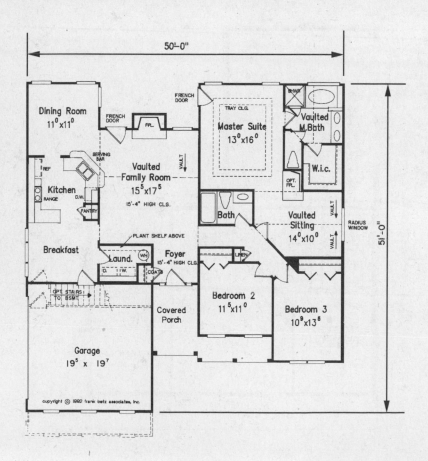

50'-0"

Dining Room
11⁰x11⁰

FRENCH DOOR

FRENCH DOOR

FPL.

TRAY CLG.

SH-WR.

Vaulted M.Bath

Master Suite
13⁰x16⁰

SERVING BAR

REF

Kitchen

D.W.

RANGE

PANTRY

Vaulted
Family Room
15⁵x17⁵

15'-4" HIGH CLG.

VAULT

OPT. FPL.

W.i.c.

PLANT SHELF ABOVE

Bath

Vaulted
Sitting
14⁰x10⁰

RADIUS WINDOW

VAULT

51'-0"

Breakfast

Laund.

D.

W.H.

W.

Foyer
15'-4" HIGH CLG.

LINEN

COATS

OPT. STAIRS TO BSMT.

Covered
Porch

Bedroom 2
11⁵x11⁰

Bedroom 3
10⁹x13⁸

Garage
19⁵ x 19⁷

copyright © 1992 frank betz associates, inc.

Special features

- Kitchen is conveniently located between the breakfast room and dining room
- Vaulted family room is centrally located
- Laundry located near garage for easy access
- 3 bedrooms, 2 baths, 2-car side entry garage
- Slab, crawl space or walk-out basement foundation, please specify when ordering

Quaint And Cozy

1,191 total square feet of living area

Price Code AA

Special features

- Energy efficient home with 2" x 6" exterior walls
- Master bedroom located near living areas for maximum convenience
- Living room has cathedral ceiling and stone fireplace
- 3 bedrooms, 2 baths, 2-car side entry garage
- Slab or crawl space foundation, please specify when ordering

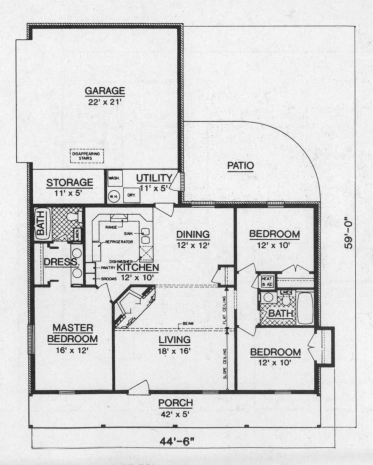

Classic Exterior Employs Innovative Planning

1,791 total square feet of living area

Price Code B

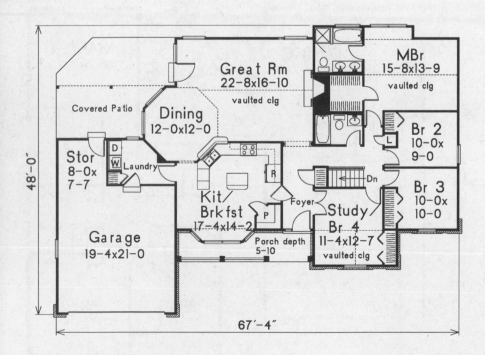

Special features

- Vaulted great room and octagon-shaped dining area enjoy views of covered patio
- Kitchen features a pass-through to dining area, center island, large walk-in pantry and breakfast room with large bay window
- Master bedroom is vaulted with sitting area
- 4 bedrooms, 2 baths, 2-car garage with storage
- Basement foundation

TO ORDER BLUEPRINTS USE THE FORM ON PAGE 15 OR CALL TOLL-FREE 1-877-671-6036
View thousands more home plans online at www.familyhandyman.com/homeplans

21

Striking Plant Shelf

1,467 total square feet of living area

Price Code C

Special features

- Vaulted ceilings, an open floor plan and a wealth of windows create an inviting atmosphere
- Efficiently arranged kitchen has an island with built-in cooktop and a snack counter
- Plentiful storage and closet space throughout this home
- 3 bedrooms, 2 baths, 2-car garage
- Crawl space foundation

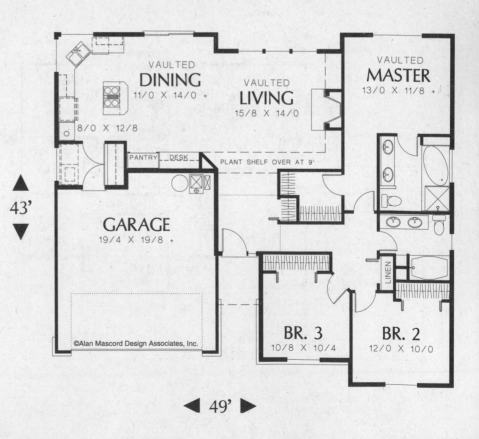

VAULTED
DINING
11/0 X 14/0 +

VAULTED
LIVING
15/8 X 14/0

VAULTED
MASTER
13/0 X 11/8 +

8/0 X 12/8

PANTRY DESK

PLANT SHELF OVER AT 9'

43'

GARAGE
19/4 X 19/8 +

LINEN

©Alan Mascord Design Associates, Inc.

BR. 3
10/8 X 10/4

BR. 2
12/0 X 10/0

◄ 49' ►

TO ORDER BLUEPRINTS USE THE FORM ON PAGE 15 OR CALL TOLL-FREE 1-877-671-6036
View thousands more home plans online at www.familyhandyman.com/homeplans

22

Country Home With Front Orientation

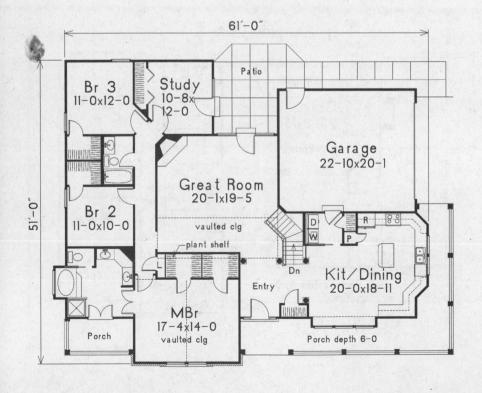

2,029 total square feet of living area

Price Code C

Special features

- Stonework, gables, roof dormer and double porches create a country flavor

- Kitchen enjoys extravagant cabinetry and counterspace in a bay, island snack bar, built-in pantry and cheery dining area with multiple tall windows

- Angled stair descends from large entry with wood columns and is open to vaulted great room with corner fireplace

- Master bedroom boasts his and hers walk-in closets, double-doors leading to an opulent master bath and private porch

- 4 bedrooms, 2 baths, 2-car side entry garage

- Basement foundation

Br 3
11-0x12-0

Study
10-8x
12-0

Patio

Garage
22-10x20-1

Great Room
20-1x19-5

vaulted clg

Br 2
11-0x10-0

plant shelf

D
W

R

P

Dn

Kit/Dining
20-0x18-11

Entry

MBr
17-4x14-0
vaulted clg

Porch

Porch depth 6-0

61'-0"

51'-0"

Ranch Offers Country Elegance

1,787 total square feet of living area

Price Code B

Special features

- Large great room with fireplace and vaulted ceiling features three large skylights and windows galore

- Cooking is sure to be a pleasure in this L-shaped well-appointed kitchen which includes bayed breakfast area with access to rear deck

- Every bedroom offers a spacious walk-in closet with a convenient laundry room just steps away

- 415 square feet of optional living area on the lower level

- 3 bedrooms, 2 baths, 2-car rear entry garage

- Walk-out basement foundation

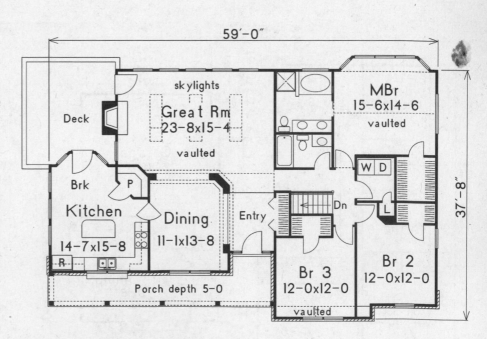

Plan #705-0803

Grand-Sized Living

3,366 total square feet of living area

Price Code F

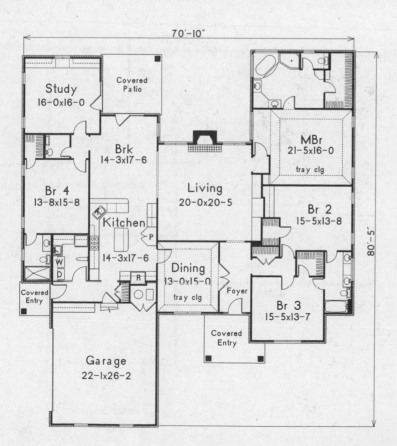

Special features

- Wonderful covered patio off secluded study and breakfast area
- Separate dining area for entertaining
- Spacious master suite has enormous private bath with walk-in closet
- 4 bedrooms, 3 1/2 baths, 2-car side entry garage
- Crawl space foundation, drawings also include slab foundation

TO ORDER BLUEPRINTS USE THE FORM ON PAGE 15 OR CALL TOLL-FREE 1-877-671-6036
View thousands more home plans online at www.familyhandyman.com/homeplans

25

Whirlpool With Skylight Above

1,911 total square feet of living area

Price Code C

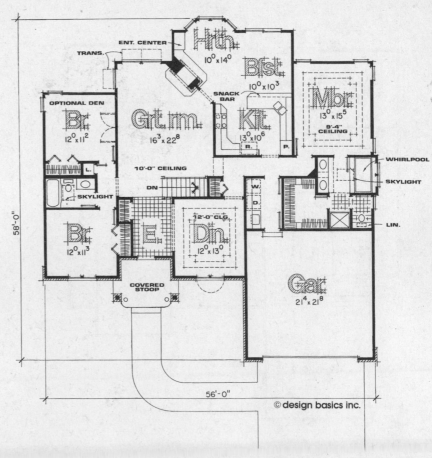

Special features

- Large entry opens into beautiful great room with angled see-through fireplace
- Terrific design includes kitchen/breakfast area with adjacent sunny bayed hearth room
- Luxury master suite has privacy from other bedrooms
- 3 bedrooms, 2 baths, 2-car garage
- Basement foundation

© design basics inc.

Second Floor Loft Is Ideal Office Area

1,702 total square feet of living area

Price Code B

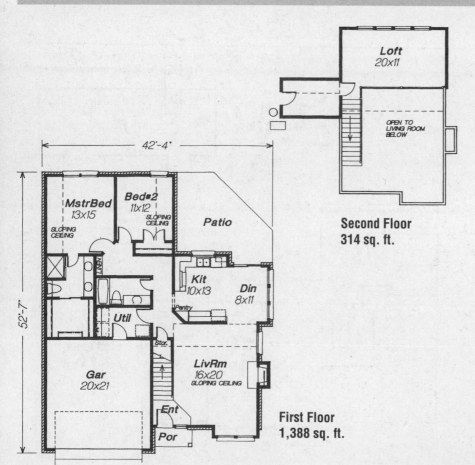

Loft
20x11

Second Floor
314 sq. ft.

OPEN TO LIVING ROOM BELOW

MstrBed
13x15

SLOPING CEILING

Bed#2
11x12
SLOPING CEILING

Patio

Kit
10x13

Din
8x11

Pantry

Util

Stor.

Gar
20x21

LivRm
16x20
SLOPING CEILING

Ent

Por

42'-4"

52'-7"

First Floor
1,388 sq. ft.

Special features

- Second floor loft has a wall of windows making this space functional and bright
- Sloped ceilings in both bedrooms
- Kitchen and dining area combine to create a terrific gathering space
- 2 bedrooms, 2 baths, 2-car garage
- Slab foundation

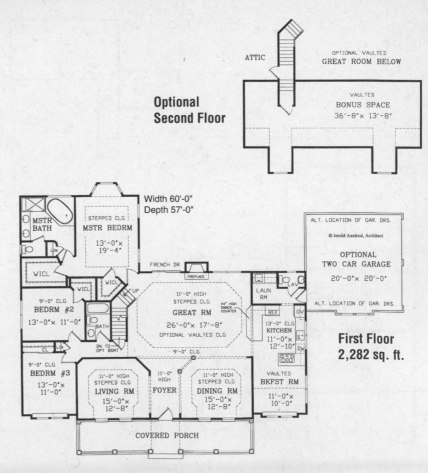

Formal Gracious Country Ranch

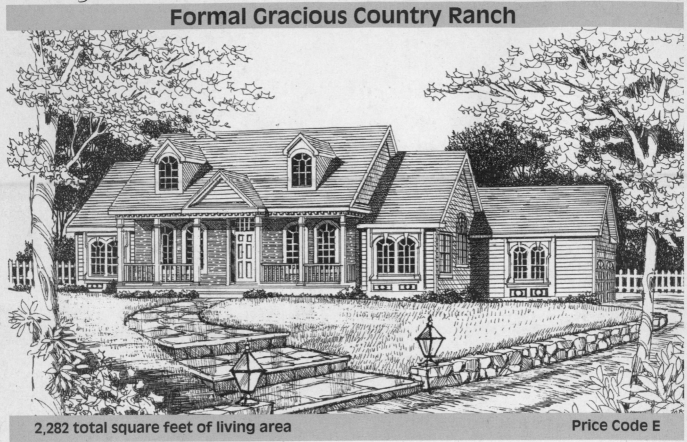

2,282 total square feet of living area

Price Code E

Special features

- Tall windows create an elegant appearance to the foyer

- Great room has 11' stepped ceiling, fireplace and French doors

- Master suite includes a stepped ceiling and two walk-in closets

- 3 bedrooms, 2 1/2 baths, optional 2-car side entry garage

- Bonus room on second floor has an additional 576 square feet of living area

- Basement, crawl space or slab foundation, please specify when ordering

Optional Second Floor

ATTIC

OPTIONAL VAULTED
GREAT ROOM BELOW

VAULTED
BONUS SPACE
36'-8" x 13'-8"

Width 60'-0"
Depth 57'-0"

MSTR BATH

STEPPED CLG
MSTR BEDRM
13'-0" x 19'-4"

WICL

FRENCH DR

FIREPLACE

ALT. LOCATION OF GAR. DRS.

© Jerold Axelrod, Architect

OPTIONAL
TWO CAR GARAGE
20'-0" x 20'-0"

ALT. LOCATION OF GAR. DRS.

WICL

WICL

UP

9'-0" CLG
BEDRM #2
13'-0" x 11'-0"

BATH

11'-0" HIGH
STEPPED CLG
GREAT RM
26'-0" x 17'-8"
OPTIONAL VAULTED CLG

44" HIGH
SNACK COUNTER

LAUN
RM

LAV

REF

13'-0" CLG
KITCHEN
11'-0" x 12'-10"

DN TO
OPT BSMT

9'-0" CLG
BEDRM #3
13'-0" x 11'-0"

9'-0" CLG

**First Floor
2,282 sq. ft.**

11'-0" HIGH
STEPPED CLG
LIVING RM
15'-0" x 12'-8"

11'-0" HIGH
FOYER

11'-0" HIGH
STEPPED CLG
DINING RM
15'-0" x 12'-8"

VAULTED
BKFST RM
11'-0" x 10'-0"

COVERED PORCH

1,721 total square feet of living area

Price Code C

Rear View

Special features

- Roof dormers add great curb appeal
- Vaulted dining and great rooms immersed in light from atrium window wall
- Breakfast room opens onto covered porch
- Functionally designed kitchen
- 3 bedrooms, 2 baths, 3-car garage
- Walk-out basement foundation, drawings also include crawl space and slab foundations

TO ORDER BLUEPRINTS USE THE FORM ON PAGE 15 OR CALL TOLL-FREE 1-877-671-6036

View thousands more home plans online at www.familyhandyman.com/homeplans

Cottage Retreat

960 total square feet of living area

Price Code AA

Special features

- Cozy, yet open floor plan is perfect for a vacation getaway or a guest house
- Spacious kitchen features peninsula cooktop with breakfast bar that overlooks the large living room
- Bath is complete with laundry facilities
- Front deck is ideal for enjoying views or outdoor entertaining
- 2 bedrooms, 1 bath
- Crawl space foundation

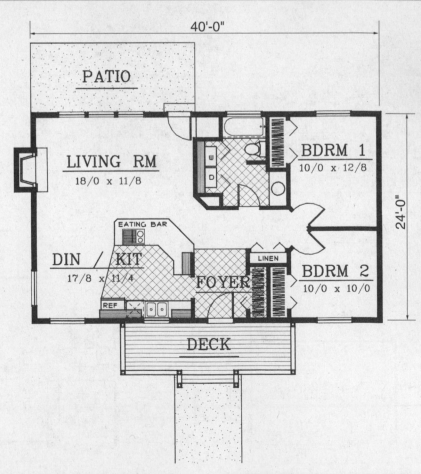

PATIO

40'-0"

LIVING RM
18/0 x 11/8

BDRM 1
10/0 x 12/8

24'-0"

EATING BAR

DIN / KIT
17/8 x 11/4

FOYER

LINEN

BDRM 2
10/0 x 10/0

REF

DECK

Layout Creates Large Open Living Area

1,285 total square feet of living area

Price Code B

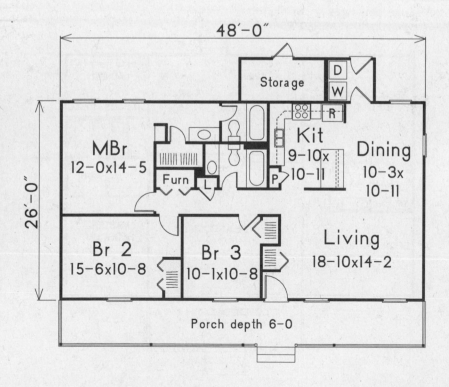

48'-0"

26'-0"

Storage

D
W

MBr
12-0x14-5

Furn

Kit
9-10x
10-11

Dining
10-3x
10-11

Br 2
15-6x10-8

Br 3
10-1x10-8

Living
18-10x14-2

Porch depth 6-0

Special features

- Accommodating home with ranch-style porch
- Large storage area on back of home
- Master bedroom includes dressing area, private bath and built-in bookcase
- Kitchen features pantry, breakfast bar and complete view to dining room
- 3 bedrooms, 2 baths
- Crawl space foundation, drawings also include basement and slab foundations

TO ORDER BLUEPRINTS USE THE FORM ON PAGE 15 OR CALL TOLL-FREE 1-877-671-6036
View thousands more home plans online at www.familyhandyman.com/homeplans

31

Perfect Home For Family Living

1,700 total square feet of living area   **Price Code B**

Special features

- Oversized laundry room has large pantry and storage area as well as access to the outdoors

- Master bedroom is separated from other bedrooms for privacy

- Raised snack bar in kitchen allows extra seating for dining

- 3 bedrooms, 2 baths

- Crawl space foundation

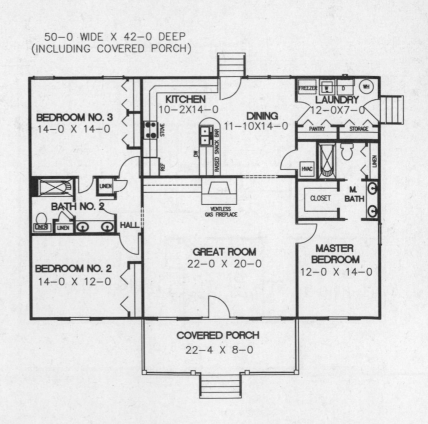

50-0 WIDE X 42-0 DEEP
(INCLUDING COVERED PORCH)

BEDROOM NO. 3
14-0 X 14-0

KITCHEN
10-2X14-0

DINING
11-10X14-0

LAUNDRY
12-0X7-0

FREEZER

PANTRY   STORAGE

HVAC

BATH NO. 2

LINEN

RAISED SNACK BAR

REF   DW   STOVE

VENTLESS
GAS FIREPLACE

CLOSET

M.
BATH

LINEN   LINEN   HALL

BEDROOM NO. 2
14-0 X 12-0

GREAT ROOM
22-0 X 20-0

MASTER
BEDROOM
12-0 X 14-0

COVERED PORCH
22-4 X 8-0

TO ORDER BLUEPRINTS USE THE FORM ON PAGE 15 OR CALL TOLL FREE 1-877-671-0030
View thousands more home plans online at www.familyhandyman.com/homeplans

Carport With Storage

1,333 total square feet of living area

Price Code A

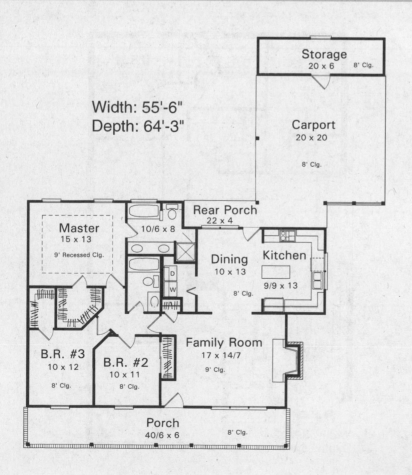

Width: 55'-6"
Depth: 64'-3"

Storage
20 x 6   8' Clg.

Carport
20 x 20

8' Clg.

Rear Porch
22 x 4

Master
15 x 13

9' Recessed Clg.

10/6 x 8

Dining
10 x 13

8' Clg.

Kitchen

9/9 x 13

D

W

B.R. #3
10 x 12

8' Clg.

B.R. #2
10 x 11

8' Clg.

Family Room
17 x 14/7

9' Clg.

Porch
40/6 x 6   8' Clg.

Special features

- Country charm with covered front porch
- Dining area looks into family room with fireplace
- Master suite has walk-in closet and private bath
- 3 bedrooms, 2 baths, 2-car attached carport
- Slab or crawl space foundation, please specify when ordering

TO ORDER BLUEPRINTS USE THE FORM ON PAGE 15 OR CALL TOLL-FREE 1-877-671-6036

View thousands more home plans online at www.familyhandyman.com/homeplans

Bedrooms With Sloped Ceilings

1,710 total square feet of living area

Price Code B

Special features

- Bedrooms have plenty of closet space
- Laundry area located near bedrooms for efficiency
- Corner fireplace warms large family room with 10' ceiling
- 4 bedrooms, 2 baths, 2-car garage
- Slab foundation

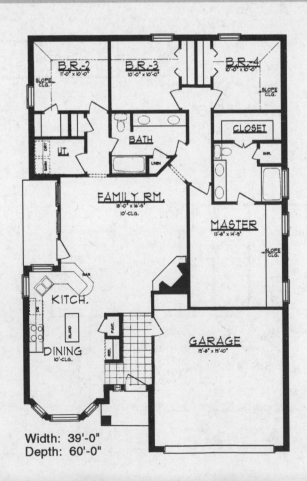

Width: 39'-0"
Depth: 60'-0"

TO ORDER BLUEPRINTS USE THE FORM ON PAGE 16 OR CALL TOLL FREE 1 877 671 6036

View thousands more home plans online at www.familyhandyman.com/homeplans

Scalloped Front Porch

1,374 total square feet of living area

Price Code A

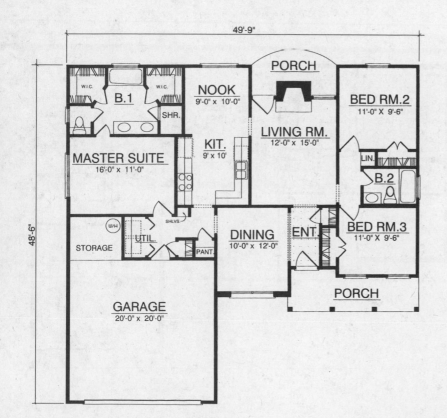

Special features

- Garage has extra storage space
- Spacious living room has fireplace
- Well-designed kitchen with adjacent breakfast nook
- Separated master suite maintains privacy
- 3 bedrooms, 2 baths, 2-car garage
- Slab or crawl space foundation, please specify when ordering

Sloped Ceilings Throughout

1,782 total square feet of living area

Price Code B

Special features

- Outstanding breakfast area accesses the outdoors through French doors
- Generous counter space and cabinets combine to create an ideal kitchen
- The master bedroom is enhanced with a beautiful bath featuring a whirlpool tub and double-bowl vanity
- 3 bedrooms, 2 baths, 2-car garage
- Basement foundation

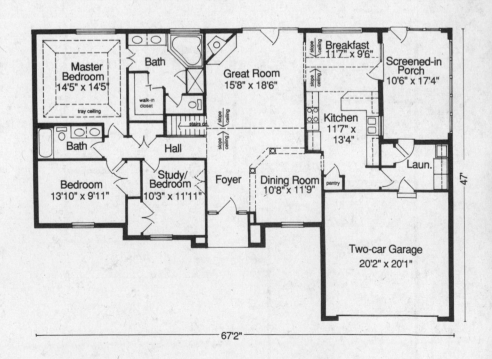

Formal Living And Dining Rooms

1,890 total square feet of living area

Price Code C

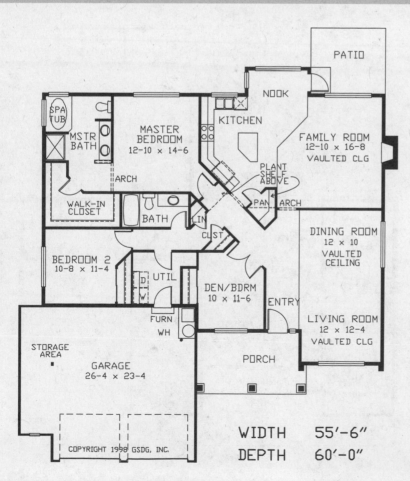

Special features

- Inviting covered porches
- Vaulted ceilings in living, dining and family rooms
- Kitchen is open to family room and nook
- Large walk-in pantry
- Arch accented master bath has spa tub, dual sinks and walk-in closet
- 3 bedrooms, 2 baths, 2-car garage
- Crawl space foundation

WIDTH 55'-6"
DEPTH 60'-0"

Open Living Areas Separate Remote Bedrooms

1,868 total square feet of living area

Price Code D

Special features

- Luxurious master bath is impressive with angled quarter-circle tub, separate vanities and large walk-in closet

- Energy efficient home with 2" x 6" exterior walls

- Dining room is surrounded by a series of arched openings which complement the open feeling of this design

- Living room has a 12' ceiling accented by skylights and a large fireplace flanked by sliding doors

- Large storage areas

- 3 bedrooms, 2 baths, 2-car side entry garage

- Slab foundation, drawings also include crawl space foundation

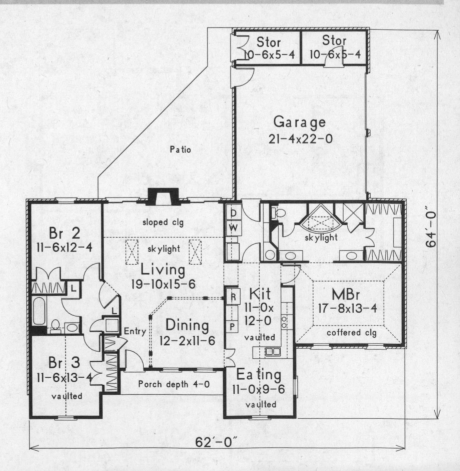

Perfect Home For A Small Family

864 total square feet of living area

Price Code AAA

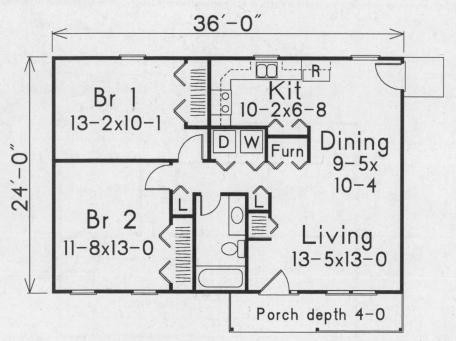

Special features

- L-shaped kitchen with convenient pantry is adjacent to dining area
- Easy access to laundry area, linen closet and storage closet
- Both bedrooms include ample closet space
- 2 bedrooms, 1 bath
- Crawl space foundation, drawings also include basement and slab foundations

TO ORDER BLUEPRINTS USE THE FORM ON PAGE 15 OR CALL TOLL-FREE 1-877-671-6036
View thousands more home plans online at www.familyhandyman.com/homeplans

39

Bayed Breakfast Nook

1,442 total square feet of living area

Price Code A

Special features

- Utility room includes counterspace and closet
- Kitchen has useful center island creating extra workspace
- Vaulted master bedroom has unique double-door entry, private bath and walk-in closet
- 3 bedrooms, 2 baths, 2-car carport
- Slab foundation

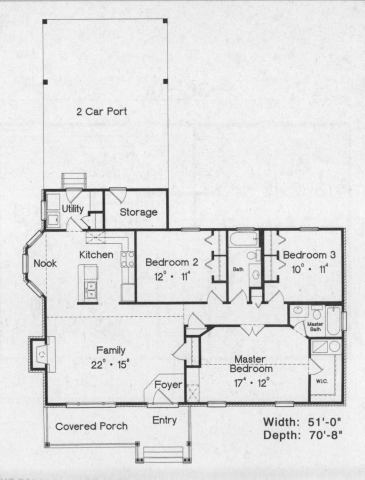

2 Car Port

Utility

Storage

Nook

Kitchen

Bedroom 2
12⁰ · 11⁴

Bath

Bedroom 3
10⁰ · 11⁴

Master Bath

Family
22⁰ · 15⁸

Master Bedroom
17⁴ · 12⁰

W.I.C.

Foyer

Entry

Covered Porch

Width: 51'-0"
Depth: 70'-8"

40

TO ORDER BLUEPRINTS USE THE FORM ON PAGE 15 OR CALL TOLL-FREE 1-877-671-6036
View thousands more home plans online at www.familyhandyman.com/homeplans

A Special Home For Views

1,684 total square feet of living area

Price Code B

Rear View

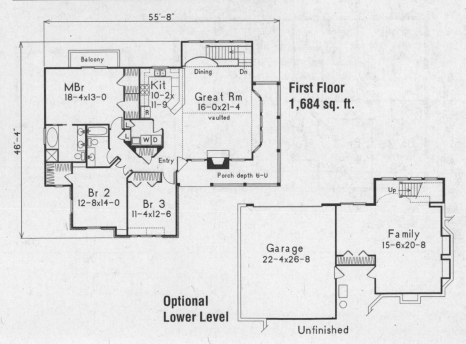

55'-8"

Balcony

MBr
18-4x13-0

Kit
10-2x
11-9

Dining   Dn

Great Rm
16-0x21-4
vaulted

46'-4"

W D

Entry

Br 2
12-8x14-0

Br 3
11-4x12-6

Porch depth 6-0

**First Floor
1,684 sq. ft.**

Up

Garage
22-4x26-8

Family
15-6x20-8

**Optional
Lower Level**

Unfinished

Special features

- Delightful wrap-around porch anchored by full masonry fireplace

- The vaulted great room includes a large bay window, fireplace, dining balcony and atrium window wall

- His and hers walk-in closets, large luxury bath and sliding doors to exterior balcony are a few fantastic features of the master bedroom

- Atrium open to 611 square feet of optional living area on the lower level

- 3 bedrooms, 2 baths, 2-car drive under garage

- Walk-out basement foundation

Sculptured Roof Line And Facade Add Charm

1,674 total square feet of living area

Price Code B

Special features

- Great room, dining area and kitchen, surrounded with vaulted ceiling, central fireplace and log bin

- Convenient laundry/mud room located between garage and family area with handy stairs to basement

- Easily expandable screened porch and adjacent patio with access from dining area

- Master bedroom features full bath with tub, separate shower and walk-in closet

- 3 bedrooms, 2 baths, 2-car garage

- Basement foundation, drawings also include crawl space and slab foundations

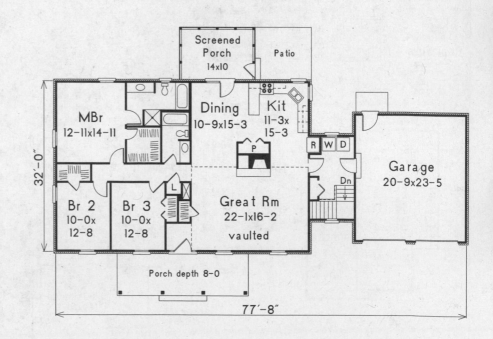

Screened Porch 14x10

Patio

Dining 10-9x15-3

Kit 11-3x 15-3

MBr 12-11x14-11

R W D

Garage 20-9x23-5

P

Dn

Br 2 10-0x 12-8

Br 3 10-0x 12-8

Great Rm 22-1x16-2 vaulted

L

32'-0"

Porch depth 8-0

77'-8"

Compact Home For Functional Living

1,220 total square feet of living area

Price Code A

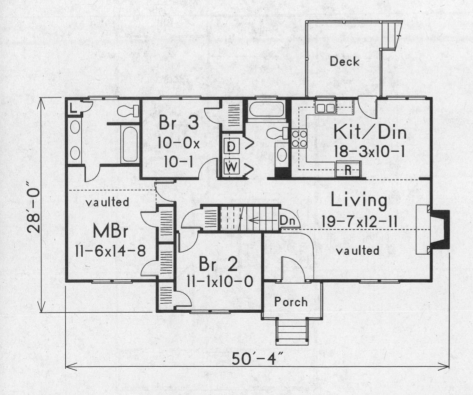

Special features

- Vaulted ceilings add luxury to living room and master suite
- Spacious living room accented with a large fireplace and hearth
- Gracious dining area is adjacent to the convenient wrap-around kitchen
- Washer and dryer handy to the bedrooms
- Covered porch entry adds appeal
- Rear sun deck adjoins dining area
- 3 bedrooms, 2 baths, 2-car drive under garage
- Basement foundation

Cozy Cottage Style

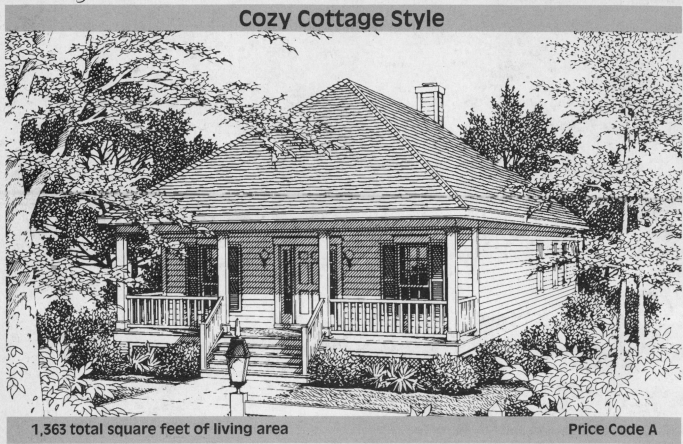

1,363 total square feet of living area

Price Code A

Special features

- Formal dining area conveniently located next to kitchen
- Master bedroom has private bath and walk-in closet
- Covered porch has patio which allows enough space for entertaining
- 3 bedrooms, 2 baths, optional 1-car carport
- Slab foundation

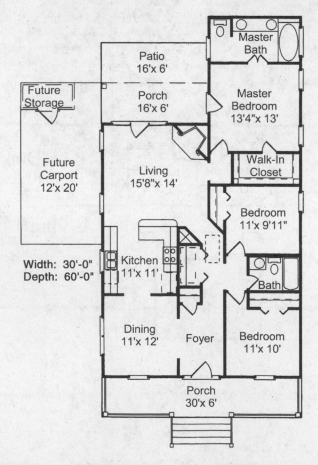

Width: 30'-0"
Depth: 60'-0"

Future Storage

Future Carport 12'x 20'

Patio 16'x 6'

Porch 16'x 6'

Master Bath

Master Bedroom 13'4"x 13'

Living 15'8"x 14'

Walk-In Closet

Bedroom 11'x 9'11"

Kitchen 11'x 11'

Bath

Dining 11'x 12'

Foyer

Bedroom 11'x 10'

Porch 30'x 6'

Spacious Room Around A Central Foyer

3,006 total square feet of living area

Price Code E

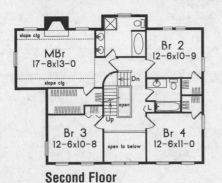

Second Floor
1,138 sq. ft.

MBr 17-8x13-0

Br 2 12-6x10-9

Br 3 12-6x10-8

Br 4 12-6x11-0

open to below

Third Floor
575 sq. ft.

Stor.

Skylt

All Purpose Room 22-0x24-0

Skylt

Skylt

Special features

- Energy efficient home with 2" x 6" exterior walls
- Large all purpose room and bath on third floor
- Efficient U-shaped kitchen includes a pantry and adjacent planning desk
- 4 bedrooms, 3 1/2 baths, 2-car side entry garage
- Basement foundation, drawings also include slab foundation

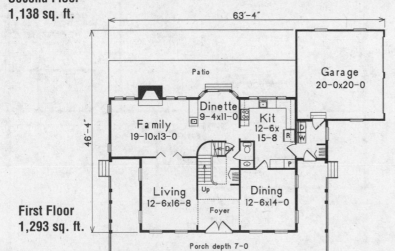

First Floor
1,293 sq. ft.

63'-4"

46'-4"

Patio

Garage 20-0x20-0

Family 19-10x13-0

Dinette 9-4x11-0

Kit 12-6x 15-8

Living 12-6x16-8

Dining 12-6x14-0

Foyer

Porch depth 7-0

TO ORDER BLUEPRINTS USE THE FORM ON PAGE 15 OR CALL TOLL-FREE 1-877-671-6036
View thousands more home plans online at www.familyhandyman.com/homeplans

45

Built-In Computer Desk

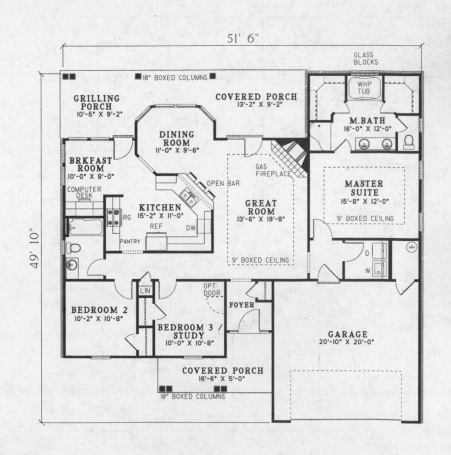

1,525 total square feet of living area   **Price Code B**

Special features

- Corner fireplace highlighted in great room
- Unique glass block window over whirlpool tub in master bath
- Open bar overlooks both the kitchen and great room
- Breakfast room leads to outdoor grilling and covered porch
- 3 bedrooms, 2 baths, 2-car garage
- Basement, walk-out basement, crawl space or slab foundation, please specify when ordering

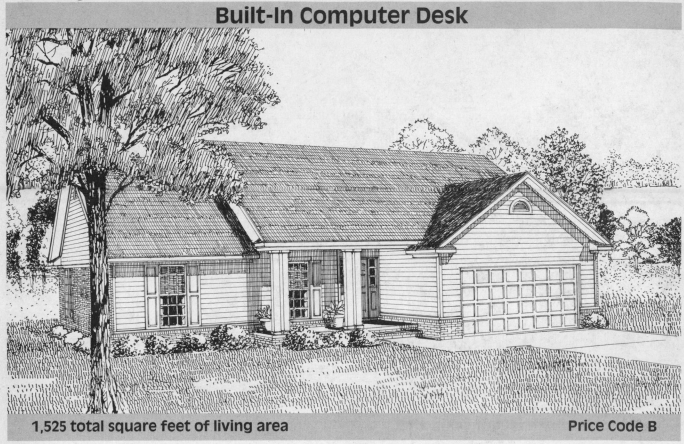

Plan #705-RDD-1895-9

Bath With Double Dressing Areas

1,895 total square feet of living area

Price Code C

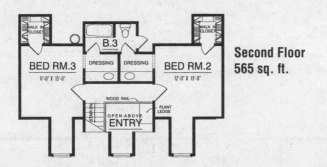

Second Floor
565 sq. ft.

WALK IN CLOSET
BED RM.3
11'-0" X 13'-0"
B.3
DRESSING DRESSING
BED RM.2
12'-0" X 13'-0"
WALK IN CLOSET
WOOD RAIL
STAIR DN
PLANT LEDGE
OPEN ABOVE
ENTRY

Special features

■ Kitchen overlooks both the breakfast nook and living room for an open floor plan

■ Living area has built-in book-shelves flanking fireplace

■ Master suite has private bath and access to covered rear porch

■ 3 bedrooms, 2 1/2 baths, 2-car garage

■ Basement, crawl space or slab foundation, please specify when ordering

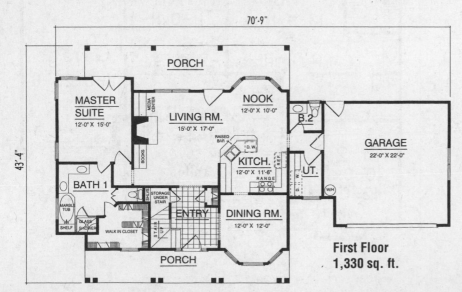

70'-9"

43'-4"

PORCH

MASTER SUITE
12'-0" X 15'-0"

MEDIA CENTER

LIVING RM.
15'-0" X 17'-0"

NOOK
12'-0" X 10'-0"

B.2

GARAGE
22'-0" X 22'-0"

BOOKS

RAISED BAR

D.W.

KITCH.
12'-0" X 11'-6"

REF.

RANGE

UT.

D.W.

W/H

BATH 1

MARBLE TUB

SHELF

GLASS SHOWER

WALK IN CLOSET

STORAGE UNDER STAIR

STAIR UP

ENTRY

DINING RM.
12'-0" X 12'-0"

PORCH

First Floor
1,330 sq. ft.

Cozy Ranch Home

950 total square feet of living area

Price Code AA

Special features

- Deck adjacent to kitchen/ breakfast area for outdoor dining

- Vaulted ceiling, open stairway and fireplace complement great room

- Secondary bedroom with sloped ceiling and box bay window can convert to den

- Master bedroom with walk-in closet, plant shelf, separate dressing area and private access to bath

- Kitchen has garage access and opens to great room

- 2 bedrooms, 1 bath, 1-car garage

- Basement foundation

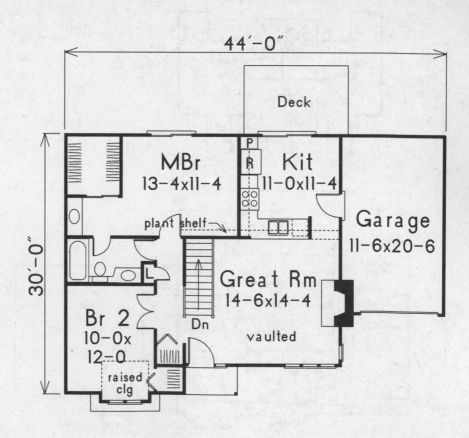

Open Floor Plan With Extra Amenities

1,680 total square feet of living area

Price Code B

**Second Floor
784 sq. ft.**

Br 2
11-8x10-9

L

Dn

MBr
11-10x15-0

Br 3
11-8x10-9

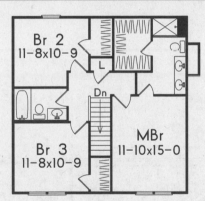

Special features

- Compact and efficient layout in an affordable package

- Second floor has three bedrooms all with oversized closets

- All bedrooms on second floor for privacy

- 3 bedrooms, 2 1/2 baths, 2-car garage

- Basement foundation

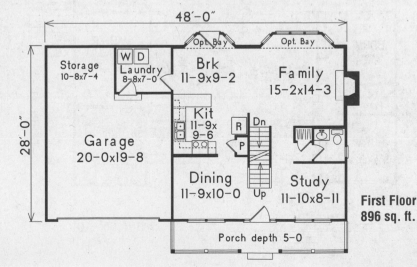

48'-0"

28'-0"

Opt. Bay   Opt. Bay

Storage
10-8x7-4

WD
Laundry
8-8x7-0

Brk
11-9x9-2

Family
15-2x14-3

Kit
11-9x
9-6

R   Dn

Garage
20-0x19-8

P

Dining
11-9x10-0

Up

Study
11-10x8-11

**First Floor
896 sq. ft.**

Porch depth 5-0

TO ORDER BLUEPRINTS USE THE FORM ON PAGE 15 OR CALL TOLL-FREE 1-877-671-6036
View thousands more home plans online at www.familyhandyman.com/homeplans

49

Country Farmhouse Appeal

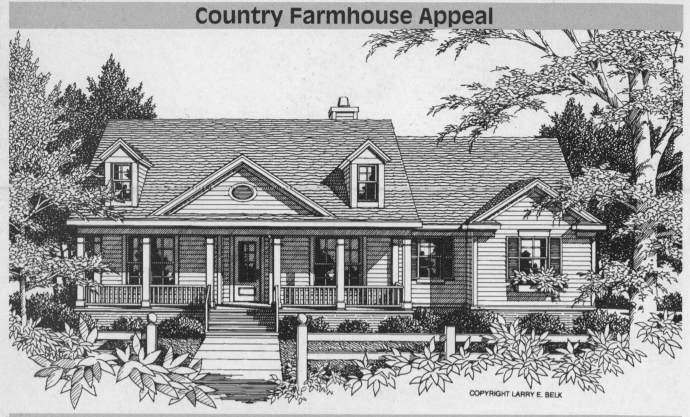

COPYRIGHT LARRY E. BELK

1,993 total square feet of living area

Price Code C

Special features

- Charming front and rear porches

- 12' ceiling in living room

- Exquisite master bath with large walk-in closet

- 3 bedrooms, 2 baths, 2-car side entry garage

- Crawl space or slab foundation, please specify when ordering

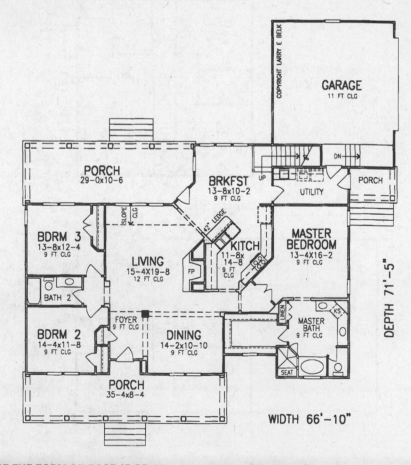

Terrific Use Of Space

© COPYRIGHT 1990 RALPH JONES & ASSOC.

1,436 total square feet of living area

Price Code A

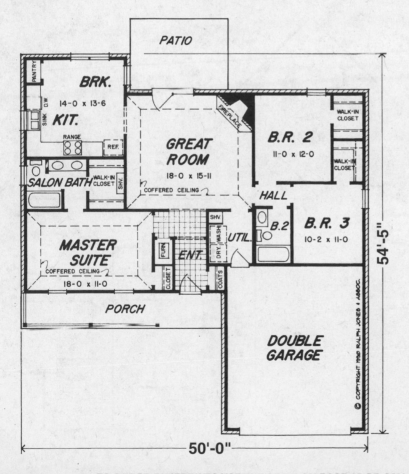

Special features

- Corner fireplace in great room warms home
- Kitchen and breakfast room combine for convenience
- Centrally located utility room
- 3 bedrooms, 2 baths, 2-car garage
- Slab foundation

Cozy Front Porch Welcomes Guests

1,393 total square feet of living area   **Price Code B**

Special features

- L-shaped kitchen features walk-in pantry, island cooktop and is convenient to laundry room and dining area

- Master bedroom features large walk-in closet and private bath with separate tub and shower

- Convenient storage/coat closet in hall

- View to the patio from the dining area

- 3 bedrooms, 2 baths, 2-car detached garage

- Crawl space foundation, drawings also include slab foundation

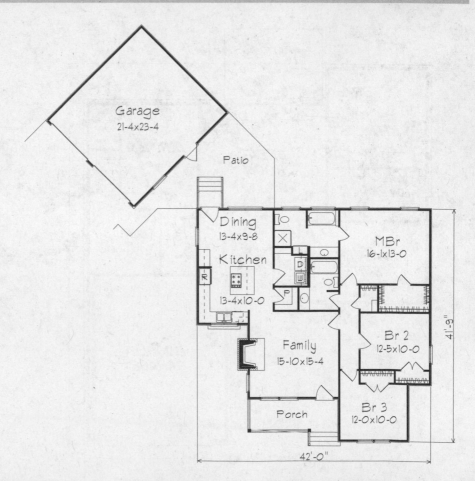

Garage
21-4x23-4

Patio

Dining
13-4x9-8

Kitchen
13-4x10-0

MBr
16-1x13-0

Family
15-10x15-4

Br 2
12-5x10-0

Porch

Br 3
12-0x10-0

41'-9"

42'-0"

Lovely, Spacious Floor Plan

1,558 total square feet of living area

Price Code B

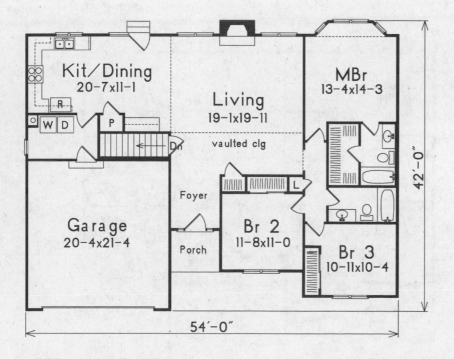

Kit/Dining
20-7x11-1

Living
19-1x19-11

vaulted clg

MBr
13-4x14-3

Foyer

Br 2
11-8x11-0

Garage
20-4x21-4

Porch

Br 3
10-11x10-4

42'-0"

54'-0"

Special features

- Spacious utility room located conveniently between garage and kitchen/dining area
- Private bedrooms separated off main living area by hallway
- Enormous living area with fireplace and vaulted ceiling opens to kitchen and dining area
- Master suite enhanced with large bay window, walk-in closet and private bath
- 3 bedrooms, 2 baths, 2-car garage
- Basement foundation

TO ORDER BLUEPRINTS USE THE FORM ON PAGE 15 OR CALL TOLL-FREE 1-877-671-6036
View thousands more home plans online at www.familyhandyman.com/homeplans

53

Classic Elegance

2,483 total square feet of living area   **Price Code D**

Special features

- A large entry porch with open brick arches and palladian door welcomes guests

- The vaulted great room features an entertainment center alcove and ideal layout for furniture placement

- Dining room is extra large with a stylish tray ceiling

- Study can easily be converted to a fourth bedroom

- 3 bedrooms, 2 baths, 2-car side entry garage

- Basement foundation

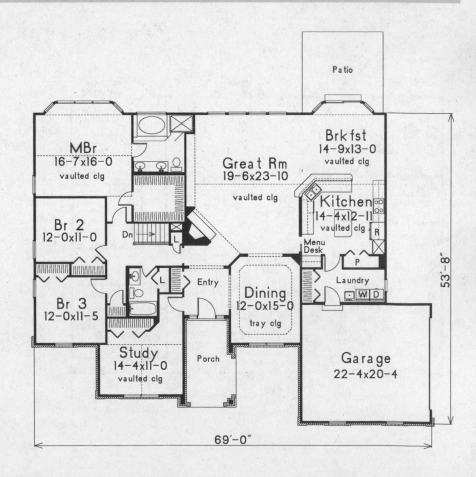

Country-Style Home With Large Front Porch

1,501 total square feet of living area

Price Code B

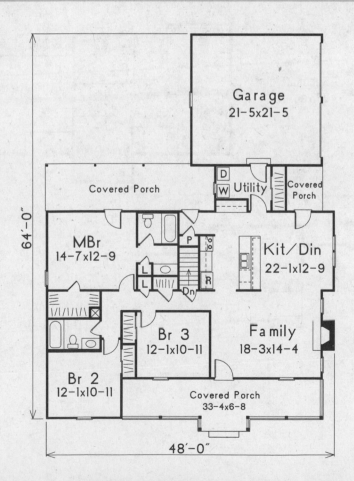

Garage
21-5x21-5

Covered Porch

D
W Utility

Covered Porch

MBr
14-7x12-9

P

Kit/Din
22-1x12-9

L
L

R

Dn

64'-0"

Br 3
12-1x10-11

Family
18-3x14-4

Br 2
12-1x10-11

Covered Porch
33-4x6-8

48'-0"

Special features

- Spacious kitchen with dining area is open to the outdoors
- Convenient utility room is adjacent to garage
- Master suite with private bath, dressing area and access to large covered porch
- Large family room creates openness
- 3 bedrooms, 2 baths, 2-car side entry garage
- Basement foundation, drawings also include crawl space and slab foundations

Plan #702-DR-3812

Perfect Farmhouse For Family Living

2,129 total square feet of living area

Price Code C

Special features

- Energy efficient home with 2" x 6" exterior walls
- Home office has a double-door entry and is secluded from other living areas
- Corner fireplace in living area is a nice focal point
- Bonus room above the garage has an additional 407 square feet of living area
- 3 bedrooms, 2 1/2 baths, 2-car side entry garage
- Basement foundation

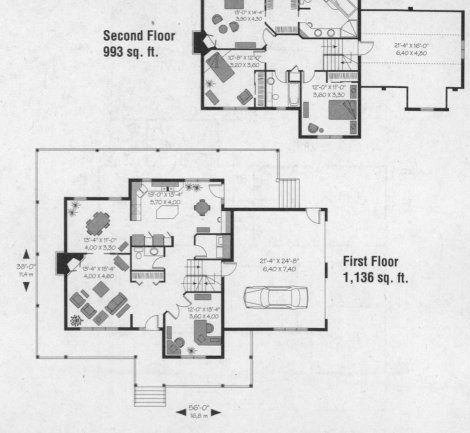

Second Floor
993 sq. ft.

13'-0" X 14'-4"
3,90 X 4,30

21'-4" X 16'-0"
6,40 X 4,80

10'-8" X 12'-0"
3,20 X 3,60

12'-0" X 11'-0"
3,60 X 3,30

First Floor
1,136 sq. ft.

19'-0" X 13'-4"
5,70 X 4,00

13'-4" X 11'-0"
4,00 X 3,30

21'-4" X 24'-8"
6,40 X 7,40

13'-4" X 15'-4"
4,00 X 4,60

12'-0" X 13'-4"
3,60 X 4,00

38'-0"
11,4 m

56'-0"
16,8 m

Well-Designed Floor Plan Has Many Extras

2,437 total square feet of living area

Price Code D

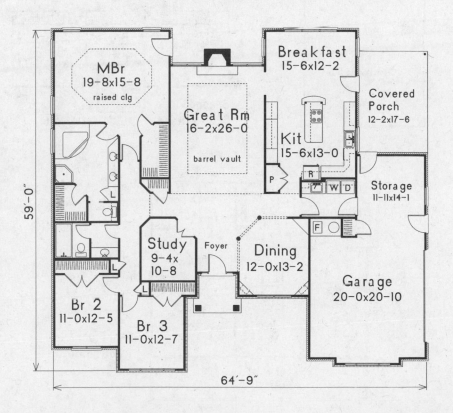

Special features

- Spacious breakfast area with access to the covered porch is adjacent to kitchen and great room

- Elegant dining area has columned entrance and built-in corner cabinets

- Cozy study has handsome double-door entrance off a large foyer

- Raised ceiling and lots of windows in master suite create a spacious, open feel

- 3 bedrooms, 2 baths, 2-car side entry garage

- Slab foundation, drawings also include crawl space foundation

Two-Story Foyer Adds Spacious Feeling

1,814 total square feet of living area

Price Code D

Special features

- Large master suite includes a spacious bath with garden tub, separate shower and large walk-in closet

- Spacious kitchen and dining area brightened by large windows and patio access

- Detached two-car garage with walkway leading to house adds charm to this country home

- Large front porch

- 3 bedrooms, 2 1/2 baths, 2-car detached garage

- Crawl space foundation, drawings also include slab foundation

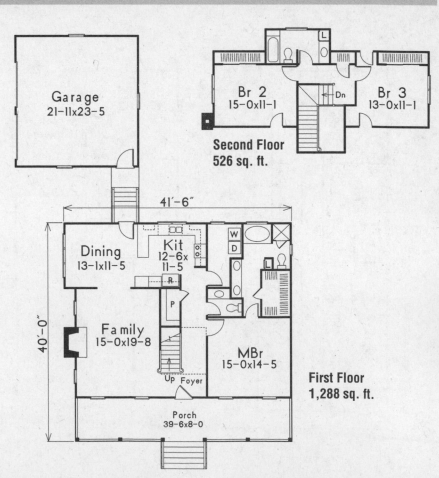

Garage
21-11x23-5

Br 2
15-0x11-1

Br 3
13-0x11-1

Second Floor
526 sq. ft.

41'-6"

40'-0"

Dining
13-1x11-5

Kit
12-6x
11-5

W
D

R

P

Family
15-0x19-8

MBr
15-0x14-5

Up Foyer

First Floor
1,288 sq. ft.

Porch
39-6x8-0

TO ORDER BLUEPRINTS USE THE FORM ON PAGE 15 OR CALL TOLL-FREE 1-877-671-6036
View thousands more home plans online at www.familyhandyman.com/homeplans

60

Pillared Front Porch Generates Charm And Warmth

1,567 total square feet of living area

Price Code B

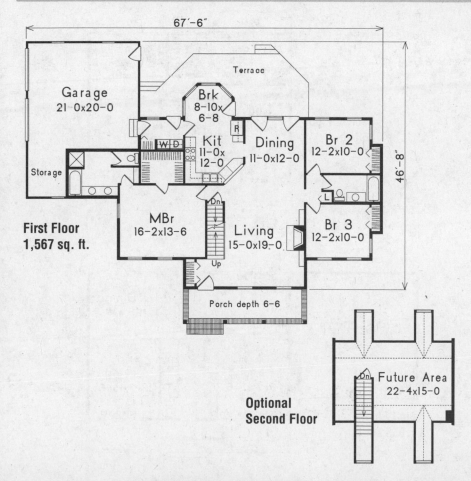

67'-6"

Garage
21-0x20-0

Storage

Terrace

Brk
8-10x
6-8

R

Kit
11-0x
12-0

W D

Dining
11-0x12-0

Br 2
12-2x10-0

46'-8"

First Floor
1,567 sq. ft.

MBr
16-2x13-6

Dn

Up

Living
15-0x19-0

Br 3
12-2x10-0

L

Porch depth 6-6

Dn

Future Area
22-4x15-0

Optional
Second Floor

Special features

- Living room flows into dining room shaped by an angled pass-through into the kitchen

- Cheerful, windowed dining area

- Future area on the second floor has an additional 338 square feet of living area

- Master suite separated from other bedrooms for privacy

- 3 bedrooms, 2 baths, 2-car side entry garage

- Basement foundation, drawings also include slab foundation

Country Classic With Modern Floor Plan

1,921 total square feet of living area

Price Code D

Special features

- Energy efficient home with 2" x 6" exterior walls
- Sunken family room includes a built-in entertainment center and coffered ceiling
- Sunken formal living room features a coffered ceiling
- Dressing area has double sinks, spa tub, shower and French door to private deck
- Large front porch adds to home's appeal
- 3 bedrooms, 2 1/2 baths, 2-car garage
- Basement foundation

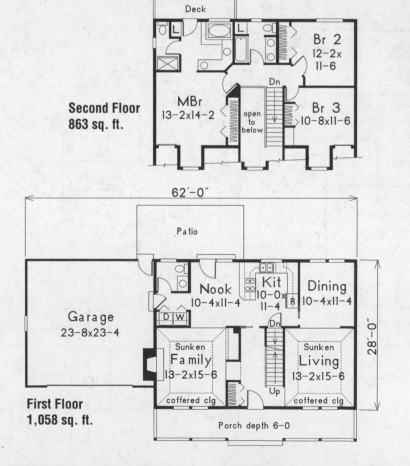

Second Floor 863 sq. ft.

Deck

Br 2
12-2x 11-6

MBr
13-2x14-2

open to below

Dn

Br 3
10-8x11-6

First Floor 1,058 sq. ft.

62'-0"

Patio

Garage
23-8x23-4

Nook
10-4x11-4

Kit
10-0x 11-4

Dining
10-4x11-4

D W

Dn

Sunken Family
13-2x15-6
coffered clg

Up

Sunken Living
13-2x15-6
coffered clg

28'-0"

Porch depth 6-0

Compact Ranch An Ideal Starter Home

988 total square feet of living area

Price Code AA

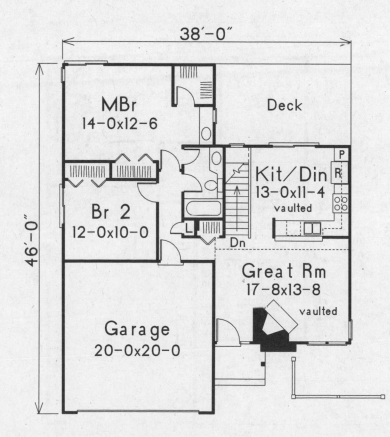

38'-0"

46'-0"

MBr
14-0x12-6

Deck

Br 2
12-0x10-0

Kit/Din
13-0x11-4
vaulted

P
R

Dn

Garage
20-0x20-0

Great Rm
17-8x13-8
vaulted

L

Special features

- Great room features corner fireplace
- Vaulted ceiling and corner windows add space and light in great room
- Eat-in kitchen with vaulted ceiling accesses deck for outdoor living
- Master bedroom features separate vanity and private access to the bath
- 2 bedrooms, 1 bath, 2-car garage
- Basement foundation

Simple Rooflines And Inviting Porch

1,389 total square feet of living area

Price Code A

Special features

- Formal living room has warming fireplace and a delightful bay window
- U-shaped kitchen shares a snack bar with the bayed family room
- Lovely master suite has its own private bath
- 3 bedrooms, 2 baths, 2-car garage
- Slab foundation

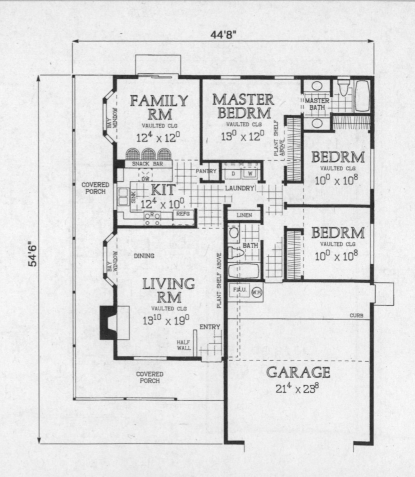

Traditional Exterior Boasts Exciting Interior

Rear View

2,531 total square feet of living area

Price Code D

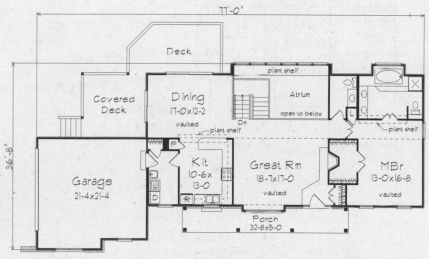

77'-0"

Deck

Covered Deck

Dining
17-0x12-2
vaulted

plant shelf

Atrium
open to below

plant shelf

36'-8"

Garage
21-4x21-4

Kit
10-6x
13-0

Great Rm
18-7x17-0
vaulted

MBr
13-0x16-8
vaulted

Porch
32-8x5-0

First Floor
1,297 sq. ft.

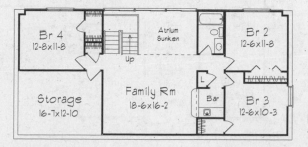

Br 4
12-8x11-8

Atrium
Sunken

Up

Br 2
12-6x11-8

Storage
16-7x12-10

Family Rm
18-6x16-2

Bar

Br 3
12-6x10-3

Lower Level
1,234 sq. ft.

Special features

- Charming porch with dormers leads into vaulted great room with atrium

- Well-designed kitchen and breakfast bar adjoins extra large laundry/mud room

- Double sinks, tub with window above and plant shelf complete vaulted master suite bath

- 4 bedrooms, 2 1/2 baths, 2-car side entry garage

- Walk-out basement foundation

Plan #705-0184

Stately Facade Features Impressive Front Balcony

2,411 total square feet of living area

Price Code D

Special features

- Elegant entrance features a two-story vaulted foyer
- Large family room enhanced by masonry fireplace and wet bar
- Master bedroom suite includes walk-in closet, oversized tub and separate shower
- Second floor study could easily convert to a fourth bedroom
- 3 bedrooms, 2 1/2 baths, 2-car garage
- Basement foundation, drawings also include slab and crawl space foundations

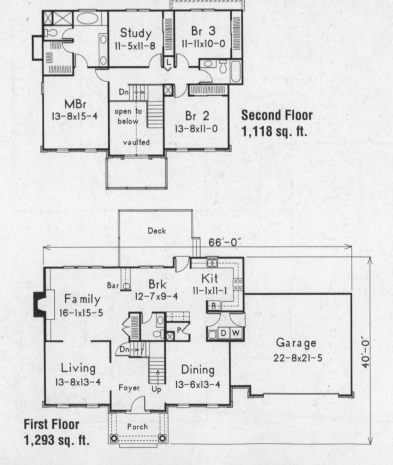

Study 11-5x11-8

Br 3 11-11x10-0

MBr 13-8x15-4

Dn open to below vaulted

Br 2 13-8x11-0

Second Floor 1,118 sq. ft.

Deck

66'-0"

Family 16-1x15-5

Bar

Brk 12-7x9-4

Kit 11-1x11-1

R

Garage 22-8x21-5

40'-0"

Living 13-8x13-4

Dn

P

D W

Dining 13-6x13-4

Foyer

Up

Porch

First Floor 1,293 sq. ft.

Inviting Gabled And Arched Brick Entry

2,109 total square feet of living area

Price Code C

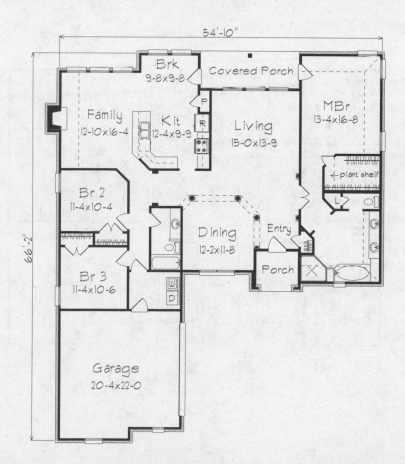

Special features

- 12' ceilings in living and dining rooms

- Kitchen designed as an integral part of the family and breakfast rooms

- Secluded and generous-sized master bedroom includes a plant shelf, walk-in closet and private bath with separate tub and shower

- Stately columns and circle-top window frame dining room

- 3 bedrooms, 2 baths, 2-car side entry garage

- Slab foundation, drawings also include crawl space foundation

Stately Covered Front Entry

2,089 total square feet of living area

Price Code C

Special features

- Family room features fireplace, built-in bookshelves and triple sliders opening to covered patio

- Kitchen overlooks family room and features pantry and desk

- Separated from the three secondary bedrooms, the master bedroom becomes a quiet retreat with patio access

- Master suite features oversized bath with walk-in closet and corner tub

- 4 bedrooms, 3 baths, 2-car garage

- Slab foundation

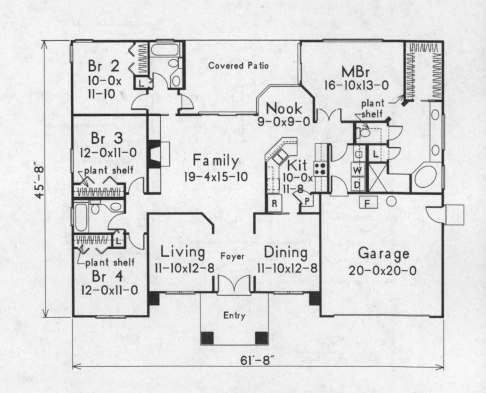

Plan #705-JFD-10-1456-2

Luxurious Master Bath

1,456 total square feet of living area

Price Code A

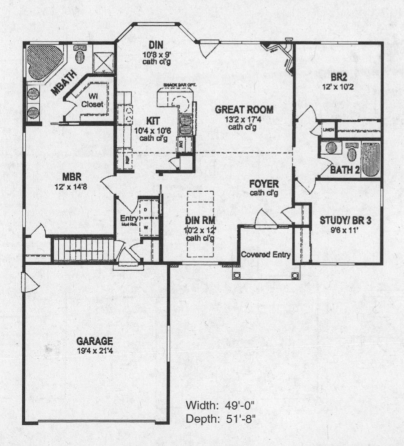

DIN
10'8 x 9'
cath cl'g

MBATH

WI Closet

KIT
10'4 x 10'6
cath cl'g

SNACK BAR OPT.

GREAT ROOM
13'2 x 17'4
cath cl'g

BR2
12' x 10'2

LINEN

BATH 2

MBR
12' x 14'8

Entry
Mud Rm.

DIN RM
10'2 x 12'
cath cl'g

FOYER
cath cl'g

STUDY/ BR 3
9'6 x 11'

Covered Entry

GARAGE
19'4 x 21'4

Width: 49'-0"
Depth: 51'-8"

Special features

- Open floor plan adds spaciousness to this design
- The study can easily be converted to a third bedroom
- Corner fireplace in great room is a terrific focal point
- 3 bedrooms, 2 baths, 2-car garage
- Basement foundation

Perfect Compact Ranch

1,738 total square feet of living area

Price Code B

Rear View

Special features

- A den in the front of the home can easily be converted to a third bedroom

- Kitchen includes an eating nook for family gatherings

- Master bedroom has an unforgettable bath with a super skylight

- Large sunken great room centralized with a cozy fireplace

- 2 bedrooms, 2 baths, 3-car garage

- Basement, crawl space or slab foundation, please specify when ordering

Crawl / Slab Option

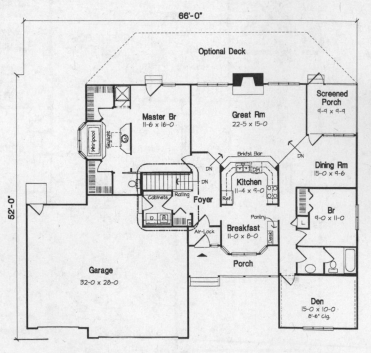

66'-0"

Optional Deck

Screened Porch
9-9 x 9-9

Master Br
11-6 x 16-0

Great Rm
22-5 x 15-0

Dining Rm
15-0 x 9-6

Brkfst Bar

Kitchen
11-4 x 9-0

Foyer

Br
9-0 x 11-0

Pantry

Breakfast
11-0 x 8-0

Air-Lock

Garage
32-0 x 28-0

Porch

52'-0"

Den
15-0 x 10-0
8'-6" Clg.

Double Bay Enhances Front Entry

1,992 total square feet of living area   **Price Code C**

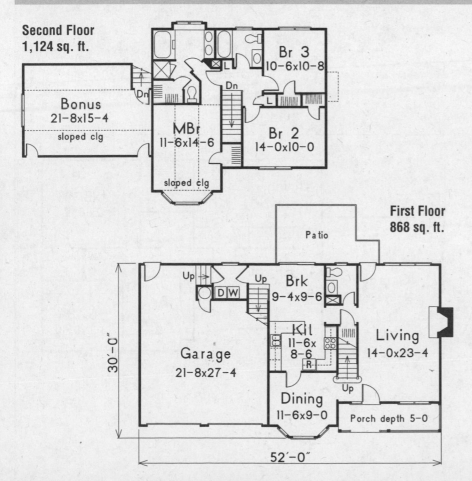

Second Floor
1,124 sq. ft.

Bonus
21-8x15-4
sloped clg

Dn

MBr
11-6x14-6
sloped clg

Br 3
10-6x10-8

Dn

Br 2
14-0x10-0

First Floor
868 sq. ft.

Patio

Up

D W

Up

Brk
9-4x9-6

Garage
21-8x27-4

Kit
11-6x
8-6

R

Living
14-0x23-4

Up

Dining
11-6x9-0

Porch depth 5-0

30'-0"

52'-0"

Special features

- Distinct living, dining and breakfast areas
- Master bedroom boasts full end bay window and a cathedral ceiling
- Storage and laundry area located adjacent to the garage
- Bonus room over the garage for future office or playroom
- 3 bedrooms, 2 1/2 baths, 2-car garage
- Crawl space foundation, drawings also include basement foundation

TO ORDER BLUEPRINTS USE THE FORM ON PAGE 15 OR CALL TOLL-FREE 1-877-671-6036
View thousands more home plans online at www.familyhandyman.com/homeplans

71

Affordable Upscale, Amenity Full

1,643 total square feet of living area

Price Code B

Special features

- Family room has vaulted ceiling, open staircase and arched windows allowing for plenty of light

- Kitchen captures full use of space, with pantry, storage, ample counter space and work island

- Large closets and storage areas throughout

- Roomy master bath has a skylight for natural lighting plus separate tub and shower

- Rear of house provides ideal location for future screened-in porch

- 3 bedrooms, 2 baths, 2-car side entry garage

- Basement foundation, drawings also include slab and crawl space foundations

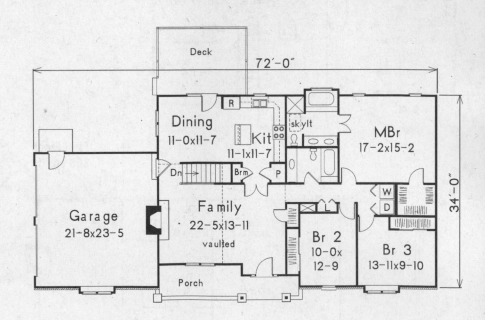

TO ORDER BLUEPRINTS USE THE FORM ON PAGE 15 OR CALL TOLL-FREE 1-877-671-6036

View thousands more home plans online at www.familyhandyman.com/homeplans

Plan #705-0747

Classic Atrium Ranch With Rooms To Spare

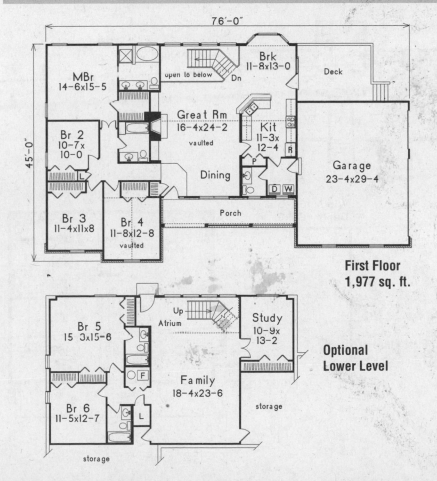

1,977 total square feet of living area

Price Code C

**First Floor
1,977 sq. ft.**

**Optional
Lower Level**

Special features

- Classic traditional exterior always in style
- Spacious great room boasts a vaulted ceiling, dining area, atrium with elegant staircase and feature windows
- Atrium open to 1,416 square feet of optional living area below which consists of an optional family room, two bedrooms, two baths and a study
- 4 bedrooms, 2 1/2 baths, 3-car side entry garage
- Walk-out basement foundation

Inviting Country Home

1,757 total square feet of living area

Price Code B

Special features

- Energy efficient home with 2" x 6" exterior walls

- First floor master bedroom has privacy as well as its own bath and walk-in closet

- Cozy living room includes fireplace for warmth

- 3 bedrooms, 2 1/2 baths, 2-car garage

- Crawl space or slab foundation, please specify when ordering

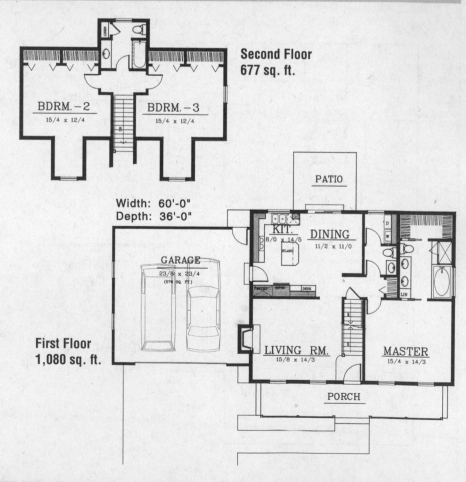

Second Floor 677 sq. ft.

BDRM.–2
15/4 x 12/4

BDRM.–3
15/4 x 12/4

Width: 60'-0"
Depth: 36'-0"

PATIO

KIT.
8/0 x 14/5

DINING
11/2 x 11/0

GARAGE
23/6 x 23/4
(576 SQ. FT.)

LIVING RM.
15/8 x 14/3

MASTER
15/4 x 14/3

First Floor 1,080 sq. ft.

PORCH

Enchanting One-Level Home

1,508 total square feet of living area

Price Code B

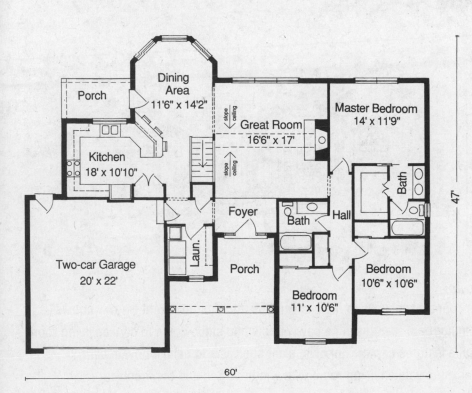

Dining Area 11'6" x 14'2"

Porch

Kitchen 18' x 10'10"

slope ceiling

Great Room 16'6" x 17'

slope ceiling

Master Bedroom 14' x 11'9"

Bath

Foyer

Bath

Hall

Laun.

Two-car Garage 20' x 22'

Porch

Bedroom 11' x 10'6"

Bedroom 10'6" x 10'6"

60'

47'

Special features

- Grand opening between rooms create a spacious effect

- Additional room for quick meals or serving a larger crowd is provided at the breakfast bar

- Sunny dining area accesses the outdoors as well

- 3 bedrooms, 2 baths, 2-car garage

- Basement or crawl space foundation, please specify when ordering

Central Living Space

Plan #705-0252

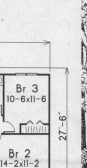

1,364 total square feet of living area   Price Code A

Special features

- Master bedroom includes full bath
- Pass-through kitchen opens into breakfast room with laundry closet and access to deck
- Adjoining dining and living rooms with vaulted ceilings and a fireplace create an open living area
- Dining room features large bay window
- 3 bedrooms, 2 baths, 2-car drive under garage
- Basement foundation

Provides Family Living At Its Best

Plan #705-0279

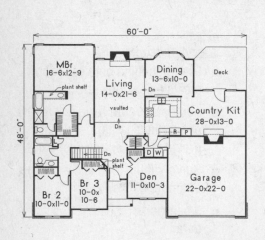

1,993 total square feet of living area   Price Code D

Special features

- Spacious country kitchen with fireplace and plenty of natural light from windows
- Formal dining room features large bay window and steps down to sunken living room
- Master suite features corner windows, plant shelves and deluxe private bath
- Entry opens into vaulted living room with windows flanking the fireplace
- 3 bedrooms, 2 baths, 2-car garage
- Basement foundation

Traditional Ranch Styling

1,167 total square feet of living area

Price Code AA

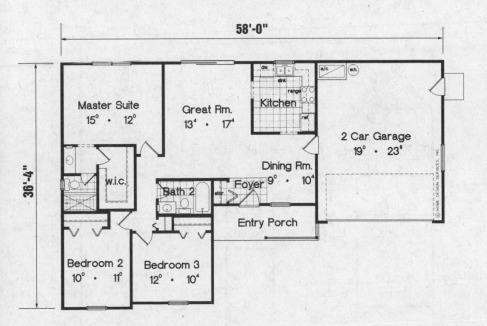

58'-0"

36'-4"

Master Suite
15⁰ • 12⁰

Great Rm.
13⁴ • 17⁴

Kitchen

w.i.c.

2 Car Garage
19⁰ • 23⁸

Dining Rm.
9⁰ • 10⁴

Bath 2

Foyer

Bedroom 2
10⁰ • 11⁰

Bedroom 3
12⁰ • 10⁴

Entry Porch

© HOME DESIGN SERVICES, INC.

Special features

- Master suite has a private bath
- Handy coat closet in foyer
- Lots of storage space through-out
- 3 bedrooms, 2 baths, 2-car garage
- Slab foundation

Central Fireplace Focuses Family Living

1,408 total square feet of living area   **Price Code A**

Special features

- Handsome see-through fireplace offers a gathering point for the family room and breakfast/kitchen area

- Vaulted ceiling and large bay window in the master bedroom add charm to this room

- A dramatic angular wall and large windows add brightness to the kitchen/breakfast area

- Family room and breakfast/kitchen area have vaulted ceilings, adding to this central living area

- 3 bedrooms, 2 baths, 2-car garage

- Crawl space foundation, drawings also include slab foundation

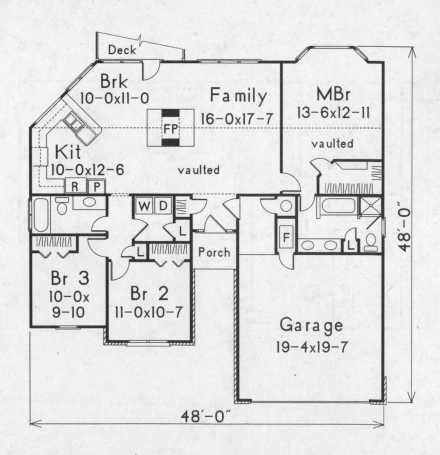

Plan #705-0441

Inviting Covered Corner Entry

1,747 total square feet of living area

Price Code B

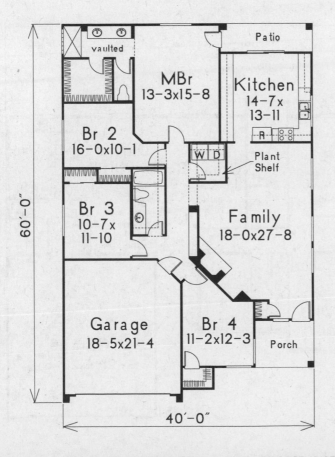

Patio

vaulted

MBr
13-3x15-8

Kitchen
14-7x
13-11

R

Br 2
16-0x10-1

W D

Plant
Shelf

Br 3
10-7x
11-10

Family
18-0x27-8

60'-0"

Garage
18-5x21-4

Br 4
11-2x12-3

Porch

40'-0"

Special features

- Entry opens into large family room with coat closet, angled fireplace and attractive plant shelf

- Kitchen and master bedroom access covered patio

- Functional kitchen includes ample workspace

- 4 bedrooms, 2 baths, 2-car garage

- Slab foundation

TO ORDER BLUEPRINTS USE THE FORM ON PAGE 15 OR CALL TOLL-FREE 1-877-671-6036
View thousands more home plans online at www.familyhandyman.com/homeplans

79

High-Style Vaulted Ranch

1,453 total square feet of living area　　　　　　**Price Code A**

Special features

- Decorative vents, window trim, shutters and brick blend to create dramatic curb appeal

- Energy efficient home with 2" x 6" exterior walls

- Kitchen opens to living area and includes salad sink in the island, pantry and handy laundry room

- Exquisite master bedroom highlighted by vaulted ceiling

- Dressing area with walk-in closet, private bath and spa tub/ shower

- 3 bedrooms, 2 baths, 2-car garage

- Basement foundation, drawings also include crawl space foundation

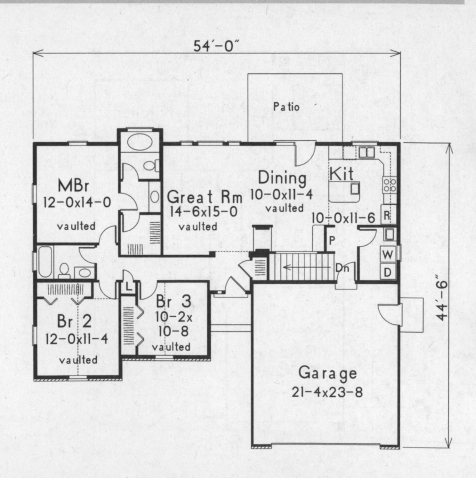

Classic Three Bedroom

2,228 total square feet of living area

Price Code D

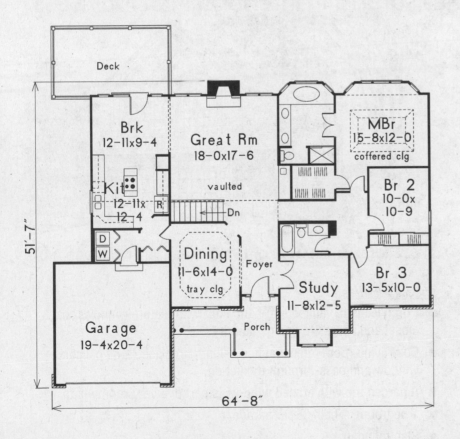

Deck

Brk
12-11x9-4

Great Rm
18-0x17-6

MBr
15-8x12-0
coffered clg

vaulted

Kit
12-11x
12-4

R

Dn

Br 2
10-0x
10-9

D
W

Dining
11-6x14-0
tray clg

Foyer

Study
11-8x12-5

Br 3
13-5x10-0

Garage
19-4x20-4

Porch

51'-7"

64'-8"

Special features

- Convenient entrance from garage into home through laundry room
- Master bedroom features walk-in closet and double-door entrance into master bath with oversized tub
- Formal dining room with tray ceiling
- Kitchen features island cooktop and adjacent breakfast room
- 3 bedrooms, 2 baths, 2-car garage
- Basement foundation

TO ORDER BLUEPRINTS USE THE FORM ON PAGE 15 OR CALL TOLL-FREE 1-877-671-6036
View thousands more home plans online at www.familyhandyman.com/homeplans

81

A Cottage With Class

Plan #705-0476

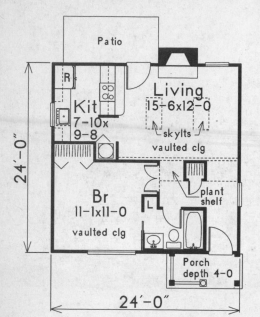

576 total square feet of living area   **Price Code AAA**

Special features

- Perfect country retreat features vaulted living room and entry with skylights and plant shelf above
- Double-doors enter a vaulted bedroom with bath access
- Kitchen offers generous storage and pass-through breakfast bar
- 1 bedroom, 1 bath
- Crawl space foundation

Apartment Garage Has Surprising Interior   Plan #705-0655

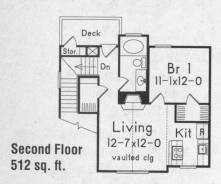

Second Floor 512 sq. ft.

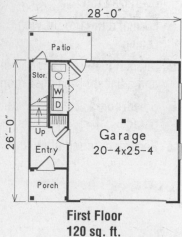

First Floor 120 sq. ft.

632 total square feet of living area   **Price Code AAA**

Special features

- Porch leads to vaulted entry and stair with feature window, coat closet and access to garage/laundry
- Cozy living room offers vaulted ceiling, fireplace, large palladian window and pass-through to kitchen
- A garden tub with arched window is part of a very roomy bath
- 1 bedroom, 1 bath, 2-car garage
- Slab foundation

Distinctive Ranch Has A Larger Look

1,360 total square feet of living area

Price Code A

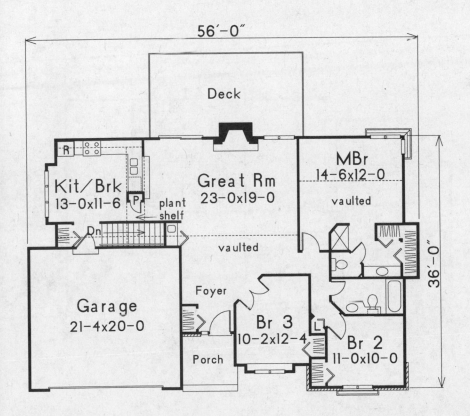

56'-0"

Deck

R

Kit/Brk
13-0x11-6

P

plant
shelf

Dn

Great Rm
23-0x19-0

MBr
14-6x12-0

vaulted

vaulted

Garage
21-4x20-0

Foyer

Br 3
10-2x12-4

Br 2
11-0x10-0

Porch

36'-0"

Special features

- Double-gabled front facade frames large windows

- Entry area is open to vaulted great room, fireplace and rear deck creating an open feel

- Vaulted ceiling and large windows add openness to kitchen/breakfast room

- Bedroom #3 easily converts to a den

- Plan easily adapts to crawl space or slab construction, with the utilities replacing the stairs

- 3 bedrooms, 2 baths, 2-car garage

- Basement foundation

Distinctive Ranch

FREILING

1,962 total square feet of living area

Price Code C

Special features

- Formal dining room has a butler's pantry for entertaining
- Open living room offers a fireplace, built-in cabinetry and exceptional views to the outdoors
- Kitchen has work island and planning desk
- 3 bedrooms, 2 1/2 baths, 3-car garage
- Basement foundation

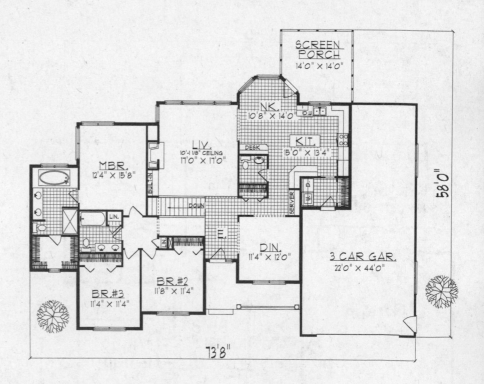

Open Living Centers On Windowed Dining Room

2,003 total square feet of living area

Price Code D

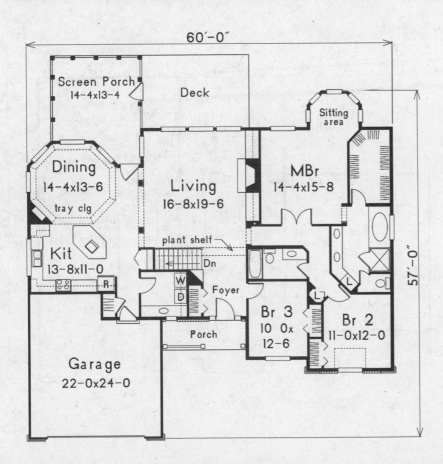

60´-0"

Screen Porch
14-4x13-4

Deck

Sitting area

Dining
14-4x13-6
tray clg

Living
16-8x19-6

MBr
14-4x15-8

Kit
13-8x11-0

plant shelf

Dn

W
D

Foyer

Br 3
10-0x
12-6

Br 2
11-0x12-0

Porch

Garage
22-0x24-0

57´-0"

Special features

- Octagon-shaped dining room with tray ceiling and deck overlook

- L-shaped island kitchen serves living and dining rooms

- Master bedroom boasts luxury bath and walk-in closet

- Living room features columns, elegant fireplace and 10' ceiling

- 3 bedrooms, 2 baths, 2-car garage

- Basement foundation

Appealing Ranch Has Attractive Front Dormers

1,642 total square feet of living area

Price Code B

Special features

- Walk-through kitchen boasts vaulted ceiling and corner sink overlooking family room

- Vaulted family room features cozy fireplace and access to rear patio

- Master bedroom includes sloped ceiling, walk-in closet and private bath

- 3 bedrooms, 2 baths, 2-car garage

- Basement foundation, drawings also include slab and crawl space foundations

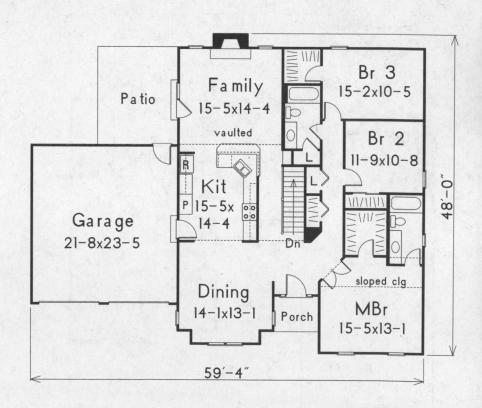

86

TO ORDER BLUEPRINTS USE THE FORM ON PAGE 15 OR CALL TOLL-FREE 1-877-671-6036
View thousands more home plans online at www.familyhandyman.com/homeplans

Gabled Front Porch Adds Charm And Value

1,443 total square feet of living area   **Price Code A**

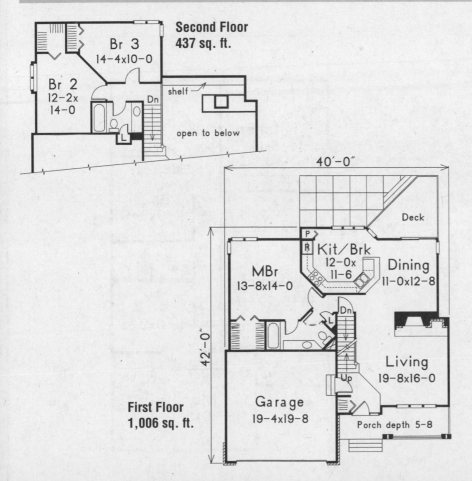

Second Floor 437 sq. ft.

Br 3 14-4x10-0

Br 2 12-2x 14-0

shelf

Dn

open to below

40'-0"

42'-0"

Deck

P
R

Kit/Brk 12-0x 11-6

Dining 11-0x12-8

MBr 13-8x14-0

Dn

Living 19-8x16-0

Up

First Floor 1,006 sq. ft.

Garage 19-4x19-8

Porch depth 5-8

Special features

- Raised foyer and cathedral ceiling in living room
- Impressive tall-wall fireplace between living and dining rooms
- Open U-shaped kitchen with breakfast bay
- Angular side deck accentuates patio and garden
- First floor master bedroom suite has a walk-in closet and a corner window
- 3 bedrooms, 2 baths, 2-car garage
- Basement foundation

Plan #705-0806

Four Bedroom Living For A Narrow Lot

1,452 total square feet of living area

Price Code A

Special features

- Large living room features cozy corner fireplace, bayed dining area and access from entry with guest closet

- Forward master bedroom suite enjoys having its own bath and linen closet

- Three additional bedrooms share a bath with double-bowl vanity

- 4 bedrooms, 2 baths

- Basement foundation

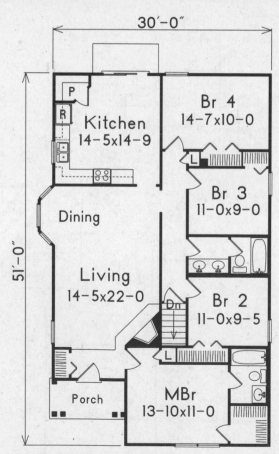

Plan #705-HP-C659

Modern Rustic Design

1,118 total square feet of living area

Price Code AA

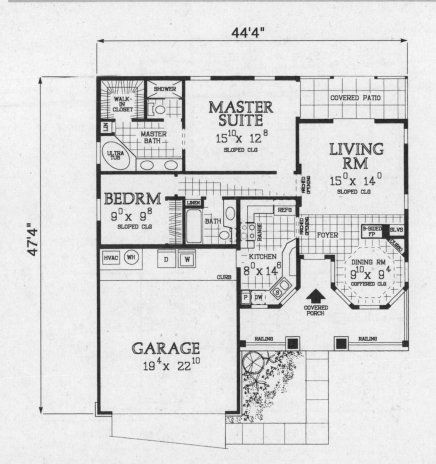

Special features

■ Great room offers a sloped ceiling, fireplace with extended hearth and built-in shelves for an entertainment center

■ Gourmet kitchen has a cooktop island counter and a morning room

■ Master suite features a sloped ceiling, cozy sitting room, walk-in closet and a private bath with whirlpool tub

■ 2 bedrooms, 2 baths, 2-car garage

■ Slab foundation

Columns And Dormers Grace Stylish Exterior

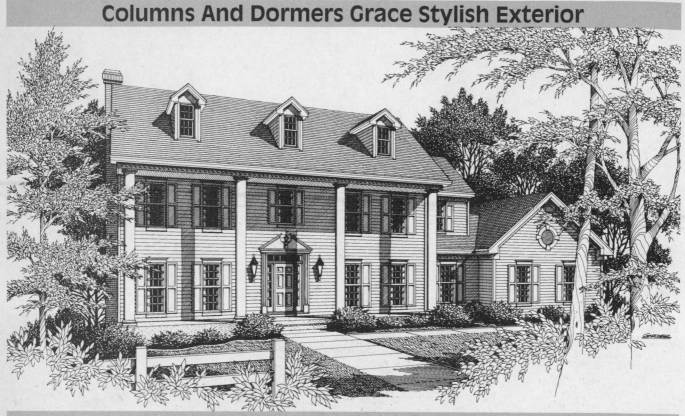

3,216 total square feet of living area

Price Code F

Special features

- All bedrooms include private full baths
- Hearth room and combination kitchen/breakfast area create large informal gathering area
- Oversized family room boasts fireplace, wet bar and bay window
- Master bath with double walk-in closets and luxurious bath
- 4 bedrooms, 4 1/2 baths, 3-car side entry garage
- Basement foundation

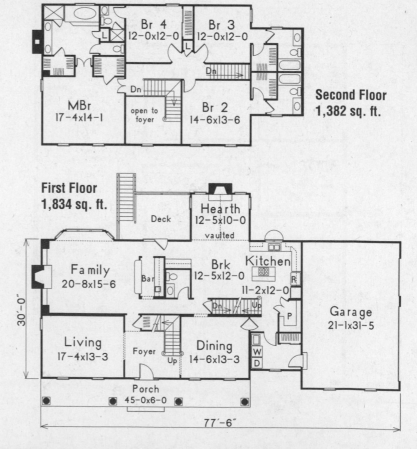

Second Floor 1,382 sq. ft.

Br 4 12-0x12-0
Br 3 12-0x12-0
MBr 17-4x14-1
open to foyer
Br 2 14-6x13-6

First Floor 1,834 sq. ft.

Deck
Hearth 12-5x10-0 vaulted
Family 20-8x15-6
Bar
Brk 12-5x12-0
Kitchen 11-2x12-0
Garage 21-1x31-5
Living 17-4x13-3
Foyer
Dining 14-6x13-3
Porch 45-0x6-0
30'-0"
77'-6"

Clean, Practical Colonial

2,328 total square feet of living area

Price Code D

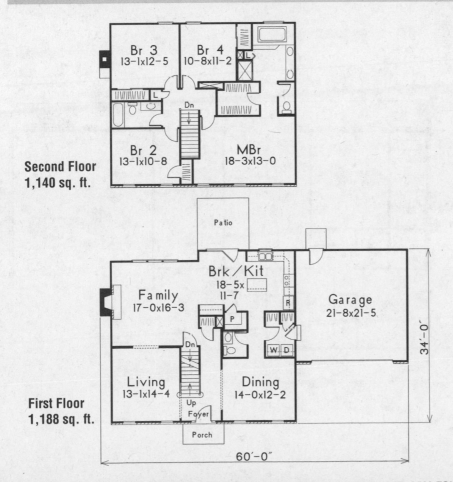

Second Floor
1,140 sq. ft.

Br 3
13-1x12-5

Br 4
10-8x11-2

Br 2
13-1x10-8

Dn

MBr
18-3x13-0

First Floor
1,188 sq. ft.

Patio

Brk/Kit
18-5x
11-7

Family
17-0x16-3

R

Garage
21-8x21-5

P

W D

Dn

Living
13-1x14-4

Up
Foyer

Dining
14-0x12-2

Porch

34'-0"

60'-0"

Special features

- Formal living and dining rooms feature floor-to-ceiling windows
- Kitchen with island counter and pantry makes cooking a delight
- Expansive master suite has luxury bath with double vanity and walk-in closet
- 4 bedrooms, 2 1/2 baths, 2-car garage
- Basement foundation, drawings also include slab and crawl space foundations

TO ORDER BLUEPRINTS USE THE FORM ON PAGE 15 OR CALL TOLL-FREE 1-877-671-6036
View thousands more home plans online at www.familyhandyman.com/homeplans

91

Pleasant Country Front Porch

1,233 total square feet of living area

Price Code A

Special features

- A versatile dressing area is featured in the full bath shared by the secondary bedrooms

- Lovely master suite has a private bath and a walk-in closet

- The foyer has a coat closet as well as an additional storage closet

- 3 bedrooms, 2 baths, 2-car garage

- Slab or crawl space foundation, please specify when ordering

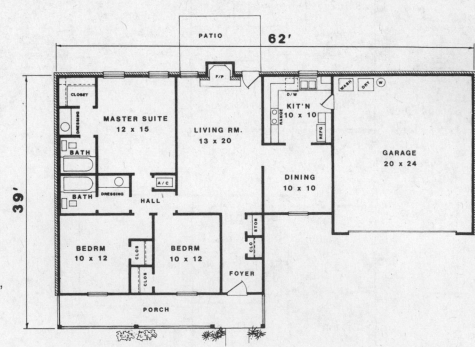

Compact Home Is Charming And Functional

1,404 total square feet of living area

Price Code A

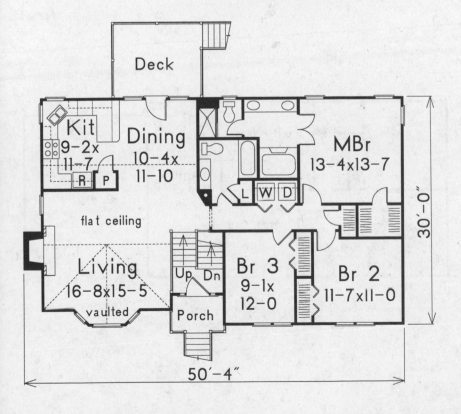

Deck

Kit
9-2x
11-7

Dining
10-4x
11-10

R P

MBr
13-4x13-7

L W D

flat ceiling

Living
16-8x15-5
vaulted

Up Dn

Br 3
9-1x
12-0

Br 2
11-7x11-0

Porch

30'-0"

50'-4"

Special features

- Split foyer entrance
- Bayed living area features unique vaulted ceiling and fireplace
- Wrap-around kitchen has corner windows for added sunlight and a bar that over-looks dining area
- Master bath features a garden tub with separate shower
- Rear deck provides handy access to dining room and kitchen
- 3 bedrooms, 2 baths, 2-car drive under garage
- Basement foundation, drawings also include partial crawl space foundation

Roomy Ranch For Easy Living

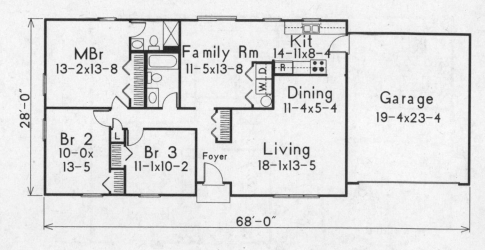

1,343 total square feet of living area

Price Code A

Special features

- Separate and convenient family and living/dining areas
- Nice-sized master bedroom suite with large closet and private bath
- Foyer with convenient coat closet opens into combined living and dining rooms
- Kitchen has access to the outdoors through sliding glass doors
- 3 bedrooms, 2 baths, 2-car garage
- Crawl space foundation, drawings also include basement foundation

Wonderful Great Room

N. HANSEN FL

1,865 total square feet of living area

Price Code D

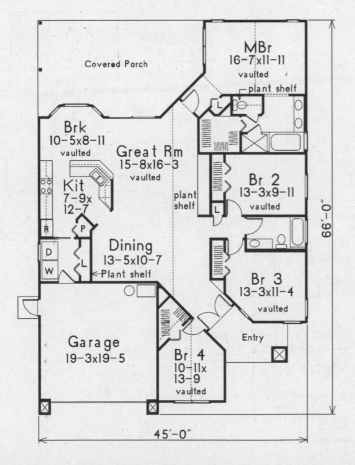

Covered Porch

MBr
16-7x11-11
vaulted

plant shelf

L

Brk
10-5x8-11
vaulted

Great Rm
15-8x16-3
vaulted

Kit
7-9x
12-7

plant shelf

Br 2
13-3x9-11
vaulted

L

66'-0"

R

D

W

P

L

Dining
13-5x10-7
Plant shelf

Br 3
13-3x11-4
vaulted

Garage
19-3x19-5

Br 4
10-11x
13-9
vaulted

Entry

45'-0"

Special features

- Large foyer opens into expansive dining area and great room
- Home features vaulted ceilings throughout
- Master suite features bath with double-bowl vanity, shower, tub and toilet in separate room for privacy
- 4 bedrooms, 2 baths, 2-car garage
- Slab foundation, drawings also include crawl space foundation

Year-Round Or Weekend Getaway Home

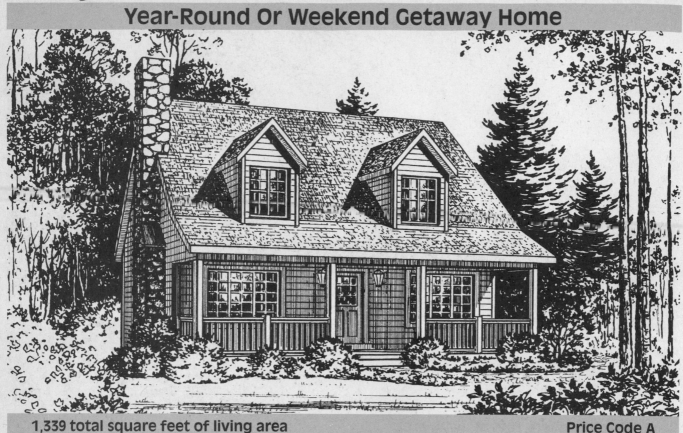

1,339 total square feet of living area

Price Code A

Special features

- Full-length covered porch enhances front facade
- Vaulted ceiling and stone fireplace add drama to family room
- Walk-in closets in bedrooms provide ample storage space
- Combined kitchen/dining area adjoins family room for perfect entertaining space
- 3 bedrooms, 2 1/2 baths
- Crawl space foundation

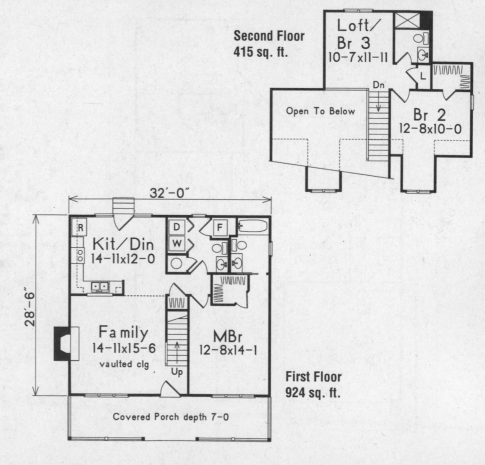

Second Floor
415 sq. ft.

Loft/Br 3
10-7x11-11

Open To Below

Dn

Br 2
12-8x10-0

32'-0"

Kit/Din
14-11x12-0

28'-6"

Family
14-11x15-6
vaulted clg

Up

MBr
12-8x14-1

First Floor
924 sq. ft.

Covered Porch depth 7-0

Brick And Siding Enhance This Traditional Home

1,170 total square feet of living area

Price Code AA

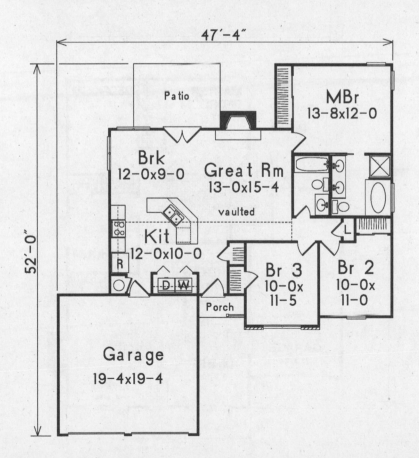

47'-4"

52'-0"

Patio

Brk
12-0x9-0

Great Rm
13-0x15-4
vaulted

Kit
12-0x10-0

MBr
13-8x12-0

Br 3
10-0x
11-5

Br 2
10-0x
11-0

Porch

Garage
19-4x19-4

D W

R

L

670

Special features

- Master bedroom enjoys privacy at the rear of this home
- Kitchen has angled bar that overlooks great room and breakfast area
- Living areas combine to create a greater sense of spaciousness
- Great room has a cozy fireplace
- 3 bedrooms, 2 baths, 2-car garage
- Slab foundation

TO ORDER BLUEPRINTS USE THE FORM ON PAGE 15 OR CALL TOLL-FREE 1-877-671-6036
View thousands more home plans online at www.familyhandyman.com/homeplans

97

Open Living Spaces

1,050 total square feet of living area

Price Code AA

Special features

- Master bedroom features a private bath and access outdoors onto a private patio
- A vaulted ceiling in the living and dining areas creates a feeling of spaciousness
- Laundry closet is convenient to all bedrooms
- Efficient U-shaped kitchen
- 3 bedrooms, 2 baths, 1-car garage
- Basement or slab foundation, please specify when ordering

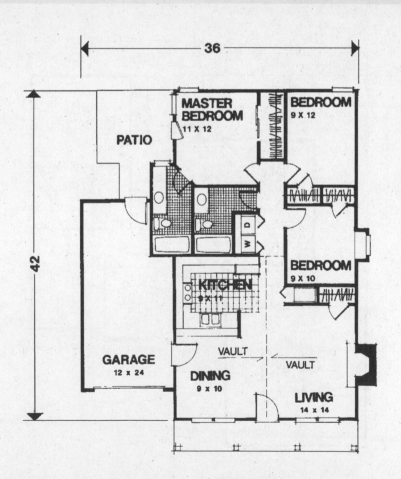

Bay Window Graces Luxury Master Bedroom

1,668 total square feet of living area

Price Code C

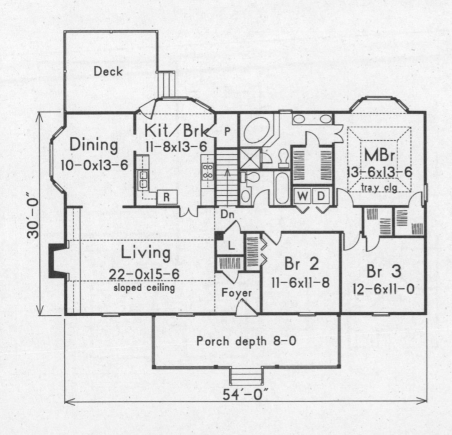

Deck

Dining
10-0x13-6

Kit/Brk
11-8x13-6

P

MBr
13-6x13-6
tray clg

W D

Dn

30'-0"

Living
22-0x15-6
sloped ceiling

L

Br 2
11-6x11-8

Br 3
12-6x11-0

Foyer

Porch depth 8-0

54'-0"

Special features

- Large bay windows in breakfast area, master bedroom and dining room

- Extensive walk-in closets and storage spaces throughout the home

- Handy entry covered porch

- Large living room has fireplace, built-in bookshelves and sloped ceiling

- 3 bedrooms, 2 baths, 2-car drive under garage

- Basement foundation

TO ORDER BLUEPRINTS USE THE FORM ON PAGE 15 OR CALL TOLL-FREE 1-877-671-6036
View thousands more home plans online at www.familyhandyman.com/homeplans

99

Unforgettable Details Throughout

2,173 total square feet of living area

Price Code D

Special features

- Enormous family room off kitchen has a fireplace surrounded by media shelves for state-of-the-art living

- The master bath has double walk-in closets as well as an oversized shower and whirlpool tub

- An arched entry graces the formal dining room

- 3 bedrooms, 2 1/2 baths, 3-car side entry garage

- Slab foundation

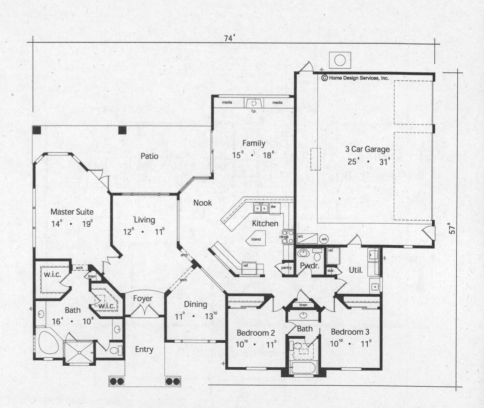

Great Traffic Flow On Both Floors

2,461 total square feet of living area

Price Code D

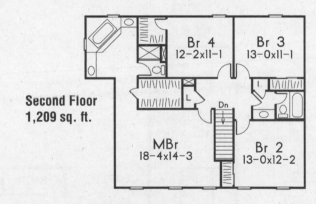

Second Floor
1,209 sq. ft.

Br 4
12-2x11-1

Br 3
13-0x11-1

L

Dn

MBr
18-4x14-3

Br 2
13-0x12-2

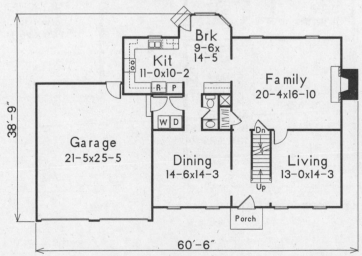

Brk
9-6x
14-5

Kit
11-0x10-2

R P

Family
20-4x16-10

W D

38'-9"

Garage
21-5x25-5

Dining
14-6x14-3

Dn

Up

Living
13-0x14-3

Porch

60'-6"

First Floor
1,252 sq. ft.

Special features

- Unique corner tub, double vanities and walk-in closet enhance the large master bedroom

- Fireplace provides focus in the spacious family room

- Centrally located half bath for guests

- 4 bedrooms, 2 1/2 baths, 2-car garage

- Basement foundation, drawings also include slab and crawl space foundations

TO ORDER BLUEPRINTS USE THE FORM ON PAGE 15 OR CALL TOLL-FREE 1-877-671-6036
View thousands more home plans online at www.familyhandyman.com/homeplans

101

Extra Large Porches

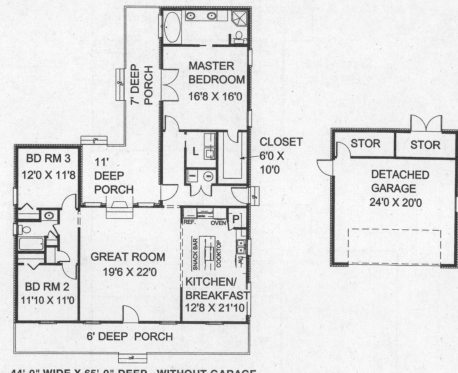

1,716 total square feet of living area

Price Code B

Special features

- Great room boasts a fireplace and access to the kitchen/ breakfast area through a large arched opening

- Master bedroom includes a huge walk-in closet and French doors that lead onto an L-shaped porch

- Bedrooms #2 and #3 share a bath and linen closet

- 3 bedrooms, 2 baths, 2-car detached garage

- Crawl space or slab foundation, please specify when ordering

7' DEEP PORCH

MASTER BEDROOM
16'8 X 16'0

CLOSET
6'0 X
10'0

BD RM 3
12'0 X 11'8

11'
DEEP
PORCH

L

REF.   OVEN   P

GREAT ROOM
19'6 X 22'0

SNACK BAR   COOKTOP

BD RM 2
11'10 X 11'0

KITCHEN/
BREAKFAST
12'8 X 21'10

6' DEEP PORCH

44'-0" WIDE X 65'-0" DEEP - WITHOUT GARAGE

STOR   STOR

DETACHED
GARAGE
24'0 X 20'0

102

TO ORDER BLUEPRINTS USE THE FORM ON PAGE 15 OR CALL TOLL-FREE 1-877-671-6036
View thousands more home plans online at www.familyhandyman.com/homeplans

Charming House, Spacious And Functional

2,505 total square feet of living area

Price Code D

Second Floor
1,069 sq. ft.

Br 2
12-6x11-6

MBr
12-9x18-0

Dn

L

Br 3
12-9x12-0

open to below

Special features

- The garage features extra storage area and ample work space

- Laundry room accessible from the garage and the outdoors

- Deluxe raised tub and immense walk-in closet grace master bath

- 3 bedrooms, 2 1/2 baths, 2-car side entry garage

- Basement foundation, drawings also include crawl space foundation

70'-0"

40'-0"

Patio

Storage
13-6x10-6

D
W

Kitchen
15-0x
14-8

Brk
9-0x
14-8

P
R

sloped clg

Family
20-6x14-8

Garage
23-4x25-0

Dining
12-9x14-2

Dn

Up

Foyer

Living
12-9x14-2

Porch depth 6-0

First Floor
1,436 sq. ft.

TO ORDER BLUEPRINTS USE THE FORM ON PAGE 15 OR CALL TOLL-FREE 1-877-671-6036
View thousands more home plans online at www.familyhandyman.com/homeplans

103

Great Views At Rear Of Home

2,197 total square feet of living area

Price Code C

Special features

- Centrally located great room opens to kitchen, breakfast nook and private backyard
- Den located off entry ideal for home office
- Vaulted master bath has spa tub, shower and double vanity
- 3 bedrooms, 2 1/2 baths, 3-car garage
- Crawl space foundation

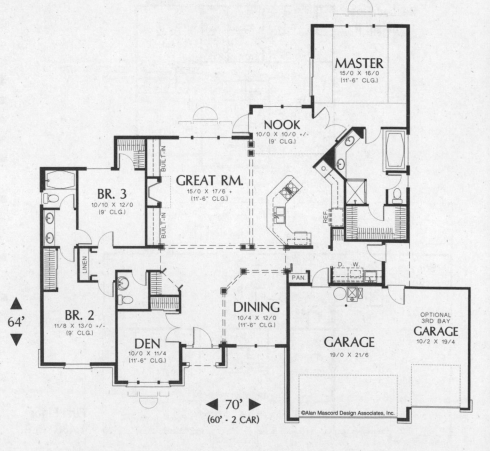

TO ORDER BLUEPRINTS USE THE FORM ON PAGE 15 OR CALL TOLL-FREE 1-877-671-6036
View thousands more home plans online at www.familyhandyman.com/homeplans

Charming Ranch With Room To Expand

2,036 total square feet of living area

Price Code C

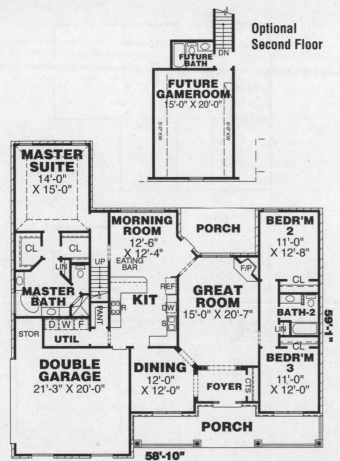

Optional Second Floor

FUTURE BATH

FUTURE GAMEROOM
15'-0" X 20'-0"

5'-0" KW

6'-8" KW

DN

MASTER SUITE
14'-0"
X 15'-0"

CL   CL

LIN

UP

MORNING ROOM
12'-6"
X 12'-4"

PORCH

BEDR'M 2
11'-0"
X 12'-8"

F/P

MASTER BATH

EATING BAR

REF

KIT

DW

S

GREAT ROOM
15'-0" X 20'-7"

CL

BATH-2

LIN

D W F

PANT

59'-1"

STOR

UTIL

CL

BEDR'M 3
11'-0"
X 12'-0"

DOUBLE GARAGE
21'-3" X 20'-0"

DINING
12'-0"
X 12'-0"

FOYER

CTS

PORCH

First Floor
2,036 sq. ft.

58'-10"

Special features

- Corner fireplace in great room adds warmth and style
- A bright and cheerful morning room is a lovely place to start the day
- Secluded master suite has an impressive bath with a whirlpool tub perfect for an escape
- Future gameroom on the second floor has an additional 370 square feet of living area
- 3 bedrooms, 2 baths, 2-car side entry garage
- Slab foundation

TO ORDER BLUEPRINTS USE THE FORM ON PAGE 15 OR CALL TOLL-FREE 1-877-671-6036
View thousands more home plans online at www.familyhandyman.com/homeplans

105

Impressive Two-Story Entry Boasts Popular T-Stair

2,336 total square feet of living area

Price Code D

Special features

- Stately sunken living room with partially vaulted ceiling and classic arched transom windows
- Family room features plenty of windows and a fireplace with flanking bookshelves
- 4 bedrooms, 2 1/2 baths, 2-car garage
- Basement foundation

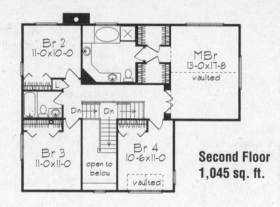

Br 2
11-0x10-0

MBr
13-0x17-8
vaulted

Dn   Dn

Br 3
11-0x11-0

Br 4
10-6x11-0

open to below

vaulted

**Second Floor
1,045 sq. ft.**

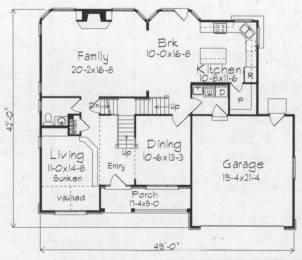

Family
20-2x16-8

Brk
10-0x16-8

Kitchen
10-8x11-6

Dn   Up

W D

P

R

Living
11-0x14-8
Sunken

vaulted

Up

Entry

Dining
10-6x13-3

Garage
19-4x21-4

Porch
17-4x5-0

42'-0"

49'-0"

**First Floor
1,291 sq. ft.**

Full-Length Front Porch

1,500 total square feet of living area

Price Code B

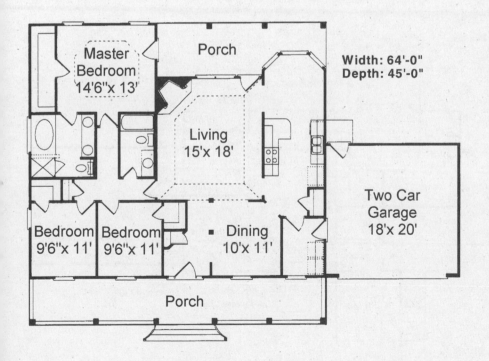

Width: 64'-0"
Depth: 45'-0"

Master Bedroom 14'6"x 13'

Porch

Living 15'x 18'

Two Car Garage 18'x 20'

Bedroom 9'6"x 11'

Bedroom 9'6"x 11'

Dining 10'x 11'

Porch

Special features

- Living room features corner fireplace adding warmth
- Master suite has all the amenities like walk-in closet, private bath and porch access
- Sunny bayed breakfast room is cheerful and bright
- 3 bedrooms, 2 baths, 2-car garage
- Slab foundation

Country Ranch With Open Interior

1,783 total square feet of living area

Price Code D

Special features

- The front to rear flow of the great room, with built-ins on one side is a furnishing delight

- Bedrooms are all quietly zoned on one side

- The master bedroom is separated for privacy

- Every bedroom features walk-in closets

- 3 bedrooms, 2 baths, 2-car side entry garage

- Basement, crawl space or slab foundation, please specify when ordering

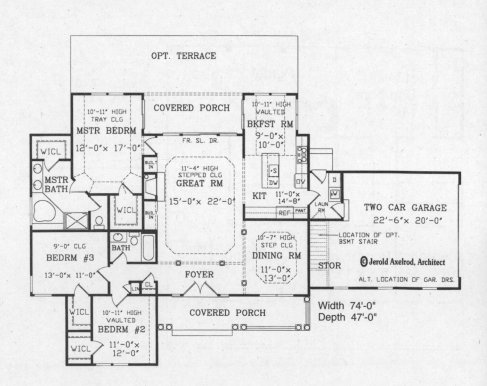

Expansive Dining Area Ideal For Entertaining

1,381 total square feet of living area

Price Code A

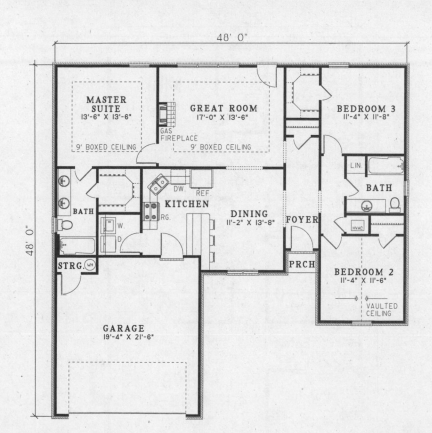

Special features

- Plenty of closet space in all bedrooms
- Kitchen has large eating bar for extra dining
- Great room has a sunny wall of windows creating a cheerful atmosphere
- 3 bedrooms, 2 baths, 2-car garage
- Slab, crawl space, walk-out basement or basement foundation, please specify when ordering

Three Bedroom Luxury In A Small Home

1,161 total square feet of living area

Price Code AA

Special features

- Brickwork and feature window add elegance to home for a narrow lot

- Living room enjoys a vaulted ceiling, fireplace and opens to kitchen area

- U-shaped kitchen offers a breakfast area with bay window, snack bar and built-in pantry

- 3 bedrooms, 2 baths

- Basement foundation

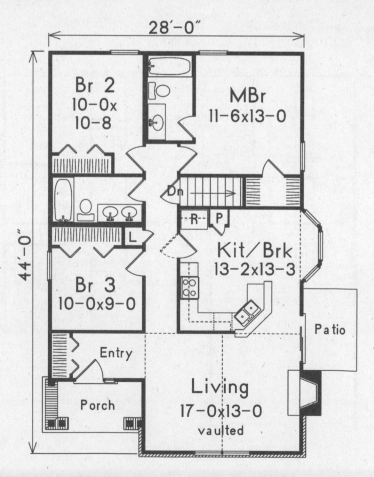

Lovely Victorian Is Ideal For A Narrow Lot

1,494 total square feet of living area

Price Code A

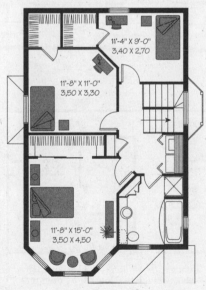

Second Floor
735 sq. ft.

11'-4" X 9'-0"
3,40 X 2,70

11'-8" X 11'-0"
3,50 X 3,30

11'-8" X 15'-0"
3,50 X 4,50

36'-0"
10,8 m

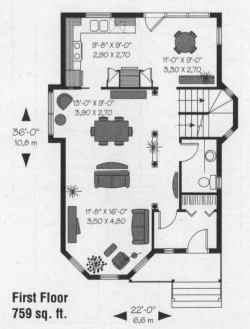

9'-8" X 9'-0"
2,90 X 2,70

11'-0" X 9'-0"
3,30 X 2,70

13'-0" X 9'-0"
3,90 X 2,70

11'-8" X 16'-0"
3,50 X 4,80

First Floor
759 sq. ft.

22'-0"
6,6 m

Special features

- Energy efficient home with 2" x 6" exterior walls
- Bay window adds excitement to living area
- Efficiently designed kitchen has plenty of storage
- Separate entry hall with closet is a nice feature
- 3 bedrooms, 1 1/2 baths
- Basement foundation

TO ORDER BLUEPRINTS USE THE FORM ON PAGE 15 OR CALL TOLL-FREE 1-877-671-6036
View thousands more home plans online at www.familyhandyman.com/homeplans

111

A Cozy Ranch With Rustic Touches

© 2003, Garrell Associates, Inc.

2,272 total square feet of living area

Price Code G

Special features

- 10' ceilings throughout first floor and 9' ceilings on the second floor
- Lots of storage area on the second floor
- First floor master bedroom has a lovely sitting area with arched entry
- Second floor bedrooms share a jack and jill bath
- 3 bedrooms, 2 1/2 baths, 2-car rear entry garage
- Slab foundation

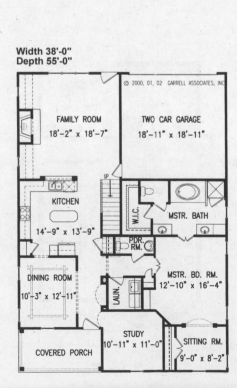

Width 38'-0"
Depth 55'-0"

© 2000, 01, 02 GARRELL ASSOCIATES, INC

FAMILY ROOM
18'-2" x 18'-7"

TWO CAR GARAGE
18'-11" x 18'-11"

KITCHEN
14'-9" x 13'-9"

UP

W.I.C.

MSTR. BATH

PDR. RM.

DINING ROOM
10'-3" x 12'-11"

LAUN.

MSTR. BD. RM.
12'-10" x 16'-4"

STUDY
10'-11" x 11'-0"

SITTING RM.
9'-0" x 8'-2"

COVERED PORCH

**First Floor
1,587 sq. ft.**

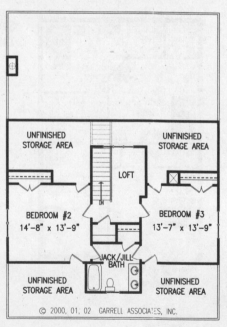

UNFINISHED STORAGE AREA

UNFINISHED STORAGE AREA

LOFT

BEDROOM #2
14'-8" x 13'-9"

BEDROOM #3
13'-7" x 13'-9"

JACK/JILL BATH

UNFINISHED STORAGE AREA

UNFINISHED STORAGE AREA

© 2000, 01, 02 GARRELL ASSOCIATES, INC.

**Second Floor
685 sq. ft.**

TO ORDER BLUEPRINTS USE THE FORM ON PAGE 15 OR CALL TOLL-FREE 1-877-671-6036

View thousands more home plans online at www.familyhandyman.com/homeplans

Country Charm With Dormers And Covered Porch

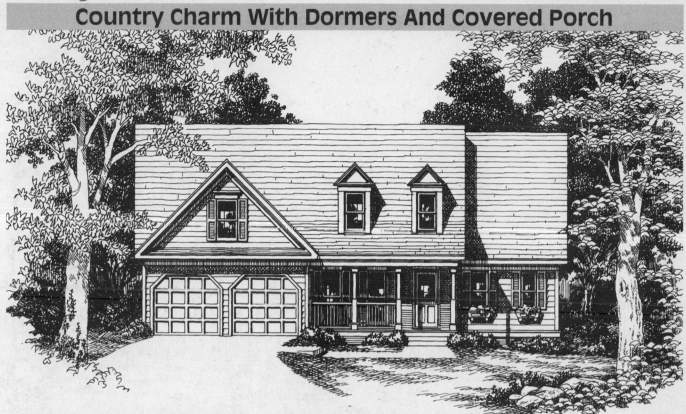

1,497 total square feet of living area

Price Code A

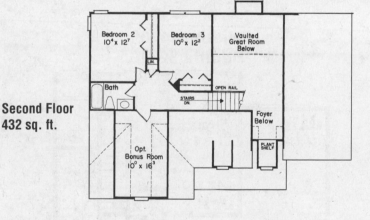

**Second Floor
432 sq. ft.**

Bedroom 2
10⁴ x 12⁷

Bedroom 3
10⁰ x 12²

Vaulted
Great Room
Below

Bath

OPEN RAIL

STAIRS DN.

Foyer
Below

PLANT SHELF

Opt. Bonus Room
10⁰ x 16³

Special features

- Master suite has private luxurious bath with spacious walk-in closet

- Formal dining room has tray ceiling and views onto front covered porch

- Bonus room on second floor has an additional 175 square feet of living area

- 3 bedrooms, 2 1/2 baths, 2-car garage

- Crawl space or walk-out basement foundation, please specify when ordering

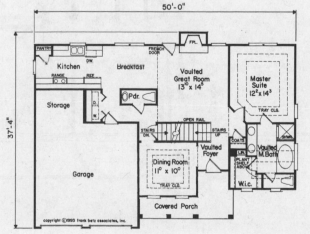

**First Floor
1,065 sq. ft.**

50'-0"

37'-4"

PANTRY

Kitchen

Breakfast

FRENCH DOOR

FPL

Vaulted
Great Room
13¹⁰ x 14⁵

Master
Suite
12² x 14³

TRAY CLG.

RANGE REF

Storage

Pdr.

STAIRS DN.

OPEN RAIL

STAIRS UP

COATS

Vaulted
M. Bath

Vaulted
Foyer

Garage

Dining Room
11⁰ x 10⁰

TRAY CLG.

PLANT SHELF ABOVE

W.i.c.

Covered Porch

copyright ©1993 frank betz associates, inc.

Easy-To-Build Plan

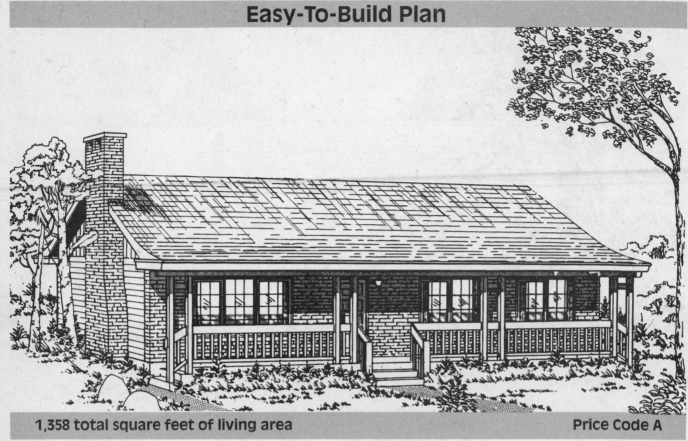

1,358 total square feet of living area

Price Code A

Special features

- Energy efficient home with 2" x 6" exterior walls
- Covered verandah invites outdoor relaxation
- Living room is warmed by masonry fireplace
- 3 bedrooms, 2 baths
- Basement or crawl space foundation, please specify when ordering

Width: 44'-0"
Depth: 32'-10"

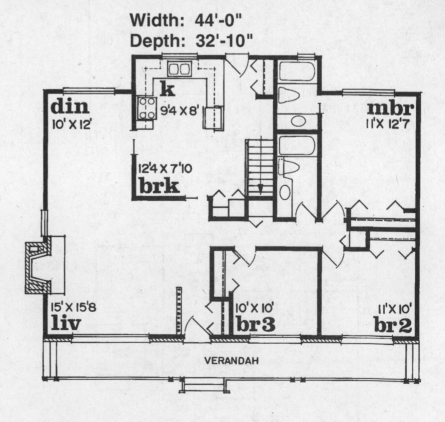

Gabled, Covered Front Porch

1,320 total square feet of living area   **Price Code A**

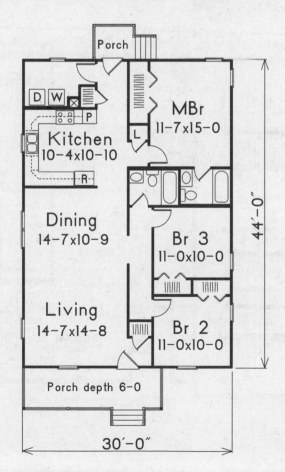

Special features

- Functional U-shaped kitchen features pantry
- Large living and dining areas join to create an open atmosphere
- Secluded master bedroom includes private full bath
- Covered front porch opens into large living area with convenient coat closet
- Utility/laundry room located near the kitchen
- 3 bedrooms, 2 baths
- Crawl space foundation

Plan #705-CHD-11-27

Lovely Ranch Home

1,123 total square feet of living area

Price Code AA

Special features

- Eating bar in kitchen extends dining area
- Dining area and great room flow together creating a sense of spaciousness
- Master suite has privacy from other bedrooms as well as a private bath
- Utility room is conveniently located near kitchen
- 3 bedrooms, 2 baths
- Crawl space or slab foundation, please specify when ordering

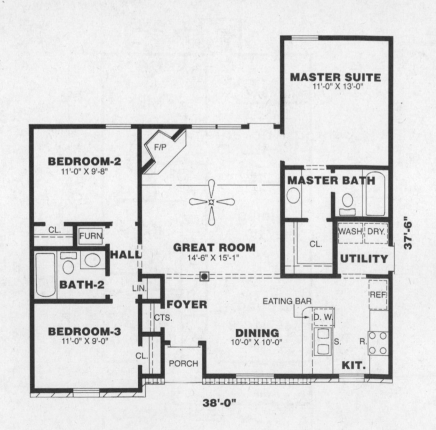

Plan #705-DBI-24035-9P

Central Laundry Area For Convenience

1,395 total square feet of living area

Price Code A

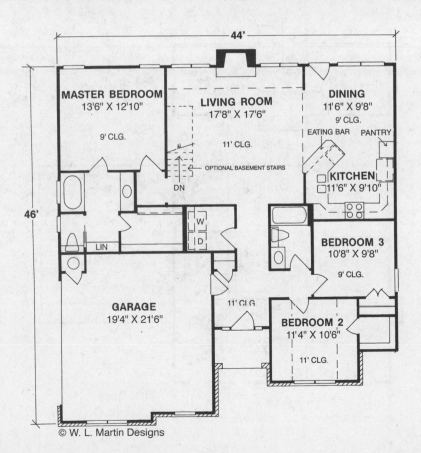

Floor plan measurements:
- Overall width: 44'
- Overall depth: 46'
- MASTER BEDROOM 13'6" X 12'10" — 9' CLG.
- LIVING ROOM 17'8" X 17'6" — 11' CLG.
- DINING 11'6" X 9'8" — 9' CLG.
- EATING BAR / PANTRY
- KITCHEN 11'6" X 9'10"
- OPTIONAL BASEMENT STAIRS — DN
- LIN
- W/D
- BEDROOM 3 10'8" X 9'8" — 9' CLG.
- BEDROOM 2 11'4" X 10'6" — 11' CLG.
- GARAGE 19'4" X 21'6"
- 11' CLG

© W. L. Martin Designs

Special features

- Dining area and kitchen separated by an angled eating bar
- 11' ceilings in entry and living room create openness
- 3 bedrooms, 2 baths, 2-car side entry garage
- Basement foundation

Plan #705-0291

Roomy Two-Story Has Screened-In Rear Porch

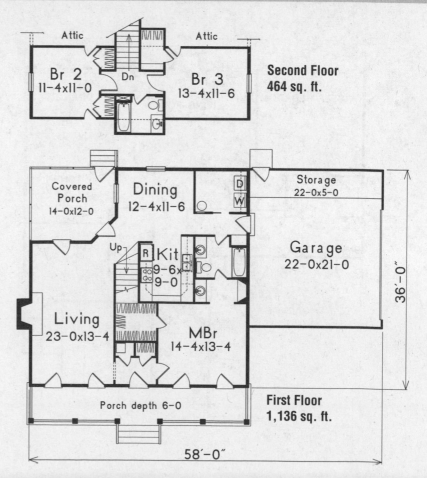

1,600 total square feet of living area

Price Code B

Special features

- Energy efficient home with 2" x 6" exterior walls

- First floor master suite accessible from two points of entry

- Master suite dressing area includes separate vanities and a mirrored make-up counter

- Second floor bedrooms with generous storage, share a full bath

- 3 bedrooms, 2 baths, 2-car side entry garage

- Crawl space foundation, drawings also include slab foundation

Attic

Br 2
11-4x11-0

Dn

Br 3
13-4x11-6

Attic

Second Floor
464 sq. ft.

Covered Porch
14-0x12-0

Dining
12-4x11-6

Storage
22-0x5-0

Up

Kit
9-6x 9-0

Garage
22-0x21-0

Living
23-0x13-4

MBr
14-4x13-4

36'-0"

Porch depth 6-0

First Floor
1,136 sq. ft.

58'-0"

Vaulted Ceilings Add Dimension

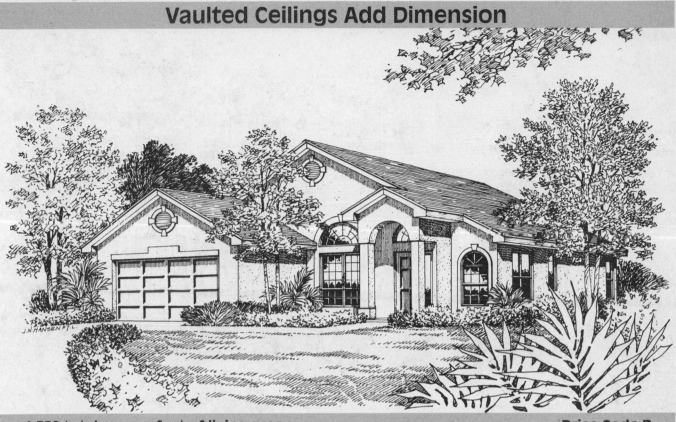

1,550 total square feet of living area

Price Code B

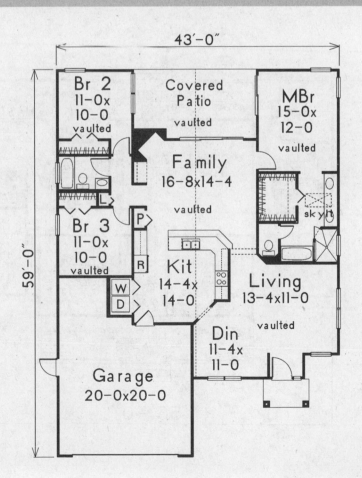

43'-0"

59'-0"

Br 2
11-0x
10-0
vaulted

Covered Patio
vaulted

MBr
15-0x
12-0
vaulted

Family
16-8x14-4
vaulted

sky lt

Br 3
11-0x
10-0
vaulted

Kit
14-4x
14-0

Living
13-4x11-0
vaulted

Din
11-4x
11-0

Garage
20-0x20-0

P
R
W
D

Special features

- Cozy corner fireplace provides focal point in family room
- Master bedroom features large walk-in closet, skylight and separate tub and shower
- Convenient laundry closet
- Kitchen with pantry and break-fast bar connects to family room
- Family room and master bedroom access covered patio
- 3 bedrooms, 2 baths, 2-car garage
- Slab foundation

Traditional Southern Style Home

1,785 total square feet of living area

Price Code B

Special features

- 9' ceilings throughout home
- Luxurious master bath includes whirlpool tub and separate shower
- Cozy breakfast area is convenient to kitchen
- 3 bedrooms, 3 baths, 2-car detached garage
- Basement, crawl space or slab foundation, please specify when ordering

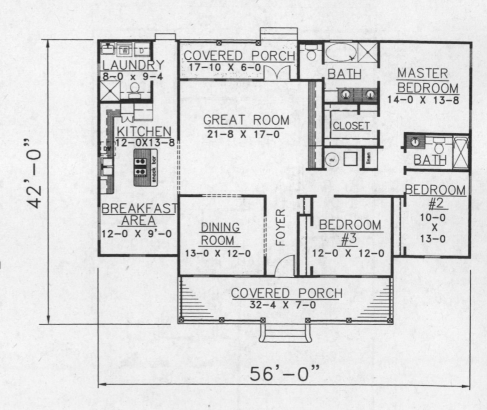

TO ORDER BLUEPRINTS USE THE FORM ON PAGE 15 OR CALL TOLL-FREE 1-877-671-6036
View thousands more home plans online at www.familyhandyman.com/homeplans

Impressive Corner Fireplace   Plan #705-0253

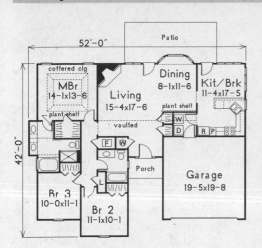

1,458 total square feet of living area   Price Code A

Special features

- Convenient snack bar joins kitchen with breakfast room
- Large living room has fireplace, plenty of windows, vaulted ceiling and nearby plant shelf
- Master bedroom offers a private bath with vaulted ceiling, walk-in closet, plant shelf and coffered ceiling
- Corner windows provide abundant light in breakfast room
- 3 bedrooms, 2 baths, 2-car garage
- Crawl space foundation, drawings also include slab foundation

Half-Round Highlights   Plan #705-0280

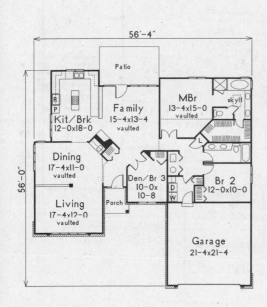

1,847 total square feet of living area   Price Code C

Special features

- Kitchen includes island cooktop and sunny breakfast area
- Master suite features vaulted ceilings and skylighted bath with large tub, separate shower and walk-in closet
- Service bar eases entertaining in vaulted dining and living rooms
- Family room, complete with corner fireplace, accesses outdoor patio
- 3 bedrooms, 2 baths, 2-car garage
- Slab foundation

Plan #705-CHD-23-10

Stucco Adds Excitement To This Traditional Ranch

2,350 total square feet of living area

Price Code D

Special features

- Luxurious master suite with large bath and enormous walk-in closet

- Built-in hutch in breakfast room is eye-catching

- Terrific study located in its own private hall with half bath includes two closets and a bookcase

- 3 bedrooms, 2 1/2 baths, 2-car side entry garage

- Walk-out basement, crawl space or slab foundation, please specify when ordering

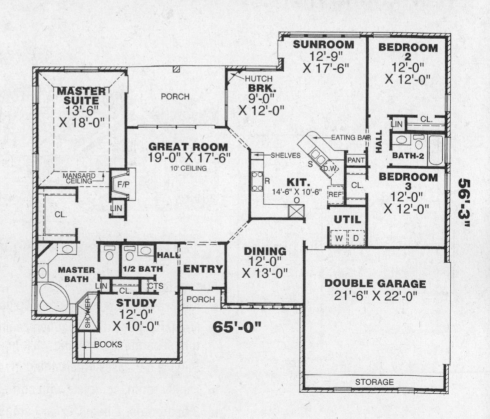

Atrium Living For Views On A Narrow Lot

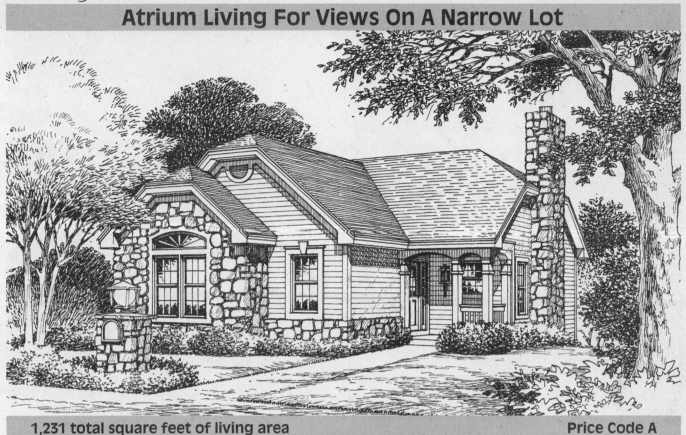

1,231 total square feet of living area

Price Code A

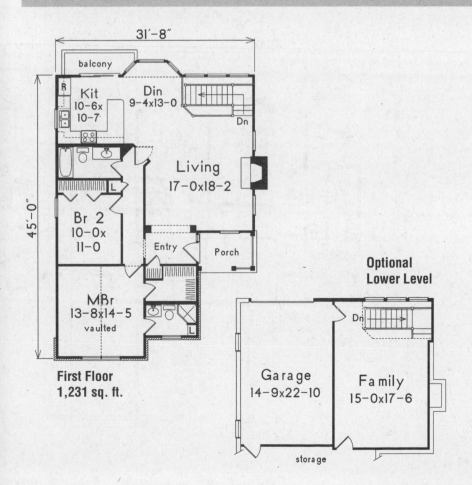

First Floor
1,231 sq. ft.

31'-8"

balcony

Kit
10-6x
10-7

Din
9-4x13-0

Dn

Living
17-0x18-2

Br 2
10-0x
11-0

Entry

Porch

MBr
13-8x14-5
vaulted

45'-0"

**Optional
Lower Level**

Dn

Garage
14-9x22-10

Family
15-0x17-6

storage

Special features

- Dutch gables and stone accents provide an enchanting appearance for a small cottage
- The spacious living room offers a masonry fireplace, atrium with window wall and is open to a dining area with bay window
- A breakfast counter, lots of cabinet space and glass sliding doors to a walk-out balcony create a sensational kitchen
- 380 square feet of optional living area available on the lower level
- 2 bedrooms, 2 baths, 1-car drive under garage
- Walk-out basement foundation

Ranch-Style Home With Many Extras

1,295 total square feet of living area

Price Code A

Special features

- Wrap-around porch is a lovely place for dining

- A fireplace gives a stunning focal point to the great room that is heightened with a sloped ceiling

- The master suite is full of luxurious touches such as a walk-in closet and a lush private bath

- 2 bedrooms, 2 baths, 2-car garage

- Basement foundation

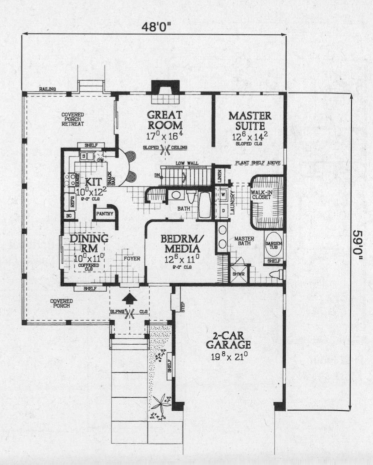

TO ORDER BLUEPRINTS USE THE FORM ON PAGE 15 OR CALL TOLL-FREE 1-877-671-6036
View thousands more home plans online at www.familyhandyman.com/homeplans

Dormers And Stone Veneer Add Exterior Appeal

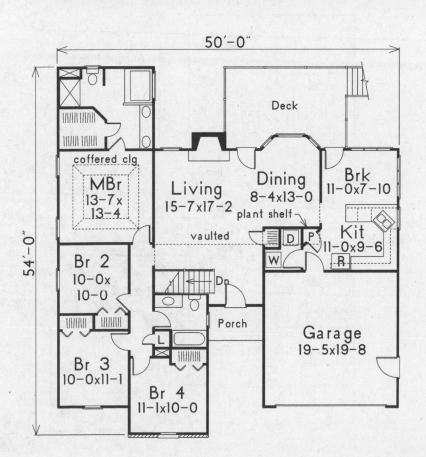

1,609 total square feet of living area   **Price Code B**

Deck

MBr
13-7 x
13-4

coffered clg

Living
15-7x17-2

vaulted

plant shelf

Dining
8-4x13-0

Brk
11-0x7-10

Kit
11-0x9-6

D P

W R

Br 2
10-0x
10-0

Dn

Porch

L

Br 3
10-0x11-1

Br 4
11-1x10-0

Garage
19-5x19-8

50'-0"

54'-0"

Special features

- Efficient kitchen with corner pantry and adjacent laundry room

- Breakfast room boasts plenty of windows and opens onto rear deck

- Master bedroom features tray ceiling and private deluxe bath

- Entry opens into large living area with fireplace

- 4 bedrooms, 2 baths, 2-car garage

- Basement foundation

Compact Design Offers Privacy

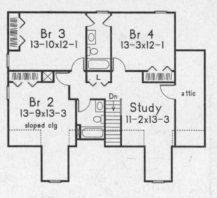

2,847 total square feet of living area

Price Code E

Second Floor
1,102 sq. ft.

Br 3
13-10x12-1

Br 4
13-3x12-1

Br 2
13-9x13-3
sloped clg

Study
11-2x13-3

attic

Dn

L

Special features

- Secluded first floor master bedroom includes an oversized window and a large walk-in closet

- Extensive attic storage and closet space

- Spacious second floor bedrooms, two of which share a private bath

- Great starter home with option to finish the second floor as needed

- 4 bedrooms, 3 1/2 baths, 2-car garage

- Basement foundation, drawings also include slab and crawl space foundations

First Floor
1,745 sq. ft.

MBr
16-2x12-1

Family
18-5x12-5

Patio

Kit
12-5x13-8

Brk
10-10x13-8

Bar

Living
16-4x12-1

Dining
11-2x13-5

Foyer

Up

Dn

Garage
22-8x23-4

W
D

P

R

Porch depth 8-0

46'-0"

65'-0"

Plan #705-0265

Economical Ranch For Easy Living

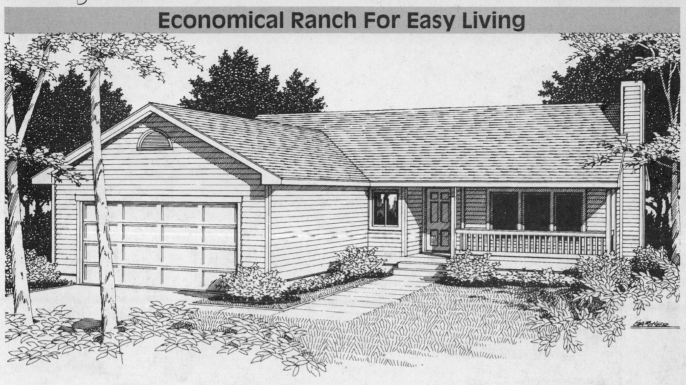

1,314 total square feet of living area　　　　**Price Code A**

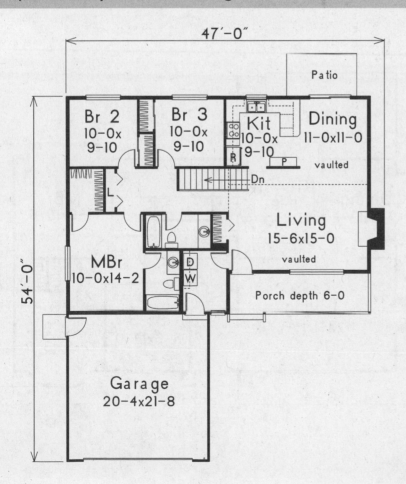

Special features

- Energy efficient home with 2" x 6" exterior walls
- Covered porch adds immediate appeal and welcoming charm
- Open floor plan combined with vaulted ceiling offers spacious living
- Functional kitchen complete with pantry and eating bar
- Cozy fireplace in the living room
- Private master bedroom features a large walk-in closet and bath
- 3 bedrooms, 2 baths, 2-car garage
- Basement foundation

Balance Of Style And Functional Design

1,698 total square feet of living area

Price Code B

Special features

- Kitchen includes walk-in pantry and corner sink that faces living area

- Breakfast room highlighted by expanse of windows and access to sun deck

- Recessed foyer opens into vaulted living room with fireplace

- Master suite features private bath with large walk-in closet

- 3 bedrooms, 2 baths, 2-car drive under garage

- Basement foundation

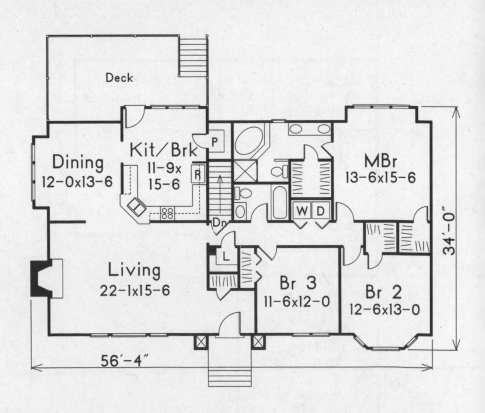

Deck

Dining
12-0x13-6

Kit/Brk
11-9x
15-6

MBr
13-6x15-6

34'-0"

Living
22-1x15-6

Br 3
11-6x12-0

Br 2
12-6x13-0

56'-4"

Home For Narrow Lot Offers Wide Open Spaces

I.N. HANSEN S.D.G.

1,492 total square feet of living area

Price Code A

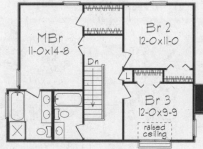

**Second Floor
732 sq. ft.**

MBr
11-0x14-8

Br 2
12-0x11-0

Dn

Br 3
12-0x9-9

raised ceiling

35'-0"

Deck

Brk
9-0x11-0

Kit

Dining
12-0x9-4

10-9x14-6

Dn

P

L

Living
15-8x14-0

Up

47'-8'

Porch

Garage
19-4x21-4

**First Floor
760 sq. ft.**

Special features

- Cleverly angled entry spills into living and dining rooms which share warmth of fireplace flanked by arched windows

- Master suite includes double-door entry, huge walk-in closet, shower and bath with picture window

- Stucco and dutch hipped roofs add warmth and charm to facade

- 3 bedrooms, 2 1/2 baths, 2-car garage

- Basement foundation

Compact Home Maximizes Space

Plan #705-0495

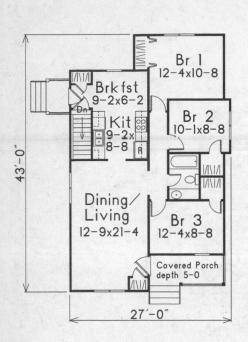

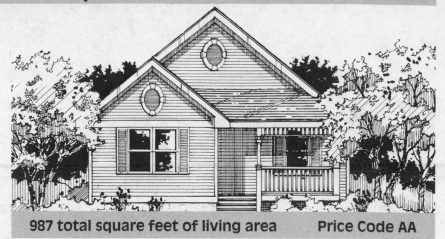

987 total square feet of living area   **Price Code AA**

Special features

- Galley kitchen opens into cozy breakfast room
- Convenient coat closets located by both entrances
- Dining/living room combined for expansive open area
- Breakfast room has access to the outdoors
- Front porch great for enjoying outdoor living
- 3 bedrooms, 1 bath
- Basement foundation

Enchanting Country Cottage

Plan #705-0477

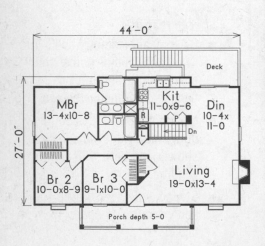

1,140 total square feet of living area   **Price Code AA**

Special features

- Open and spacious living and dining areas for family gatherings
- Well-organized kitchen with an abundance of cabinetry and a built-in pantry
- Roomy master bath features double-bowl vanity
- 3 bedrooms, 2 baths, 2-car drive under garage
- Basement foundation

TO ORDER BLUEPRINTS USE THE FORM ON PAGE 15 OR CALL TOLL-FREE 1-877-671-6036
View thousands more home plans online at www.familyhandyman.com/homeplans

Sunny Dining Room

1,735 total square feet of living area

Price Code B

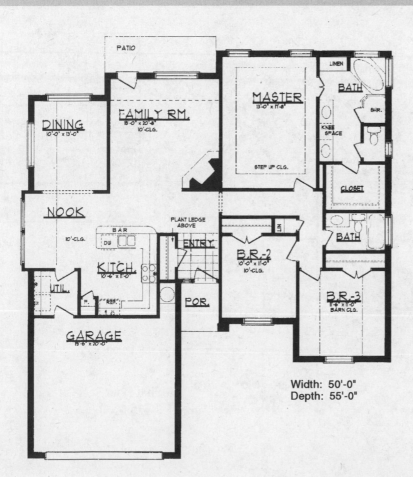

PATIO

DINING
10'-0" x 13'-0"

FAMILY RM.
13'-0" x 20'-8"
10'-CLG.

MASTER
13'-0" x 17'-8"

LINEN

BATH

KNEE SPACE

STEP UP CLG.

CLOSET

NOOK

10'-CLG.

PLANT LEDGE ABOVE

BAR

DW

ENTRY

B.R.-2
10'-0" x 11'-0"
10'-CLG.

BATH

KITCH.
10'-6" x 11'-0"

REF.

POR.

B.R.-3
11'-8" x 11'-0"
BARN CLG.

UTIL.

GARAGE
19'-6" x 20'-0"

Width: 50'-0"
Depth: 55'-0"

Special features

- Luxurious master bath has spa tub, shower, double vanity and large walk-in closet
- Peninsula in kitchen has sink and dishwasher
- Massive master bedroom has step up ceiling and private location
- 3 bedrooms, 2 baths, 2-car garage
- Slab foundation

Inviting Double French Doors

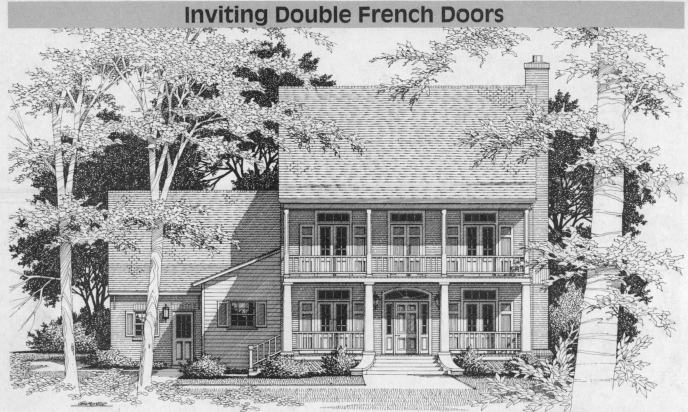

2,327 total square feet of living area

Price Code D

Special features

- 9' ceilings throughout
- Covered porches on both floors create outside living space
- Secondary bedrooms share full bath
- L-shaped kitchen features island cooktop and convenient laundry room
- 3 bedrooms, 2 1/2 baths, 2-car side entry garage
- Basement foundation

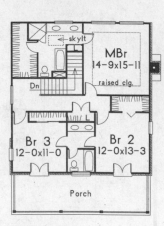

Second Floor
1,011 sq. ft.

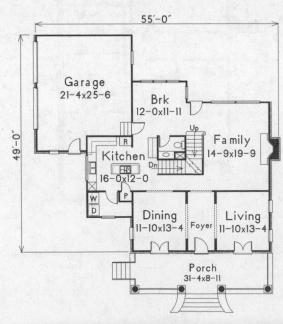

First Floor
1,316 sq. ft.

Double Gables Accent Facade

© COPYRIGHT MCMXCVI · RALPH JONES

1,497 total square feet of living area

Price Code A

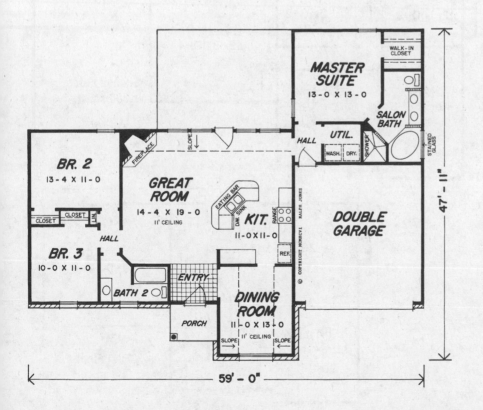

BR. 2
13-4 X 11-0

GREAT ROOM
14-4 X 19-0
11' CEILING

BR. 3
10-0 X 11-0

HALL

BATH 2

ENTRY

PORCH

DINING ROOM
11-0 X 13-0
11' CEILING

KIT.
11-0 X 11-0

EATING BAR

DOUBLE GARAGE

MASTER SUITE
13-0 X 13-0

WALK-IN CLOSET

SALON BATH

UTIL.
WASH. DRY.

HALL

SHOWER

STAINED GLASS

FIREPLACE

SLOPE

© COPYRIGHT MCMXCVI RALPH JONES

59' - 0"

47' - 11"

Special features

- Open living area with kitchen counter overlooking a cozy great room with fireplace
- Sloped ceiling accents dining room
- Master suite has privacy from other bedrooms
- 3 bedrooms, 2 baths, 2-car garage
- Slab foundation

Double Gables Create Appealing Facade

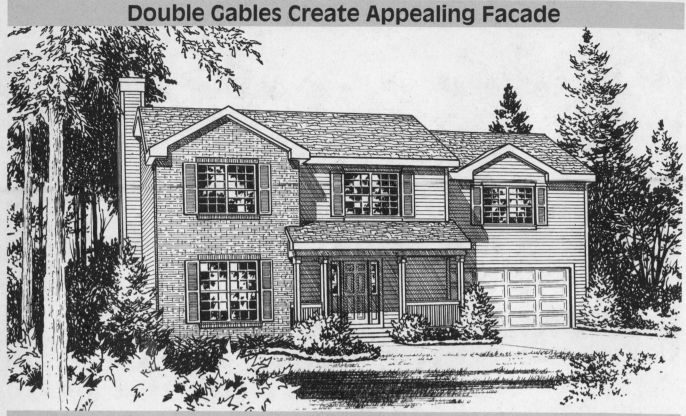

2,200 total square feet of living area

Price Code D

Special features

- Open first floor features convenient access to laundry area
- Second floor captures space above garage for large recreation area or future bedrooms
- Oversized country kitchen has plenty of space for entertaining
- 3 bedrooms, 2 1/2 baths, 2-car garage
- Basement foundation

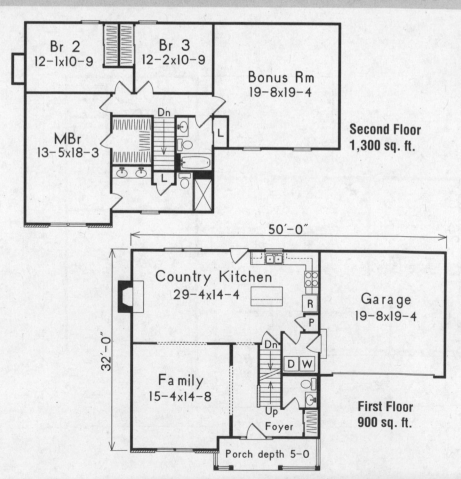

Br 2
12-1x10-9

Br 3
12-2x10-9

Bonus Rm
19-8x19-4

MBr
13-5x18-3

Dn

**Second Floor
1,300 sq. ft.**

50'-0"

Country Kitchen
29-4x14-4

Garage
19-8x19-4

R

P

32'-0"

Dn

D W

Family
15-4x14-8

Up
Foyer

**First Floor
900 sq. ft.**

Porch depth 5-0

TO ORDER BLUEPRINTS USE THE FORM ON PAGE 15 OR CALL TOLL-FREE 1-877-671-6036
View thousands more home plans online at www.familyhandyman.com/homeplans

Gables Add Style To This Ranch

988 total square feet of living area

Price Code AA

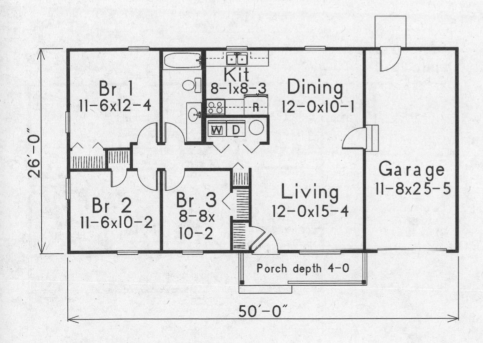

Br 1
11-6x12-4

Kit
8-1x8-3

Dining
12-0x10-1

26'-0"

Br 2
11-6x10-2

Br 3
8-8x
10-2

Living
12-0x15-4

Garage
11-8x25-5

W D R

Porch depth 4-0

50'-0"

Special features

- Pleasant covered porch entry
- The kitchen, living and dining areas are combined to maximize space
- Entry has convenient coat closet
- Laundry closet is located adjacent to bedrooms
- 3 bedrooms, 1 bath, 1-car garage
- Basement foundation, drawings also include crawl space foundation

Vaulted Ceilings Add A Sense Of Spaciousness

1,408 total square feet of living area

Price Code A

Special features

- A bright country kitchen boasts an abundance of counterspace and cupboards

- The front entry is sheltered by a broad verandah

- A spa tub is brightened by a box bay window in the master bath

- 3 bedrooms, 2 baths, 2-car side entry garage

- Basement or crawl space foundation, please specify when ordering

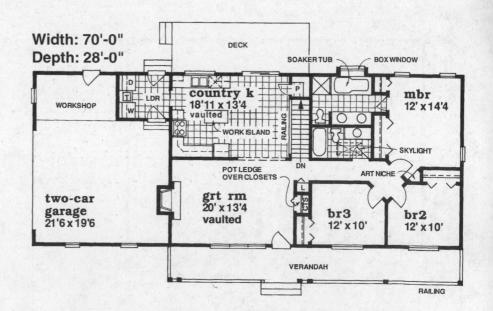

Width: 70'-0"
Depth: 28'-0"

DECK

SOAKER TUB   BOX WINDOW

WORKSHOP   LDR   **country k** 18'11 x 13'4 vaulted   P   **mbr** 12' x 14'4

D   WORK ISLAND   RAILING

T   W

SKYLIGHT

POT LEDGE OVER CLOSETS   DN   ART NICHE

two-car garage 21'6 x 19'6   **grt rm** 20' x 13'4 vaulted   **br3** 12' x 10'   **br2** 12' x 10'

VERANDAH

RAILING

Spectacular View From The Great Room

3,796 total square feet of living area

Price Code F

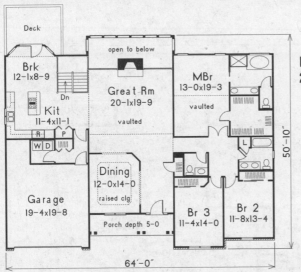

Deck

Brk
12-1x8-9

open to below

MBr
13-0x19-3
vaulted

**First Floor
2,436 sq. ft.**

Kit
11-4x11-1

Dn

Great Rm
20-1x19-9
vaulted

R   P
W D

Dining
12-0x14-0
raised clg.

Garage
19-4x19-8

Br 3
11-4x14-0

Br 2
11-8x13-4

Porch depth 5-0

50'-10"

64'-0"

L

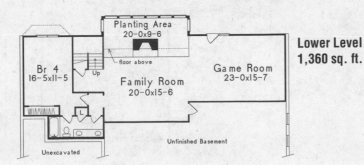

Planting Area
20-0x9-6

floor above

**Lower Level
1,360 sq. ft.**

Br 4
16-5x11-5

Up

Family Room
20-0x15-6

Game Room
23-0x15-7

L

Unexcavated

Unfinished Basement

Special features

- Entry foyer leads directly to great room with fireplace and wonderful view through wall of windows

- Kitchen/breakfast room features large island cooktop, pantry and easy access outdoors

- Master suite includes vaulted ceiling and pocket door entrance into master bath that features double-bowl vanity and large tub

- 4 bedrooms, 3 1/2 baths, 2-car garage

- Basement foundation

Bedrooms Separated From Living Areas

1,734 total square feet of living area

Price Code B

Special features

- Large entry with coffered ceiling and display niches
- Sunken great room has 10' ceiling
- Kitchen island includes eating counter
- 9' ceiling in master bedroom
- Master bath features corner tub and double sinks
- 3 bedrooms, 2 baths, 2-car garage
- Crawl space foundation

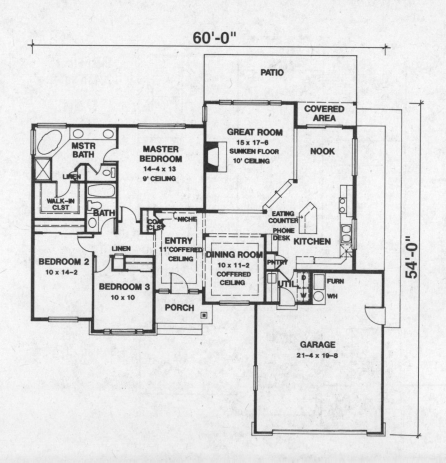

Spacious Foyer Welcomes Guests

1,593 total square feet of living area

Price Code B

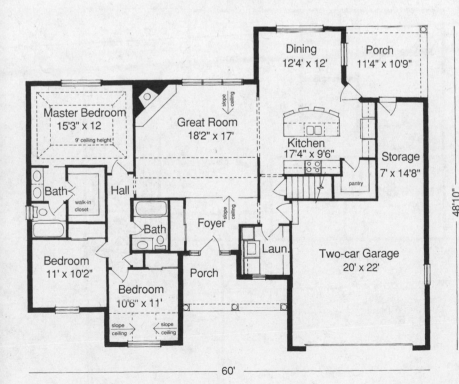

Special features

- The rear porch is a pleasant surprise and perfect for enjoying the outdoors
- Great room is filled with extras like a corner fireplace, sloping ceiling and view to the outdoors
- Separating the kitchen from the dining area is a large island with seating
- 3 bedrooms, 2 baths, 2-car garage
- Basement foundation

Rustic Styling With All The Comforts

J.N. HANSEN, D.C.

1,885 total square feet of living area

Price Code C

Special features

- Enormous covered patio
- Dining and great rooms combine to create one large and versatile living area
- Utility room directly off kitchen for convenience
- 3 bedrooms, 2 baths, 2-car side entry garage
- Basement foundation

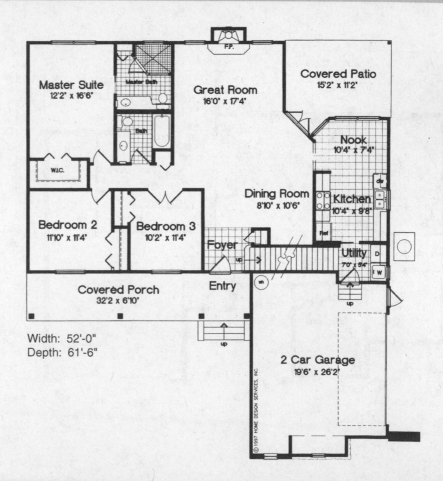

Master Suite
12'2" x 16'6"

Master Bath

Great Room
16'0" x 17'4"

Covered Patio
15'2" x 11'2"

Bath

Nook
10'4" x 7'4"

W.I.C.

Dining Room
8'10" x 10'6"

Kitchen
10'4" x 9'8"

Ref

Bedroom 2
11'10" x 11'4"

Bedroom 3
10'2" x 11'4"

Foyer

Utility
7'0" x 5'4"

up

Covered Porch
32'2" x 6'10"

Entry

Width: 52'-0"
Depth: 61'-6"

© 1997 HOME DESIGN SERVICES, INC.

2 Car Garage
19'6" x 26'2"

Serving Bar In Kitchen

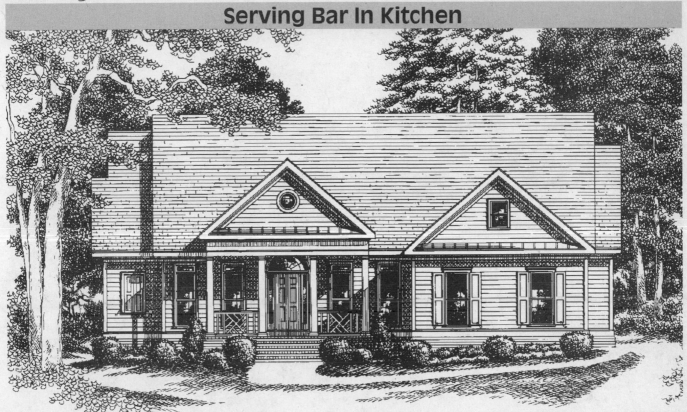

2,072 total square feet of living area

Price Code C

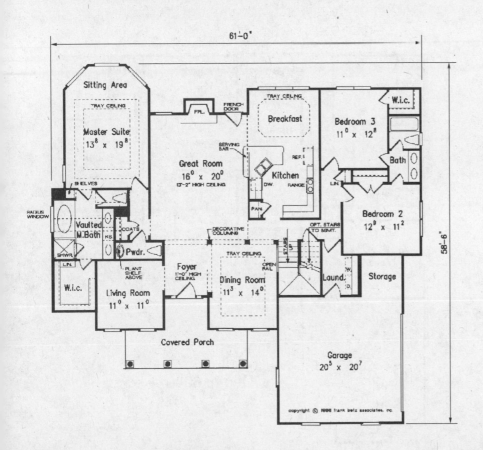

Special features

- Master suite has large bay sitting area, private vaulted bath and enormous walk-in closet

- Tray ceiling in breakfast room and dining room is a charming touch

- Great room has a centered fireplace and a French door leading outdoors

- 3 bedrooms, 2 1/2 baths, 2-car side entry garage

- Walk-out basement or crawl space foundation, please specify when ordering

Office Or Fourth Bedroom

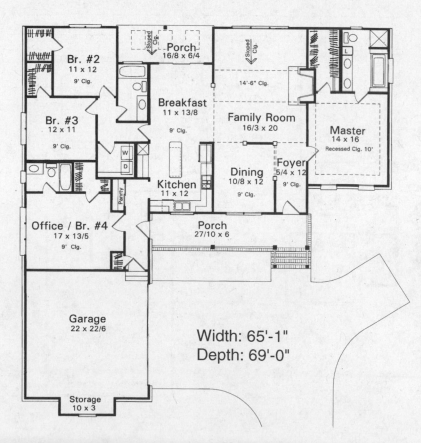

2,158 total square feet of living area

Price Code C

Special features

- Private master suite has walk-in closet and bath
- Sloped ceiling in family room adds drama
- Secondary bedrooms include 9' ceilings and walk-in closets
- Covered porch adds a charming touch
- 4 bedrooms, 3 baths, 2-car side entry garage
- Crawl space or slab foundation, please specify when ordering

Br. #2
11 x 12
9' Clg.

Porch
16/8 x 6/4

Sloped Clg.

Sloped Clg.

Br. #3
12 x 11
9' Clg.

Breakfast
11 x 13/8
9' Clg.

14'-6" Clg.

Family Room
16/3 x 20

Master
14 x 16
Recessed Clg. 10'

Kitchen
11 x 12

Dining
10/8 x 12
9' Clg.

Foyer
5/4 x 12
9' Clg.

W D

Pantry

Office / Br. #4
17 x 13/5
9' Clg.

Porch
27/10 x 6

Garage
22 x 22/6

Width: 65'-1"
Depth: 69'-0"

Storage
10 x 3

Simple Roofline Makes Home Economical To Build

1,792 total square feet of living area

Price Code B

Rear View

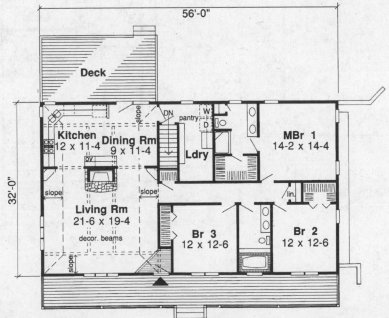

56'-0"

32'-0"

Deck

Kitchen
12 x 11-4

Dining Rm
9 x 11-4

slope

DN

pantry

W
D

Ldry

MBr 1
14-2 x 14-4

slope

slope

slope

Living Rm
21-6 x 19-4

decor. beams

lin.

slope

Br 3
12 x 12-6

Br 2
12 x 12-6

Special features

- Master bedroom has a private bath and large walk-in closet

- A central stone fireplace and windows on two walls are focal points in the living room

- Decorative beams and sloped ceiling add interest to the kitchen, living and dining rooms

- 3 bedrooms, 2 baths, 2-car drive under garage

- Basement foundation

Covered Rear Porch

1,253 total square feet of living area

Price Code A

Special features

- Sloped ceiling and fireplace in family room adds drama
- U-shaped kitchen efficiently designed
- Large walk-in closets are found in all the bedrooms
- 3 bedrooms, 2 baths, 2-car garage
- Crawl space or slab foundation, please specify when ordering

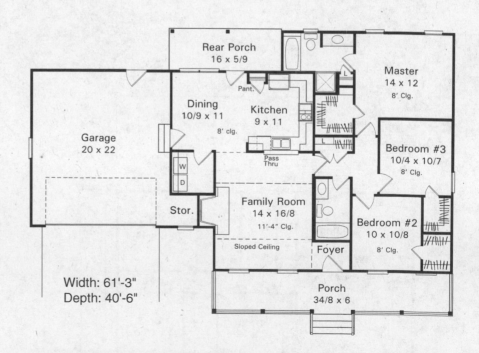

Rear Porch
16 x 5/9

Pant.

Dining
10/9 x 11
8' clg.

Kitchen
9 x 11

Master
14 x 12
8' Clg.

Garage
20 x 22

Bedroom #3
10/4 x 10/7
8' Clg.

W D

Pass Thru

Stor.

Family Room
14 x 16/8
11'-4" Clg.

Bedroom #2
10 x 10/8
8' Clg.

Sloped Ceiling

Foyer

Width: 61'-3"
Depth: 40'-6"

Porch
34/8 x 6

Open Ranch Design Gives Expansive Look

1,630 total square feet of living area

Price Code B

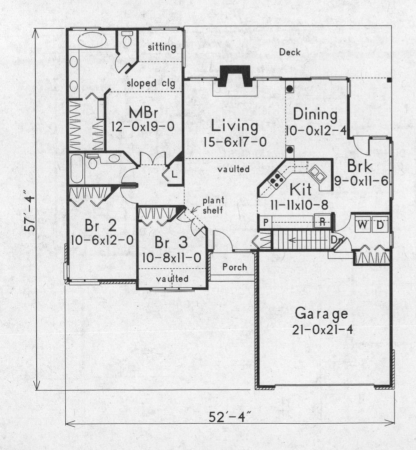

Special features

- Crisp facade and full windows front and back offer open viewing
- Wrap-around rear deck is accessible from breakfast room, dining room and master bedroom
- Vaulted ceiling in living room and master bedroom
- Sitting area and large walk-in closet complement master bedroom
- 3 bedrooms, 2 baths, 2-car garage
- Basement foundation

Spacious Ranch Style

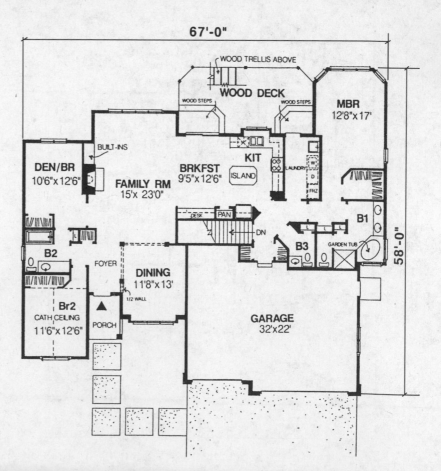

© Urban Design Group, Inc.

2,086 total square feet of living area

Price Code C

Special features

- Corner garden tub graces private master bath
- Kitchen and breakfast room have terrific placement connecting to family room which creates a feeling of openness
- Secluded den makes an ideal office space
- 9' ceilings throughout this home
- 3 bedrooms, 2 1/2 baths, 3-car garage
- Basement foundation

Dramatic Cathedral Ceilings

1,436 total square feet of living area

Price Code A

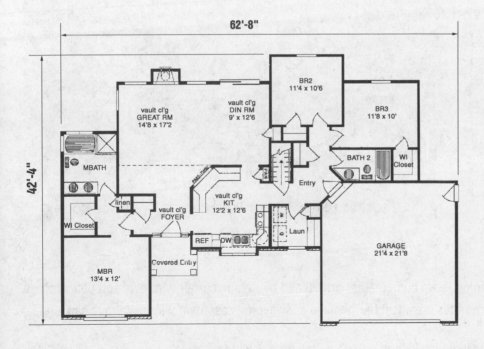

62'-8"

42'-4"

vault cl'g
GREAT RM
14'8 x 17'2

vault cl'g
DIN RM
9' x 12'6

BR2
11'4 x 10'6

BR3
11'8 x 10'

MBATH

BATH 2

WI Closet

linen

PANTRY

Entry

vault cl'g
KIT
12'2 x 12'6

WI Closet

vault cl'g
FOYER

REF | DW

Laun

GARAGE
21'4 x 21'8

MBR
13'4 x 12'

Covered Entry

Special features

- Covered entry is inviting
- Kitchen has handy breakfast bar which overlooks great room and dining room
- Private master suite with bath and walk-in closet is separate from other bedrooms
- 3 bedrooms, 2 baths, 2-car garage
- Basement foundation

Stylish Ranch With Rustic Charm — Plan #705-0515

Special features

- Family/dining room has sliding door
- Master bedroom includes private bath with shower
- Hall bath includes double vanity for added convenience
- Kitchen features U-shaped design, large pantry and laundry area
- 3 bedrooms, 2 baths, 2-car garage
- Crawl space foundation, drawings also include basement and slab foundations

1,344 total square feet of living area — **Price Code A**

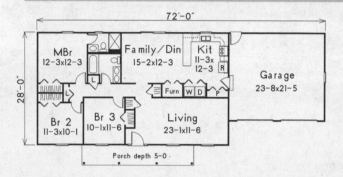

72'-0"
28'-0"

MBr 12-3x12-3
Family/Din 15-2x12-3
Kit 11-3x 12-3
Garage 23-8x21-5

Furn W D P

Br 2 11-3x10-1
Br 3 10-1x11-6
Living 23-1x11-6

Porch depth 5-0

Organized Kitchen, Center Of Activity — Plan #705-0419

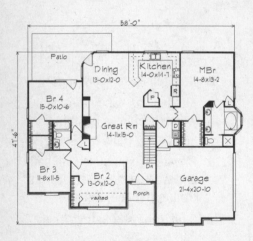

58'-0"
41'-6"

Patio

Dining 13-0x12-0
Kitchen 14-0x14-7
MBr 14-8x13-2

Br 4 15-0x10-6

Great Rm 14-11x15-0

Br 3 11-8x11-5
Br 2 13-0x12-0
vaulted
Porch
Garage 21-4x20-10

Dn

1,882 total square feet of living area — **Price Code C**

Special features

- Handsome brick facade
- Spacious great room and dining room combination brightened by unique corner windows and patio access
- Well-designed kitchen incorporates breakfast bar peninsula, sweeping casement window above sink and walk-in pantry island
- Master suite features large walk-in closet and private bath with bay window
- 4 bedrooms, 2 baths, 2-car side entry garage
- Basement foundation

Comfortable One-Story Country Home

1,367 total square feet of living area

Price Code A

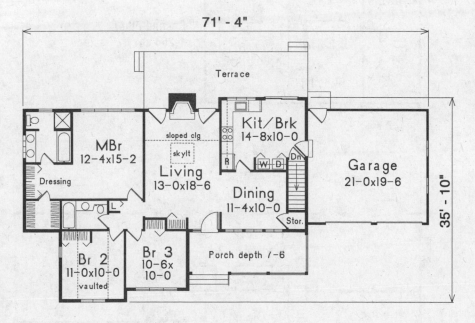

71' - 4"

Terrace

MBr
12-4x15-2

Dressing

sloped clg

skylt

Living
13-0x18-6

Kit/Brk
14-8x10-0

R

W D Dn

Dining
11-4x10-0

Stor.

Garage
21-0x19-6

35' - 10"

Br 2
11-0x10-0
vaulted

Br 3
10-6x
10-0

Porch depth 7-6

Special features

- Neat front porch shelters the entrance
- Dining room has full wall of windows and a convenient storage area
- Breakfast area leads to the rear terrace through sliding doors
- Large living room with high ceiling, skylight and fireplace
- 3 bedrooms, 2 baths, 2-car garage
- Basement foundation, drawings also include slab foundation

TO ORDER BLUEPRINTS USE THE FORM ON PAGE 15 OR CALL TOLL-FREE 1-877-671-6036
View thousands more home plans online at www.familyhandyman.com/homeplans

149

Stately Country Home For The "Spacious Age"

2,727 total square feet of living area

Price Code E

Special features

- Wrap-around porch and large foyer create an impressive entrance

- A state-of-the-art vaulted kitchen has walk-in pantry and is open to the breakfast room and adjoining screened porch

- A walk-in wet bar, fireplace bay window and deck access are features of the family room

- Vaulted master bedroom suite enjoys a luxurious bath with skylight and an enormous 13' deep walk-in closet

- 4 bedrooms, 2 1/2 baths, 2-car side entry garage

- Walk-out basement foundation

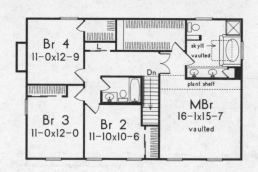

**Second Floor
1,204 sq. ft.**

Br 4
11-0x12-9

MBr
16-1x15-7
vaulted

Br 3
11-0x12-0

Br 2
11-10x10-6

plant shelf

skylt
vaulted

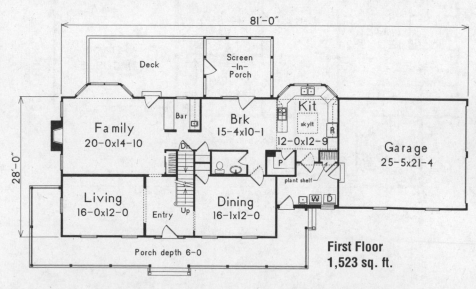

81'-0"

28'-0"

Deck

Screen
-In-
Porch

Kit
12-0x12-9
skylt

Bar

Family
20-0x14-10

Brk
15-4x10-1

Garage
25-5x21-4

plant shelf

Living
16-0x12-0

Entry

Up

Dining
16-1x12-0

W D

Porch depth 6-0

**First Floor
1,523 sq. ft.**

TO ORDER BLUEPRINTS USE THE FORM ON PAGE 15 OR CALL TOLL-FREE 1-877-671-6036
View thousands more home plans online at www.familyhandyman.com/homeplans

Spacious Interior For Open Living

1,400 total square feet of living area

Price Code A

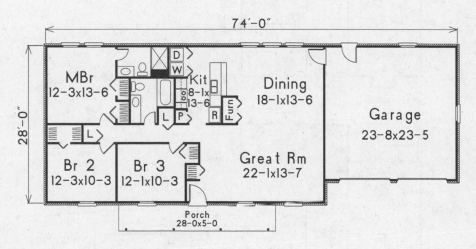

74'-0"

MBr
12-3x13-6

Kit
8-1x
13-6

Dining
18-1x13-6

Garage
23-8x23-5

28'-0"

Br 2
12-3x10-3

Br 3
12-1x10-3

Great Rm
22-1x13-7

Porch
28-0x5-0

Special features

- Front porch offers warmth and welcome
- Large great room opens into dining room creating an open living atmosphere
- Kitchen features convenient laundry area, pantry and breakfast bar
- 3 bedrooms, 2 baths, 2-car garage
- Crawl space foundation, drawings also include basement and slab foundations

TO ORDER BLUEPRINTS USE THE FORM ON PAGE 15 OR CALL TOLL-FREE 1-877-671-6036
View thousands more home plans online at www.familyhandyman.com/homeplans

151

Charming Two-Story With Dormers And Porch

1,711 total square feet of living area

Price Code B

Special features

- U-shaped kitchen joins break-fast and family rooms for open living atmosphere

- Master bedroom has secluded covered porch and private bath

- Balcony overlooks family room that features a fireplace and accesses deck

- 3 bedrooms, 2 1/2 baths, 2-car garage

- Basement foundation

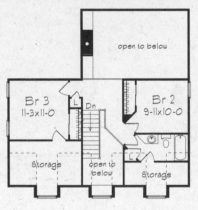

Second Floor
483 sq. ft.

Br 3
11-3x11-0

Br 2
9-11x10-0

open to below

Storage

open to below

Storage

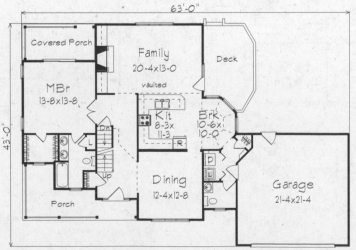

First Floor
1,228 sq. ft.

63'-0"

43'-0"

Covered Porch

Family
20-4x13-0
vaulted

Deck

MBr
13-8x13-8

Kit
8-3x11-3

Brk
10-6x10-0

Dining
12-4x12-8

Garage
21-4x21-4

Porch

Sensational Ranch

1,472 total square feet of living area

Price Code A

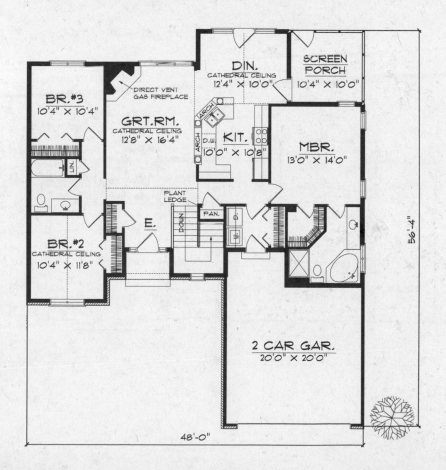

Special features

- Inviting screened porch at the rear of the home has direct access to the dining room with cathedral ceilings

- Columns and arches help separate the kitchen from the great room

- Spectacular great room has lots of windows and a terrific corner fireplace

- 3 bedrooms, 2 baths, 2-car garage

- Basement foundation

Sunny Eating Area

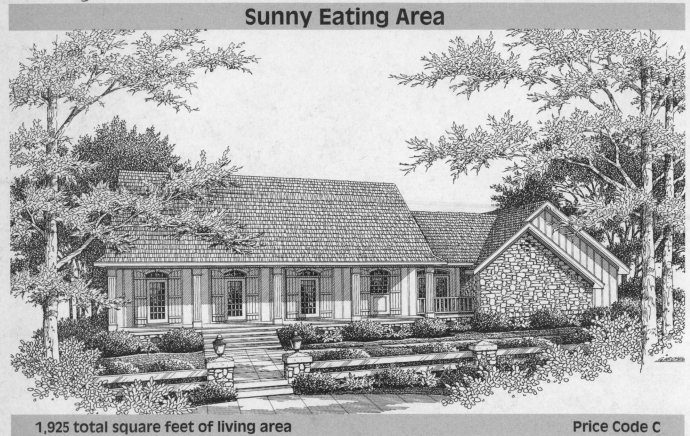

1,925 total square feet of living area

Price Code C

Special features

- Energy efficient home with 2" x 6" exterior walls
- Balcony off eating area adds character
- Master suite has dressing room, bath, walk-in closet and access to utility room
- 3 bedrooms, 2 baths, 2-car side entry garage
- Crawl space or slab foundation, please specify when ordering

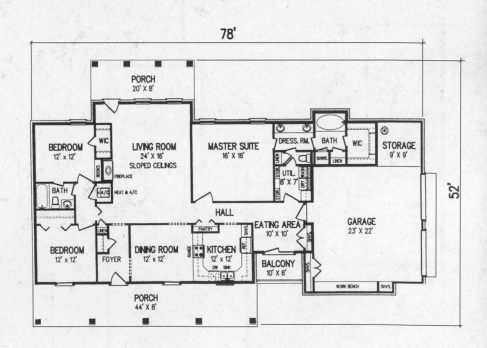

Bedrooms Separate From Rest Of Home

1,849 total square feet of living area

Price Code C

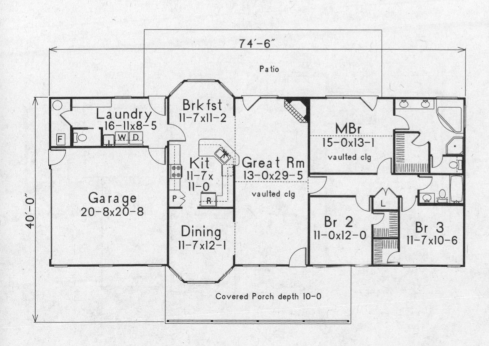

Special features

- Enormous laundry/mud room has many extras including storage area and half bath
- Lavish master bath has corner jacuzzi tub, double sinks, separate shower and walk-in closet
- Secondary bedrooms include walk-in closets
- Kitchen has wrap-around eating counter and is positioned between formal dining area and breakfast room for convenience
- 3 bedrooms, 2 1/2 baths, 2-car side entry garage
- Slab foundation, drawings also include crawl space foundation

Plan #705-0410

Distinctive Turret Surrounds The Dining Bay

1,742 total square feet of living area

Price Code B

Special features

- Efficient kitchen combines with breakfast area and great room creating a spacious living area
- Master bedroom includes private bath with huge walk-in closet, shower and corner tub
- Great room boasts a fireplace and access outdoors
- Laundry room conveniently located near kitchen and garage
- 3 bedrooms, 2 baths, 2-car garage
- Slab foundation, drawings also include crawl space foundation

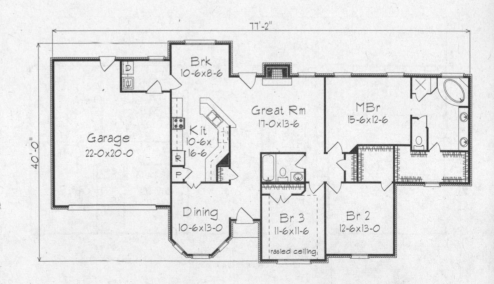

Large Front Porch

Plan #705-0241

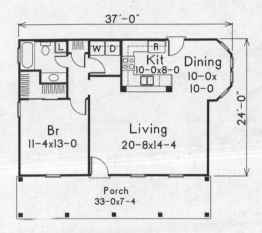

829 total square feet of living area   **Price Code AAA**

Special features

- U-shaped kitchen opens into living area by a 42" high counter
- Oversized bay window and French door accent dining room
- Gathering space is created by the large living room
- Convenient utility room and linen closet
- 1 bedroom, 1 bath
- Slab foundation

Quaint Country Home Is Ideal

Plan #705-0462

Second Floor
300 sq. ft.

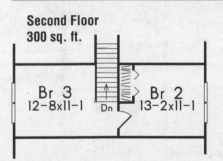

First Floor
728 sq. ft.

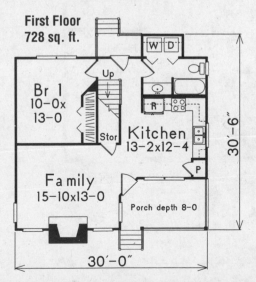

1,028 total square feet of living area   **Price Code AA**

Special features

- Master bedroom conveniently located on first floor
- Well-designed bath contains laundry facilities
- L-shaped kitchen has a handy pantry
- Tall windows flank family room fireplace
- Cozy covered porch provides unique angled entry into home
- 3 bedrooms, 1 bath
- Crawl space foundation

Quaint And Compact

1,018 total square feet of living area

Price Code AA

Special features

- Bayed living room provides charm while dining room offers access to patio area
- Well-defined use of space is a plus in this home
- Two-car garage offers space for washer and dryer
- 3 bedrooms, 2 baths, 2-car garage
- Basement, crawl space or slab foundation, please specify when ordering

Width: 43'-6"
Depth: 49'-0"

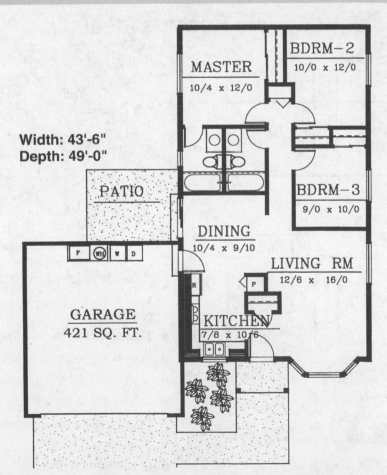

Open Floor Plan Makes Home Feel Larger

1,277 total square feet of living area   **Price Code A**

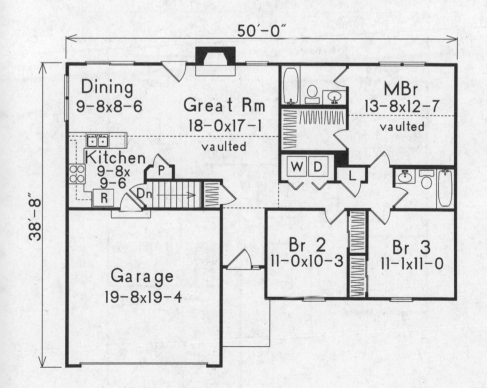

50'-0"

38'-8"

Dining
9-8x8-6

Great Rm
18-0x17-1
vaulted

MBr
13-8x12-7
vaulted

Kitchen
9-8x
9-6

W D

L

P

R

Dn

Garage
19-8x19-4

Br 2
11-0x10-3

Br 3
11-1x11-0

Special features

- Vaulted ceilings in master bedroom, great room, kitchen and dining room
- Laundry closet located near bedrooms for convenience
- Compact but efficient kitchen
- 3 bedrooms, 2 baths, 2-car garage
- Basement foundation

Large Great Room Perfect For Entertaining

1,862 total square feet of living area

Price Code C

Special features

- Master bedroom includes tray ceiling, bay window, access to patio and a private bath with oversized tub and generous closet space

- Corner sink and breakfast bar faces into breakfast area and great room

- Spacious great room features vaulted ceiling, fireplace and access to rear patio

- 3 bedrooms, 2 baths, 2-car garage

- Slab foundation, drawings also include crawl space foundation

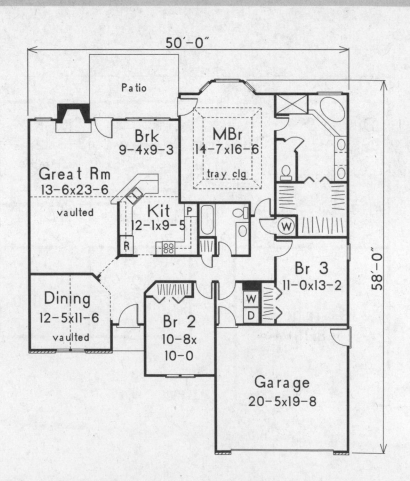

Open Living Spaces

1,000 total square feet of living area

Price Code AA

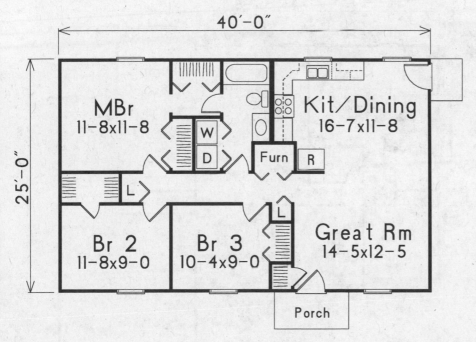

40'-0"

25'-0"

MBr
11-8x11-8

W
D

Kit/Dining
16-7x11-8

Furn   R

L

Br 2
11-8x9-0

Br 3
10-4x9-0

L

Great Rm
14-5x12-5

Porch

Special features

- Bath includes convenient closeted laundry area
- Master bedroom includes double closets and private access to bath
- Foyer features handy coat closet
- L-shaped kitchen provides easy access outdoors
- 3 bedrooms, 1 bath
- Crawl space foundation, drawings also include basement and slab foundations

Plan #705-0162

Traditional Exterior, Handsome Accents

1,882 total square feet of living area   **Price Code D**

Special features

- Wide, handsome entrance opens to the vaulted great room with fireplace
- Living and dining areas are conveniently joined but still allow privacy
- Private covered porch extends breakfast area
- Practical passageway runs through laundry and mud room from garage to kitchen
- Vaulted ceiling in master bedroom
- 3 bedrooms, 2 baths, 2-car garage
- Basement foundation

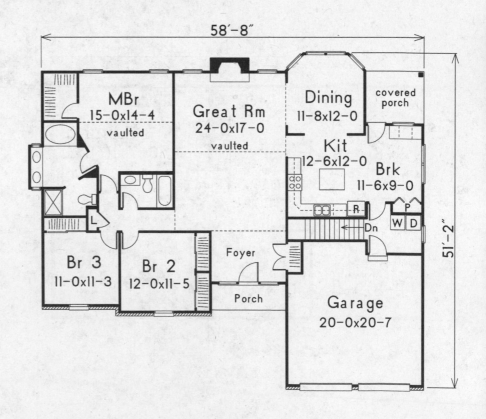

Bright Spacious Living Area

1,844 total square feet of living area

Price Code C

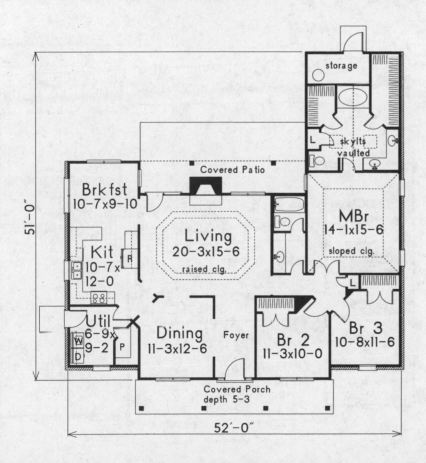

Br kfst
10-7x9-10

Kit
10-7x
12-0

Util
6-9x
9-2

Living
20-3x15-6
raised clg.

Dining
11-3x12-6

Foyer

Br 2
11-3x10-0

storage

Covered Patio

skylts
vaulted

MBr
14-1x15-6
sloped clg.

Br 3
10-8x11-6

Covered Porch
depth 5-3

51'-0"

52'-0"

Special features

- Luxurious master bath is impressive with vaulted ceiling, large walk-in closets and an oversized tub
- Living room has high ceiling and large windows that flank the fireplace
- Front and rear covered porches create homey feel
- Cozy breakfast room is adjacent to kitchen for easy access
- Spacious utility room includes pantry and is accessible to both the kitchen and the outdoors
- 3 bedrooms, 2 baths
- Slab foundation

Plan #705-AP-1812

Ranch With Lots To Offer

1,886 total square feet of living area

Price Code C

Special features

- Enter double-doors in master bedroom to find vaulted ceilings, double closets and a luxurious private bath

- Large covered deck can be accessed by the family room, bedroom #2 and the master bedroom

- Sunny breakfast room is convenient to the kitchen

- 3 bedrooms, 2 baths, 2-car side entry garage

- Basement, crawl space or slab foundation, please specify when ordering

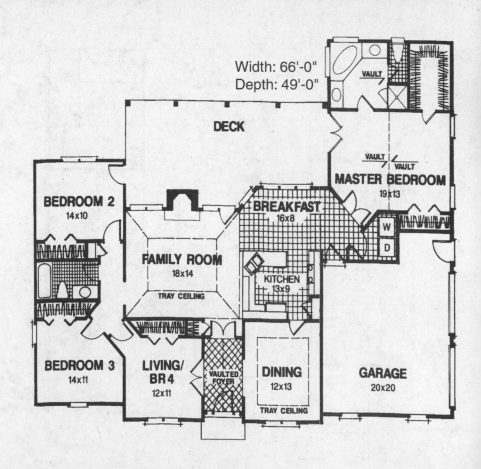

Width: 66'-0"
Depth: 49'-0"

DECK

BEDROOM 2
14x10

FAMILY ROOM
18x14
TRAY CEILING

BREAKFAST
16x8

KITCHEN
13x9

MASTER BEDROOM
19x13

VAULT

W
D

BEDROOM 3
14x11

LIVING/
BR 4
12x11

VAULTED
FOYER

DINING
12x13
TRAY CEILING

GARAGE
20x20

Whirlpool Tub In Master Bath

1,571 total square feet of living area

Price Code B

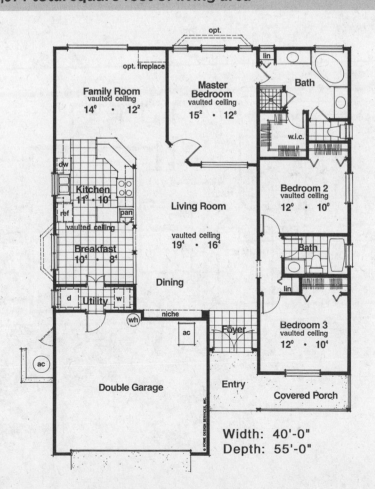

opt.

opt. fireplace

Family Room
vaulted ceiling
14⁰ • 12²

Master Bedroom
vaulted ceiling
15² • 12⁶

lin

Bath

w.i.c.

dw

Kitchen
11⁰ • 10⁴

ref

pan

vaulted ceiling

Living Room
vaulted ceiling
19⁴ • 16⁴

Bedroom 2
vaulted ceiling
12⁰ • 10⁰

Breakfast
10⁴ • 8⁴

Dining

Bath

lin

d **Utility** w

wh

niche

ac

Foyer

ac

Bedroom 3
vaulted ceiling
12⁰ • 10⁴

ac

Double Garage

Entry

Covered Porch

Width: 40'-0"
Depth: 55'-0"

Special features

- Bedrooms #2 and #3 share a bath in their own private hall
- Kitchen counter overlooks family room
- Open living area adds appeal with vaulted ceiling and display niche
- 3 bedrooms, 2 baths, 2-car garage
- Slab foundation

Inviting Covered Verandas

1,830 total square feet of living area

Price Code C

Special features

- Inviting covered verandas in the front and rear of the home
- Great room has fireplace and cathedral ceiling
- Handy service porch allows easy access
- Master suite has vaulted ceiling and private bath
- 3 bedrooms, 2 baths, 3-car side entry garage
- Basement, crawl space or slab foundation, please specify when ordering

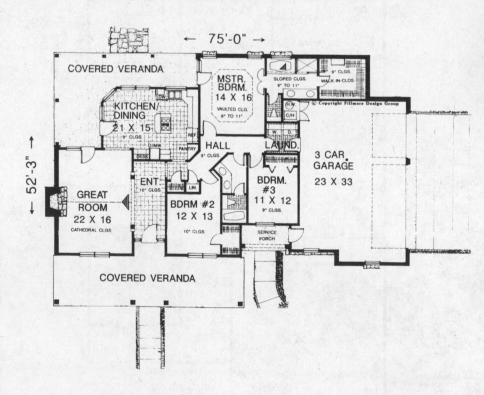

Full Pillared Porch Makes A Grand Entrance

1,800 total square feet of living area

Price Code C

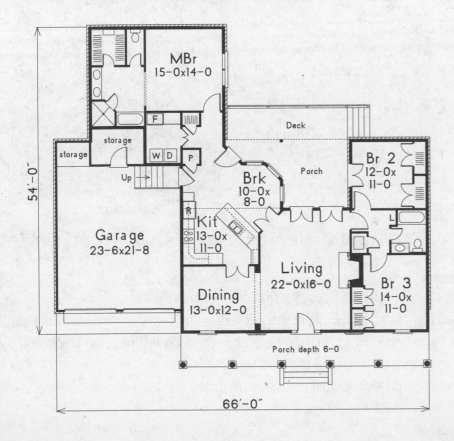

Special features

- Stylish kitchen and breakfast area feature large windows that allow great views outdoors
- Covered front and rear porches provide an added dimension to this home's living space
- Generous storage areas and large utility room
- Energy efficient home with 2" x 6" exterior walls
- Large separate master suite and adjoining bath with large tub and corner shower
- 3 bedrooms, 2 baths, 2-car garage
- Crawl space foundation, drawings also include slab foundation

Central Fireplace Brightens Family Living   Plan #705-0225

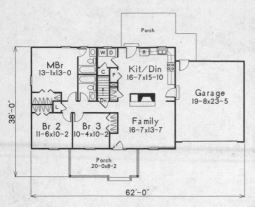

1,260 total square feet of living area   Price Code A

Special features

- Spacious kitchen and dining area features large pantry, storage area, easy access to garage and laundry room
- Pleasant covered front porch adds a practical touch
- Master bedroom with a private bath adjoins two other bedrooms, all with plenty of closet space
- 3 bedrooms, 2 baths, 2-car garage
- Basement foundation, drawings also include crawl space and slab foundations

A Trim Arrangement Of Living Areas   Plan #705-0214

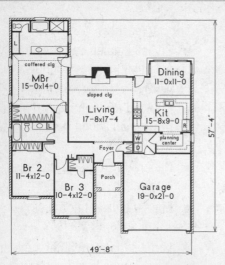

1,770 total square feet of living area   Price Code B

Special features

- Distinctive covered entrance leads into spacious foyer
- Master bedroom, living and dining rooms, all feature large windows for plenty of light
- Oversized living room has a high ceiling and large windows that flank the fireplace
- Kitchen includes pantry and large planning center
- Master bedroom has high vaulted ceiling, deluxe bath, and private access outdoors
- 3 bedrooms, 2 baths, 2-car garage
- Slab foundation

Compact Home With Functional Design

1,396 total square feet of living area

Price Code A

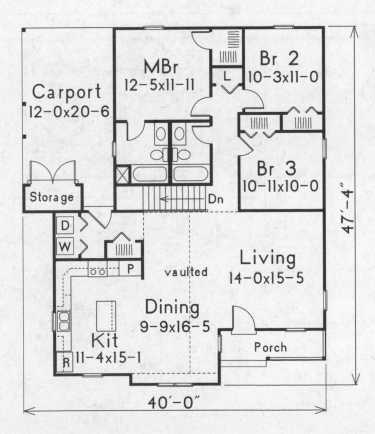

Special features

- Gabled front adds interest to facade
- Living and dining rooms share a vaulted ceiling
- Master bedroom features a walk-in closet and private bath
- Functional kitchen with a center work island and convenient pantry
- 3 bedrooms, 2 baths, 1-car carport
- Basement foundation, drawings also include crawl space foundation

Gracious Atrium Ranch

2,218 total square feet of living area

Price Code D

Rear View

Special features

- Great room has arched entry, bay windowed atrium with staircase and a fireplace

- Breakfast room offers bay window and snack bar open to kitchen with laundry nearby

- Atrium open to 1,217 square feet of optional living area below

- 4 bedrooms, 2 baths, 2-car garage

- Walk-out basement foundation

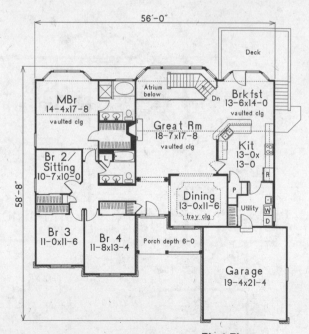

56'-0"

Deck

MBr
14-4x17-8
vaulted clg

Atrium
below

Brk fst
13-6x14-0
vaulted clg

Great Rm
18-7x17-8
vaulted clg

Kit
13-0x
13-0

Br 2/
Sitting
10-7x10-0

Dining
13-0x11-6
tray clg

Utility

Br 3
11-0x11-6

Br 4
11-8x13-4

Porch depth 6-0

Garage
19-4x21-4

58'-8"

**First Floor
2,218 sq. ft.**

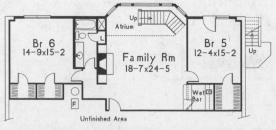

Up
Atrium

Br 6
14-9x15-2

Family Rm
18-7x24-5

Br 5
12-4x15-2

Up

Wet
Bar

F

Unfinished Area

**Optional
Lower Level**

Bayed Dining Room

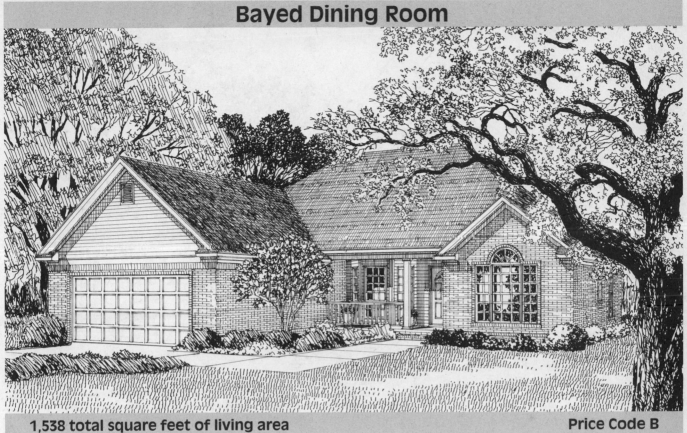

1,538 total square feet of living area

Price Code B

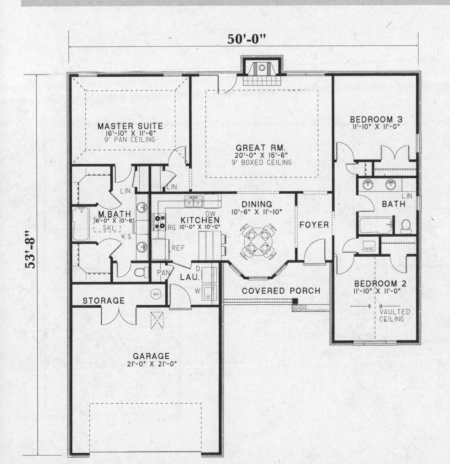

50'-0"

53'-8"

MASTER SUITE
16'-10" X 11'-6"
9' PAN CEILING

GREAT RM.
20'-0" X 15'-6"
9' BOXED CEILING

BEDROOM 3
11'-10" X 11'-0"

LIN

LIN

BATH

LIN

M.BATH
16'-0" X
SKL
K.S.

KITCHEN
10'-0" X 10'-0"

DW

DINING
10'-6" X 11'-10"

FOYER

RG

REF

HVAC

PAN

LAU.

D

W

BEDROOM 2
11'-10" X 11'-0"

STORAGE

WH

COVERED PORCH

VAULTED
CEILING

GARAGE
21'-0" X 21'-0"

Special features

- Dining and great rooms high-lighted in this design
- Master suite has many amenities
- kitchen and laundry are accessible from any room in the house
- 3 bedrooms, 2 baths, 2-car garage
- Basement, walk-out basement, crawl space or slab foundation, please specify when ordering

Central Living Area Keeps Bedrooms Private

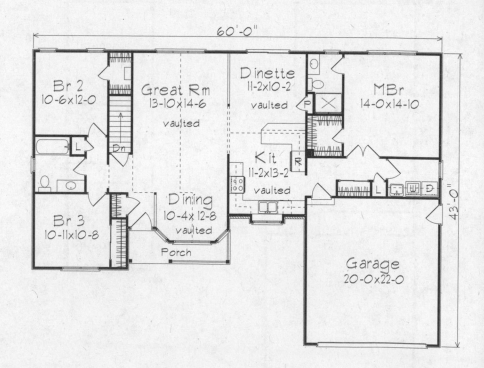

1,546 total square feet of living area

Price Code B

Special features

- Spacious, open rooms create casual atmosphere
- Master suite secluded for privacy
- Dining room features large bay window
- Kitchen and dinette combine for added space and includes access to the outdoors
- Large laundry room includes convenient sink
- 3 bedrooms, 2 baths, 2-car garage
- Basement foundation

TO ORDER BLUEPRINTS USE THE FORM ON PAGE 15 OR CALL TOLL-FREE 1-877-671-6036

View thousands more home plans online at www.familyhandyman.com/homeplans

Handsome Ranch Design

2,096 total square feet of living area

Price Code C

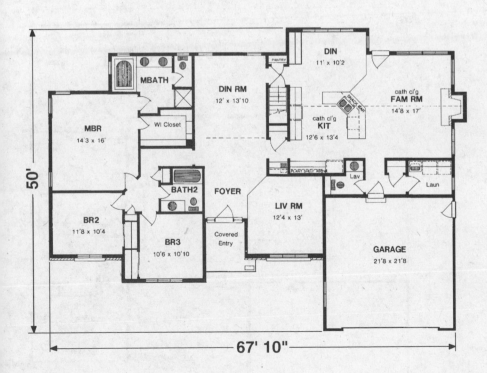

Special features

- Family room with cathedral ceiling and fireplace overlooks backyard
- Efficiently arranged kitchen has island with sink, dishwasher and eating area
- Secluded bedrooms maintain privacy
- 3 bedrooms, 2 1/2 baths, 2-car garage
- Basement foundation

Charming Design Features Home Office

2,452 total square feet of living area

Price Code D

Special features

- Cheery and spacious home office room with private entrance and bath, two closets, vaulted ceiling and transomed window perfect shown as a home office or a fourth bedroom

- Delightful great room with vaulted ceiling, fireplace, extra storage closets and patio doors to sundeck

- Extra-large kitchen features walk-in pantry, cooktop island and bay window

- Vaulted master suite includes transomed windows, walk-in closet and luxurious bath

- 4 bedrooms, 2 1/2 baths, 3-car garage

- Basement foundation

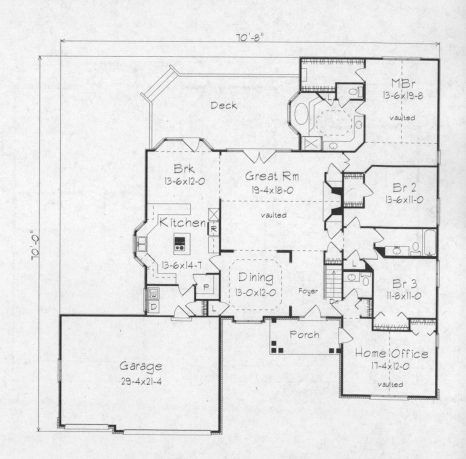

Spacious Rooms Throughout

3,035 total square feet of living area

Price Code E

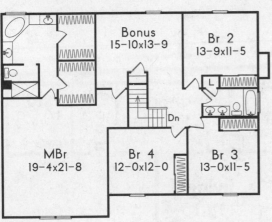

Bonus
15-10x13-9

Br 2
13-9x11-5

L

MBr
19-4x21-8

Br 4
12-0x12-0

Br 3
13-0x11-5

Dn

**Second Floor
1,712 sq. ft.**

Special features

- Master suite features two walk-in closets and a luxury bath
- Second floor has four bedrooms plus a bonus area ideal as an additional family area
- Unique version of traditional two-story with rooms located around central staircase
- 4 bedrooms, 2 1/2 baths, 2-car garage
- Basement foundation

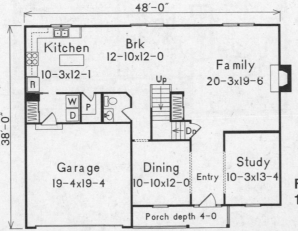

48'-0"

Kitchen
10-3x12-1

Brk
12-10x12-0

Family
20-3x19-6

Up

W P
D

38'-0"

Garage
19-4x19-4

Dining
10-10x12-0

Entry

Study
10-3x13-4

Dn

**First Floor
1,323 sq. ft.**

Porch depth 4-0

TO ORDER BLUEPRINTS USE THE FORM ON PAGE 15 OR CALL TOLL-FREE 1-877-671-6036
View thousands more home plans online at www.familyhandyman.com/homeplans

175

Gable Roof And Large Porch Create A Cozy Feel

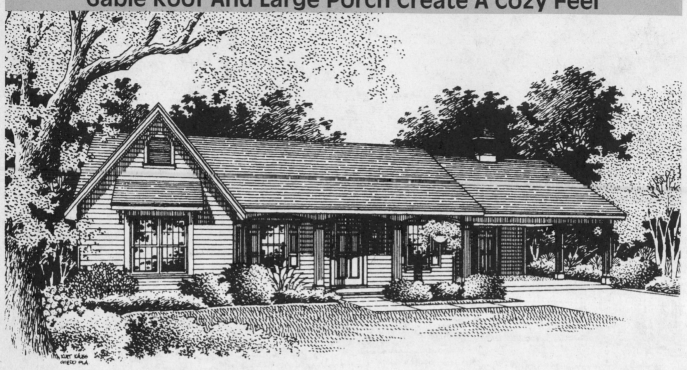

1,375 total square feet of living area

Price Code A

Special features

- Master bedroom has private bath and walk-in closet
- Kitchen and dining room located conveniently near utility and living rooms
- Cathedral ceiling in living room adds spaciousness
- 3 bedrooms, 2 baths, 2-car carport
- Slab foundation

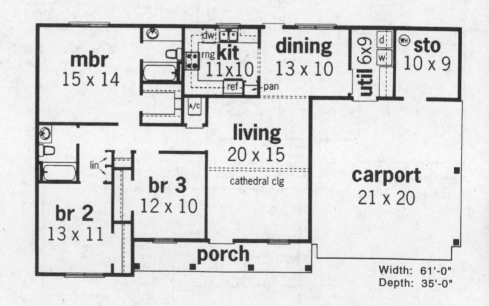

mbr 15 x 14

kit 11x10

dining 13 x 10

util 6x9

sto 10 x 9

living 20 x 15

cathedral clg

br 3 12 x 10

carport 21 x 20

br 2 13 x 11

porch

Width: 61'-0"
Depth: 35'-0"

Cozy Corner Fireplace

1,994 total square feet of living area

Price Code D

Second Floor
882 sq. ft.

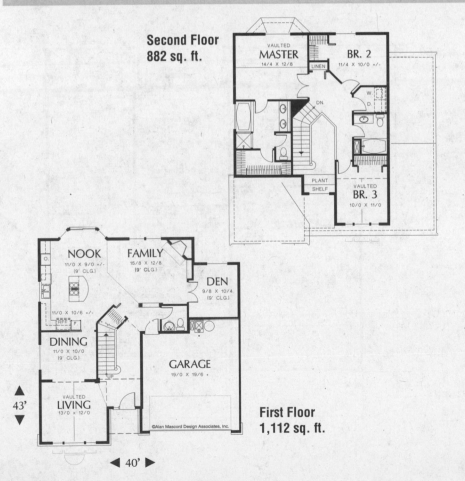

First Floor
1,112 sq. ft.

©Alan Mascord Design Associates, Inc.

43'

40'

Special features

- Breakfast nook overlooks kitchen and great room creating an airy feeling
- Enter double-doors to find a cozy den ideal as a home office
- Master suite has walk-in closet and private bath
- 3 bedrooms, 2 1/2 baths, 2-car garage
- Crawl space foundation

TO ORDER BLUEPRINTS USE THE FORM ON PAGE 15 OR CALL TOLL-FREE 1-877-671-6036
View thousands more home plans online at www.familyhandyman.com/homeplans

177

Great Design

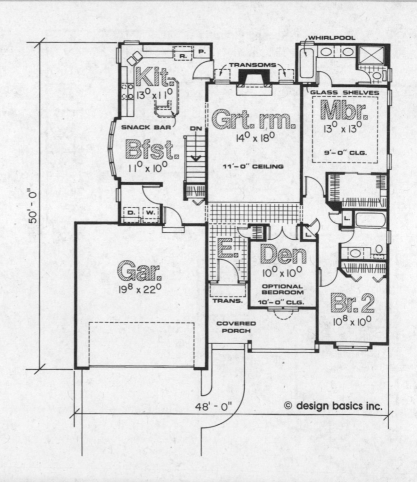

1,479 total square feet of living area

Price Code A

Special features

- Centrally located great room enhanced with fireplace
- Den can easily convert to a third bedroom
- Master bedroom has private bath with large walk-in closet
- Sunny kitchen/breakfast room enjoys view into great room
- 2 bedrooms, 2 baths, 2-car garage
- Basement foundation

WHIRLPOOL

Kit.
13⁰ x 11⁰

R. P.

TRANSOMS

Grt. rm.
14⁰ x 18⁰

GLASS SHELVES

Mbr.
13⁰ x 13⁰

9'-0" CLG.

SNACK BAR

DN

Bfst.
11⁰ x 10⁰

11'-0" CEILING

D. W.

L

50' - 0"

Gar.
19⁸ x 22⁰

E.

Den
10⁰ x 10⁰

OPTIONAL
BEDROOM
10'-0" CLG.

Br. 2
10⁸ x 10⁰

TRANS.

COVERED
PORCH

48' - 0"

© design basics inc.

Charming Two-Story With Covered Entry

2,013 total square feet of living area

Price Code C

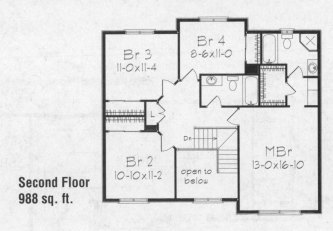

Second Floor 988 sq. ft.

Br 3
11-0x11-4

Br 4
8-6x11-0

Br 2
10-10x11-2

open to below

Dn

MBr
13-0x16-10

L

Special features

- Sliding doors in dinette allow convenient access outdoors

- Family room includes cozy fireplace for informal gathering

- All bedrooms located on second floor for privacy

- Master bath includes dressing area, walk-in closet and separate tub and shower

- 4 bedrooms, 2 1/2 baths, 2-car garage

- Basement foundation

56'-0"

30'-0"

Garage
19-4x21-4

Kit
9-4x11-6

Dinette
10-4x11-4

Family
13-0x15-4

Dining
11-2x11-4

Foyer

up

Living
11-4x13-0

Porch

First Floor 1,025 sq. ft.

Fabulous Curb Appeal

1,588 total square feet of living area

Price Code B

Special features

- Workshop in garage ideal for storage and projects

- 12' vaulted master suite has his and hers closets as well as a lovely bath with bayed soaking tub and compartmentalized shower and toilet area

- Lovely arched entry to 14' vaulted great room that flows open to the dining room and sky-lit kitchen

- 3 bedrooms, 2 baths, 2-car garage

- Basement foundation

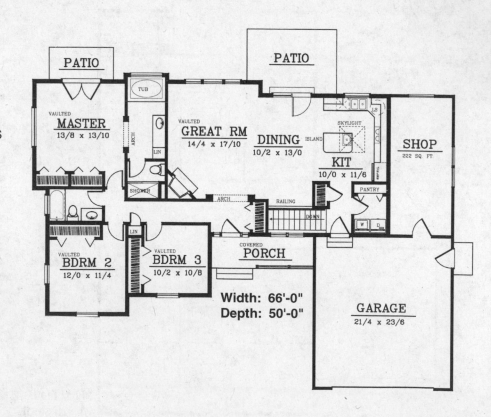

Width: 66'-0"
Depth: 50'-0"

TO ORDER BLUEPRINTS USE THE FORM ON PAGE 15 OR CALL TOLL-FREE 1-877-671-6036

View thousands more home plans online at www.familyhandyman.com/homeplans

Handsome Facade, Spacious Living Arrangement

2,396 total square feet of living area

Price Code D

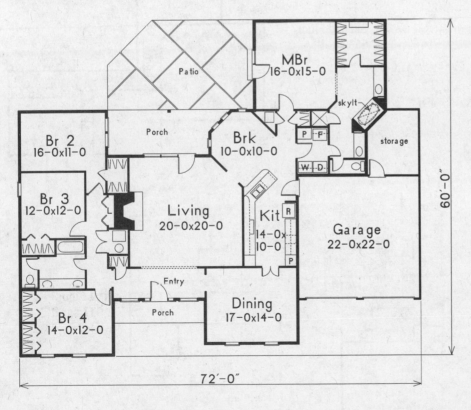

Special features

- Generously wide entry welcomes guests
- Central living area with a 12' ceiling and large fireplace serves as a convenient traffic hub
- Kitchen is secluded, yet has easy access to the living, dining and breakfast areas
- Deluxe master bedroom suite has a walk-in closet, oversized tub, shower and other amenities
- Energy efficient home with 2" x 6" exterior walls
- 4 bedrooms, 2 baths, 2-car garage
- Slab foundation, drawings also include basement and crawl space foundations

Plan #705-AX-93305

Inviting Covered Porch

2,567 total square feet of living area

Price Code F

Special features

- Breakfast room has a 12' cathedral ceiling and a bayed area full of windows

- Great room has a stepped ceiling, built-in media center and a corner fireplace

- Bonus room on the second floor has an additional 300 square feet of living area

- 4 bedrooms, 3 baths, 2-car side entry garage

- Basement, crawl space or slab foundation, please specify when ordering

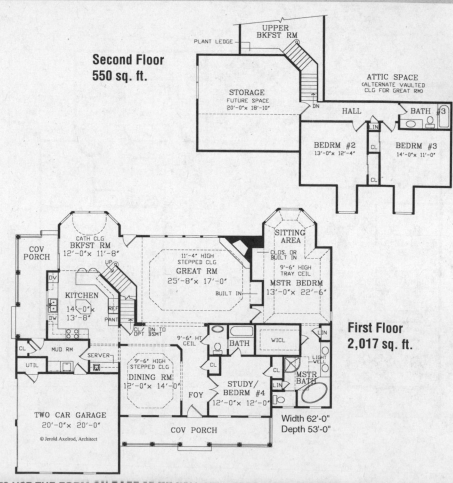

Second Floor 550 sq. ft.

First Floor 2,017 sq. ft.

Width 62'-0"
Depth 53'-0"

TO ORDER BLUEPRINTS USE THE FORM ON PAGE 15 OR CALL TOLL-FREE 1-877-671-0036

View thousands more home plans online at www.familyhandyman.com/homeplans

Peaceful Shaded Front Porch

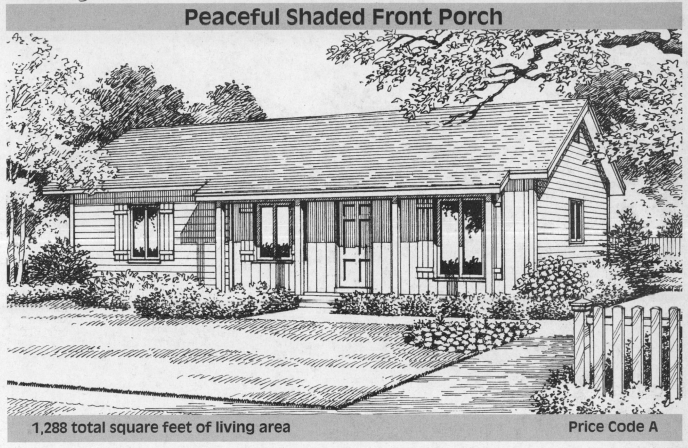

1,288 total square feet of living area

Price Code A

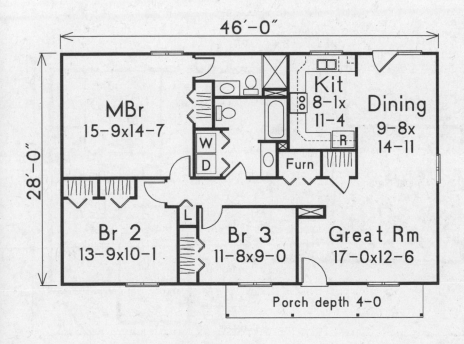

46'-0"

28'-0"

MBr
15-9x14-7

W
D

Kit
8-1x
11-4

Dining
9-8x
14-11

Furn

L

Br 2
13-9x10-1

Br 3
11-8x9-0

Great Rm
17-0x12-6

Porch depth 4-0

Special features

- Kitchen, dining area and great room join to create an open living space
- Master bedroom includes private bath
- Secondary bedrooms include ample closet space
- Hall bath features convenient laundry closet
- Dining room accesses the outdoors
- 3 bedrooms, 2 baths
- Crawl space foundation, drawings also include basement and slab foundations

Open And Spacious Feel To This Home

1,611 total square feet of living area

Price Code B

Special features

- Sliding doors lead to a delightful screened porch creating a wonderful summer retreat

- Master bedroom has a lavishly appointed dressing room and large walk-in closet

- The kitchen offers an abundance of cabinets and counter space with convenient access to the laundry room and garage

- 3 bedrooms, 2 baths, 2-car side entry garage

- Basement foundation

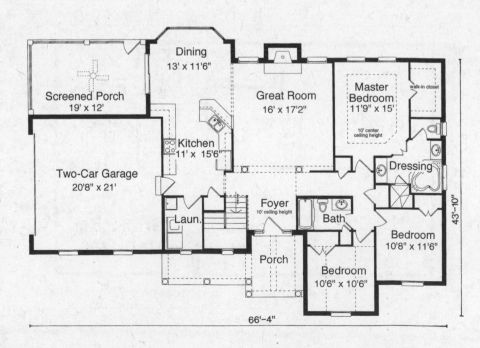

Screened Porch
19' x 12'

Two-Car Garage
20'8" x 21'

Dining
13' x 11'6"

Kitchen
11' x 15'6"

Great Room
16' x 17'2"

Master Bedroom
11'9" x 15'
10' center ceiling height

walk-in closet

Dressing

Laun.

Foyer
10' ceiling height

Bath

Porch

Bedroom
10'6" x 10'6"

Bedroom
10'8" x 11'6"

43'-10"

66'-4"

Country Charm

Plan #705-0498

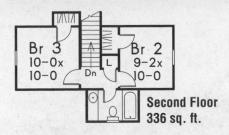

Second Floor 336 sq. ft.

First Floor 618 sq. ft.

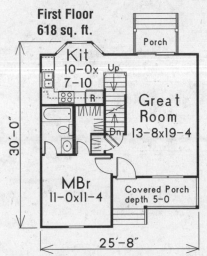

954 total square feet of living area   **Price Code AA**

Special features

- Kitchen has cozy bayed eating area
- Master bedroom has a walk-in closet and private bath
- Large great room has access to the back porch
- Convenient coat closet near front entry
- 3 bedrooms, 2 baths
- Basement foundation

Innovative Ranch

Plan #705-0478

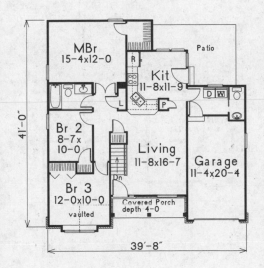

1,092 total square feet of living area   **Price Code AA**

Special features

- Box window and inviting porch with dormers create a charming facade
- Eat-in kitchen offers a pass-through breakfast bar, corner window wall to patio, pantry and convenient laundry with half bath
- Master bedroom features double entry doors and walk-in closet
- 3 bedrooms, 1 1/2 baths, 1-car garage
- Basement foundation

Open Living In This Ranch

COPYRIGHT 1991 LARRY E. BELK

1,575 total square feet of living area

Price Code B

Special features

- Decorative columns separate dining room from living room and foyer
- Kitchen has plenty of workspace
- Spacious walk-in closet in master bedroom
- 3 bedrooms, 2 baths, 2-car garage
- Slab or crawl space foundation, please specify when ordering

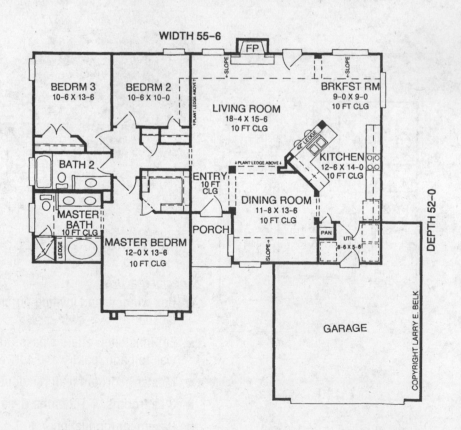

WIDTH 55-6

BEDRM 3
10-6 X 13-6

BEDRM 2
10-6 X 10-0

LIVING ROOM
18-4 X 15-6
10 FT CLG

BRKFST RM
9-0 X 9-0
10 FT CLG

BATH 2

KITCHEN
12-6 X 14-0
10 FT CLG

MASTER
BATH
10 FT CLG

ENTRY
10 FT
CLG

DINING ROOM
11-8 X 13-6
10 FT CLG

MASTER BEDRM
12-0 X 13-6
10 FT CLG

PORCH

PAN

UTIL
8-6 X 5-6

DEPTH 52-0

GARAGE

COPYRIGHT LARRY E. BELK

Vaulted Rooms Throughout

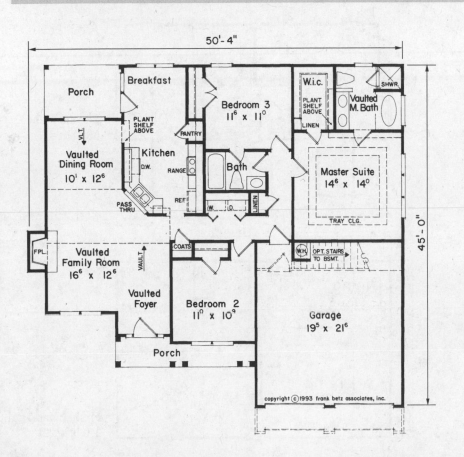

1,373 total square feet of living area

Price Code A

Special features

- 9' ceilings throughout this home
- Sunny breakfast room is very accessible to kitchen
- Kitchen has pass-through to vaulted family room
- 3 bedrooms, 2 baths, 2-car garage
- Crawl space or walk-out basement foundation, please specify when ordering

Front Dormers Add Light, Space And Appeal

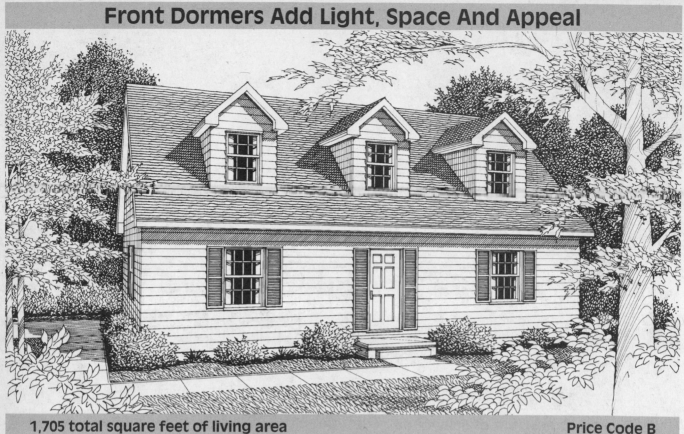

1,705 total square feet of living area

Price Code B

Special features

- Cozy design includes two bedrooms on first floor and two bedrooms on second floor for added privacy

- L-shaped kitchen provides easy access to dining room and outdoors

- Convenient first floor laundry area

- 4 bedrooms, 2 baths

- Crawl space foundation, drawings also include basement and slab foundations

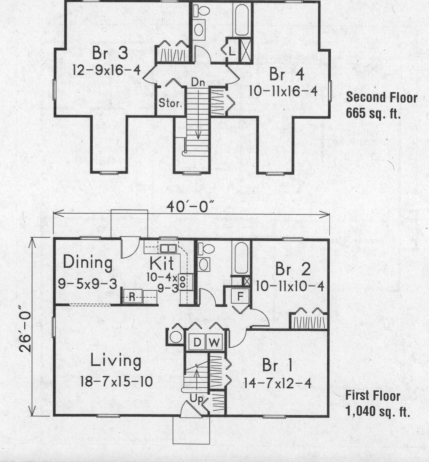

Br 3
12-9x16-4

Br 4
10-11x16-4

Dn

Stor.

Second Floor 665 sq. ft.

40'-0"

26'-0"

Dining
9-5x9-3

Kit
10-4x
9-3

R

Br 2
10-11x10-4

F

D W

Living
18-7x15-10

Br 1
14-7x12-4

Up

First Floor 1,040 sq. ft.

Smart Floor Plan Makes Efficient Design

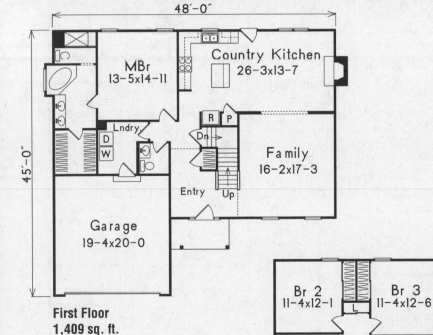

2,179 total square feet of living area

Price Code C

First Floor
1,409 sq. ft.

48'-0"

45'-0"

MBr
13-5x14-11

Country Kitchen
26-3x13-7

Lndry

D
W

R P

Dn

Family
16-2x17-3

Entry   Up

Garage
19-4x20-0

Second Floor
770 sq. ft.

Br 2
11-4x12-1

Br 3
11-4x12-6

L

Dn

plant
shelf →

open to
below

Br 4
13-9x12-6

Special features

- Open floor plan and minimal halls eliminate wasted space and create efficiency

- First floor master suite is conveniently located near large kitchen

- Three bedrooms on the second floor share large bath with nearby linen closet

- 4 bedrooms, 2 1/2 baths, 2-car garage

- Basement foundation

TO ORDER BLUEPRINTS USE THE FORM ON PAGE 15 OR CALL TOLL-FREE 1-877-671-6036

View thousands more home plans online at www.familyhandyman.com/homeplans

Classic Rural Farmhouse

2,363 total square feet of living area

Price Code D

Special features

- Covered porches provide outdoor seating areas
- Corner fireplace becomes focal point of family room
- Kitchen features island cooktop and adjoining nook
- Energy efficient home with 2" x 6" exterior walls
- 3 bedrooms, 2 1/2 baths, 2-car garage
- Partial basement/crawl space foundation

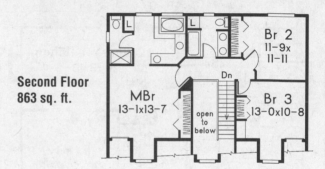

Second Floor 863 sq. ft.

Br 2
11-9x 11-11

MBr
13-1x13-7

open to below

Dn

Br 3
13-0x10-8

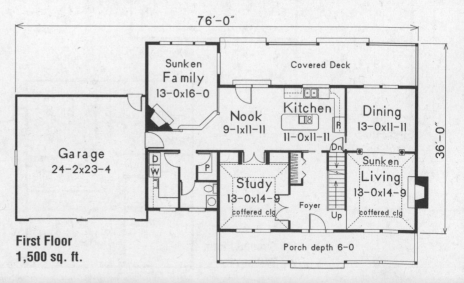

76'-0"

Sunken Family
13-0x16-0

Covered Deck

Garage
24-2x23-4

Nook
9-1x11-11

Kitchen
11-0x11-11

Dining
13-0x11-11

Dn

Study
13-0x14-9
coffered clg

Foyer

Sunken Living
13-0x14-9
coffered clg

Up

36'-0"

First Floor 1,500 sq. ft.

Porch depth 6-0

Circle-Top Windows Grace The Facade Of This Home

1,672 total square feet of living area

Price Code C

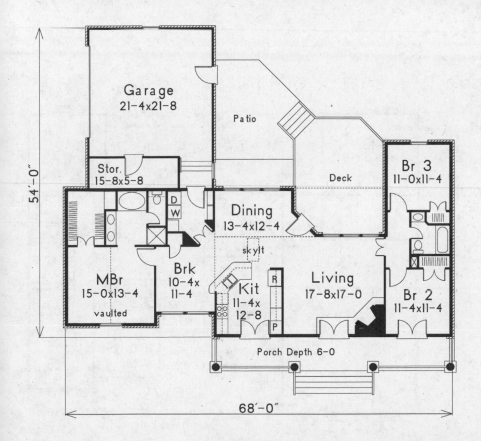

Garage 21-4x21-8

Patio

Deck

Stor. 15-8x5-8

Br 3 11-0x11-4

Dining 13-4x12-4

sky lt

MBr 15-0x13-4

vaulted

Brk 10-4x 11-4

Kit 11-4x 12-8

R

P

Living 17-8x17-0

Br 2 11-4x11-4

Porch Depth 6-0

54'-0"

68'-0"

Special features

■ Vaulted master suite features walk-in closet and adjoining bath with separate tub and shower

■ Energy efficient home with 2" x 6" exterior walls

■ Covered front and rear porches

■ 12' ceilings in living room, kitchen and front secondary bedroom

■ Kitchen complete with pantry, angled bar and adjacent eating area

■ Sloped ceiling in dining room

■ 3 bedrooms, 2 baths, 2-car side entry garage

■ Crawl space foundation, drawings also include basement and slab foundations

Appealing Gabled Front Facade

2,412 total square feet of living area

Price Code D

Special features

- Coffered ceiling in dining room adds character and spaciousness

- Great room enhanced by vaulted ceiling and atrium window wall

- Spacious well-planned kitchen includes breakfast bar and overlooks breakfast room and beyond to deck

- Luxurious master suite features enormous walk-in closet, private bath and easy access to laundry area

- 4 bedrooms, 2 baths, 3-car side entry garage

- Walk-out basement foundation

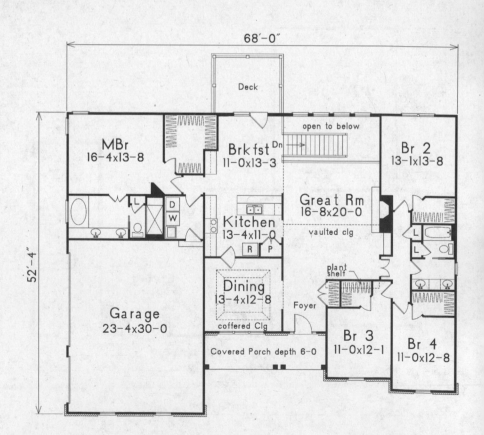

68'-0"

52'-4"

Deck

open to below

MBr
16-4x13-8

Brk fst Dn
11-0x13-3

Br 2
13-1x13-8

Great Rm
16-8x20-0
vaulted clg

Kitchen
13-4x11-0

plant shelf

Dining
13-4x12-8
coffered Clg

Foyer

Garage
23-4x30-0

Br 3
11-0x12-1

Br 4
11-0x12-8

Covered Porch depth 6-0

Excellent Ranch For Country Setting

2,758 total square feet of living area

Price Code E

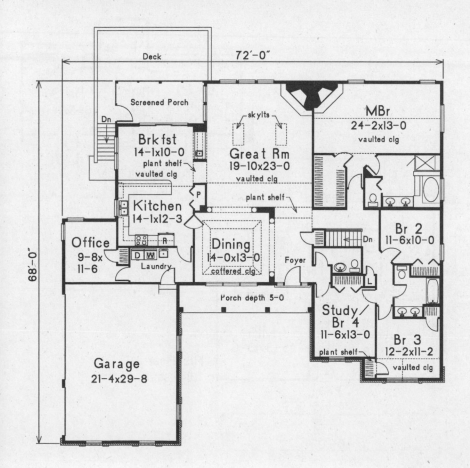

Deck

72'-0"

Screened Porch

Dn

Brkfst
14-1x10-0
plant shelf
vaulted clg

skylts

Great Rm
19-10x23-0
vaulted clg

MBr
24-2x13-0
vaulted clg

Kitchen
14-1x12-3

plant shelf

P

Office
9-8x
11-6

D W
R

Laundry

Dining
14-0x13-0
coffered clg

Foyer

Dn

Br 2
11-6x10-0

L

Porch depth 5-0

Study/
Br 4
11-6x13-0
plant shelf

Br 3
12-2x11-2
vaulted clg

Garage
21-4x29-8

68'-0"

Special features

- Vaulted great room excels with fireplace, wet bar, plant shelves and skylights

- Fabulous master suite enjoys a fireplace, large bath, walk-in closet and vaulted ceiling

- Trendsetting kitchen/breakfast room adjoins spacious screened porch

- Convenient office near kitchen is perfect for computer room, hobby enthusiast or fifth bedroom

- 4 bedrooms, 2 1/2 baths, 3-car side entry garage

- Basement foundation

TO ORDER BLUEPRINTS USE THE FORM ON PAGE 15 OR CALL TOLL-FREE 1-877-671-6036
View thousands more home plans online at www.familyhandyman.com/homeplans

193

Quaint Exterior, Full Front Porch

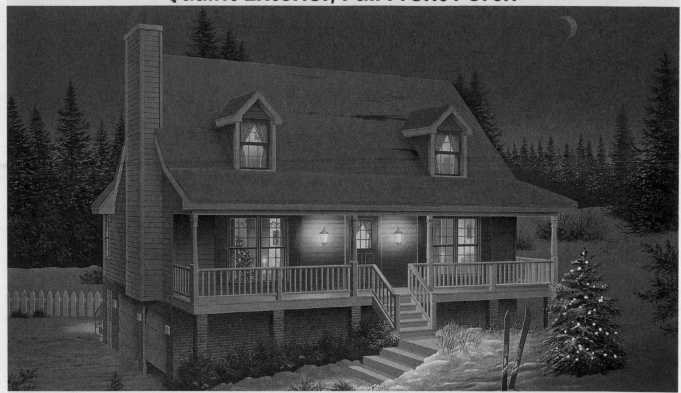

1,657 total square feet of living area

Price Code B

Special features

- Stylish pass-through between living and dining areas
- Master bedroom is secluded from living area for privacy
- Large windows in breakfast and dining areas
- 3 bedrooms, 2 1/2 baths, 2-car drive under garage
- Basement foundation

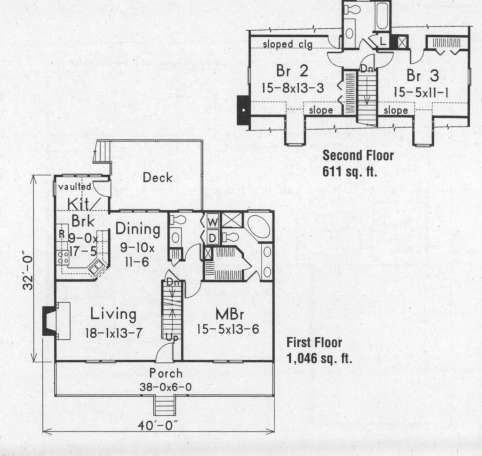

**Second Floor
611 sq. ft.**

**First Floor
1,046 sq. ft.**

TO ORDER BLUEPRINTS USE THE FORM ON PAGE 15 OR CALL TOLL-FREE 1-877-671-6036
View thousands more home plans online at www.familyhandyman.com/homeplans

Smaller Home Offers Stylish Exterior

1,700 total square feet of living area

Price Code B

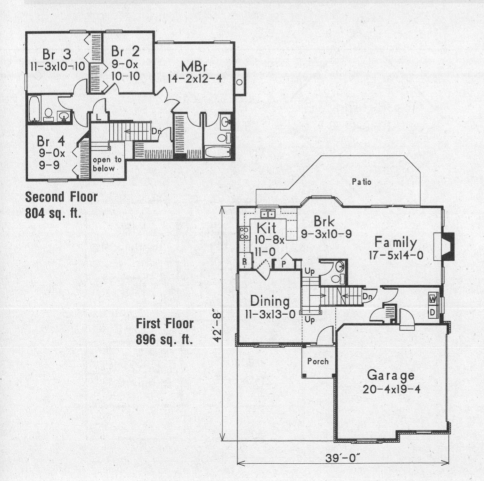

Second Floor
804 sq. ft.

Br 3
11-3x10-10

Br 2
9-0x
10-10

MBr
14-2x12-4

Br 4
9-0x
9-9

open to
below

First Floor
896 sq. ft.

42'-8"

39'-0"

Patio

Kit
10-8x
11-0

Brk
9-3x10-9

Family
17-5x14-0

Dining
11-3x13-0

Up

Up

Dn

W
D

Porch

Garage
20-4x19-4

Special features

- Two-story entry with T-stair is illuminated with decorative oval window
- Skillfully designed U-shaped kitchen has a built-in pantry
- All bedrooms have generous closet storage and are common to spacious hall with walk-in cedar closet
- 4 bedrooms, 2 1/2 baths, 2-car side entry garage
- Basement foundation

TO ORDER BLUEPRINTS USE THE FORM ON PAGE 15 OR CALL TOLL-FREE 1-877-671-6036
View thousands more home plans online at www.familyhandyman.com/homeplans

195

Rambling Country Bungalow

1,475 total square feet of living area

Price Code B

Special features

- Family room features a high ceiling and prominent corner fireplace
- Kitchen with island counter and garden window makes a convenient connection between the family and dining rooms
- Hallway leads to three bedrooms all with large walk-in closets
- Covered breezeway joins main house and garage
- Full-width covered porch entry lends a country touch
- 3 bedrooms, 2 baths, 2-car side entry garage
- Slab foundation, drawings also include crawl space foundation

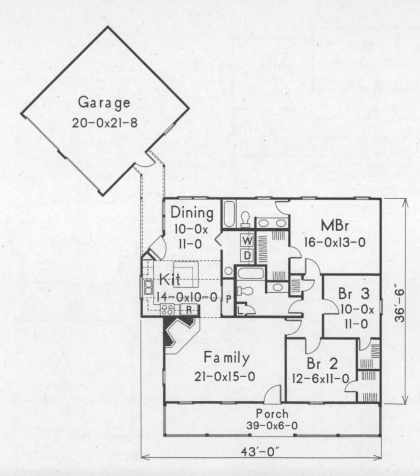

Garage
20-0x21-8

Dining
10-0x
11-0

MBr
16-0x13-0

Kit
14-0x10-0

Br 3
10-0x
11-0

Family
21-0x15-0

Br 2
12-6x11-0

Porch
39-0x6-0

36'-6"

43'-0"

Nostalgic Porch And Charming Interior

1,040 total square feet of living area

Price Code B

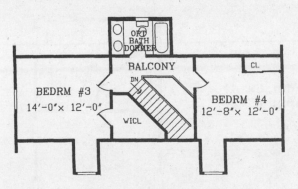

Optional Second Floor

BEDRM #3
14'-0" × 12'-0"

BALCONY

BEDRM #4
12'-8" × 12'-0"

OPT BATH DORMER

CL

WICL

DN

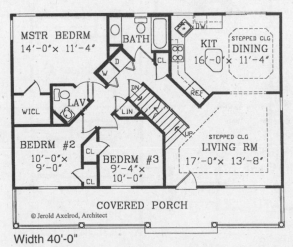

MSTR BEDRM
14'-0" × 11'-4"

BATH

KIT

STEPPED CLG
DINING
16'-0" × 11'-4"

WICL

LAV

LIN

BEDRM #2
10'-0" × 9'-0"

BEDRM #3
9'-4" × 10'-0"

STEPPED CLG
LIVING RM
17'-0" × 13'-8"

COVERED PORCH

© Jerold Axelrod, Architect

**First Floor
1,040 sq. ft.**

Width 40'-0"
Depth 32'-0"

Special features

- Affordable home has the ability to accommodate a small or large family
- An island in the kitchen greatly simplifies your food preparation efforts
- A wide archway joins the formal living room to the dramatic angled kitchen and dining room
- Optional second floor has an additional 597 square feet of living area
- 4 bedrooms, 2 baths
- Basement, crawl space or slab foundation, please specify when ordering

Open Ranch Living

1,704 total square feet of living area

Price Code B

Special features

- Open floor plan combines foyer, dining and living rooms together for an open airy feeling
- Kitchen has island that adds workspace and storage
- Bedrooms are situated together and secluded from the rest of the home
- 3 bedrooms, 2 baths
- Slab foundation

Width: 58'-4"
Depth: 45'-0"

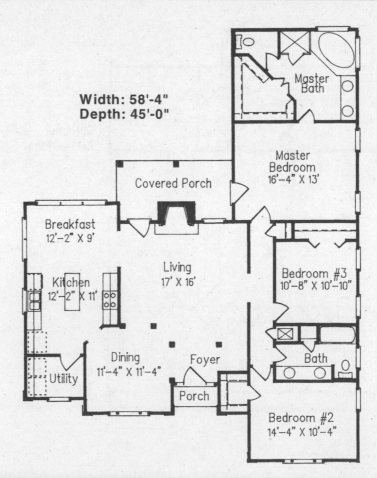

Classic Ranch Has Grand Appeal With Expansive Porch

1,400 total square feet of living area

Price Code A

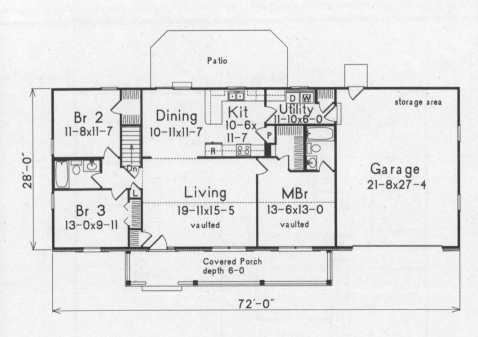

Patio

Br 2
11-8x11-7

Dining
10-11x11-7

Kit
10-6x
11-7

Utility
11-10x6-0

storage area

28'-0"

Br 3
13-0x9-11

Living
19-11x15-5
vaulted

MBr
13-6x13-0
vaulted

Garage
21-8x27-4

Covered Porch
depth 6-0

72'-0"

Special features

- Master bedroom is secluded for privacy
- Large utility room with additional cabinet space
- Covered porch provides an outdoor seating area
- Roof dormers add great curb appeal
- Vaulted ceilings in living room and master bedroom
- Oversized two-car garage with storage
- 3 bedrooms, 2 baths, 2-car garage
- Basement foundation, drawings also include crawl space foundation

TO ORDER BLUEPRINTS USE THE FORM ON PAGE 15 OR CALL TOLL-FREE 1-877-671-6036
View thousands more home plans online at www.familyhandyman.com/homeplans

199

Lots Of Details In This Modest Ranch

1,312 total square feet of living area

Price Code A

Special features

- A beamed ceiling and fireplace create an exciting feel to the living room
- Box window behind double sink in kitchen is a nice added feature
- Private bath and generous closet space in the master bedroom
- 3 bedrooms, 2 baths, 2-car garage
- Basement or crawl space foundation, please specify when ordering

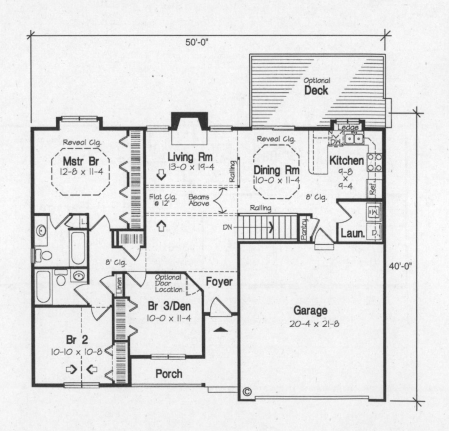

Combined Kitchen And Dining Room

1,092 total square feet of living area

Price Code AA

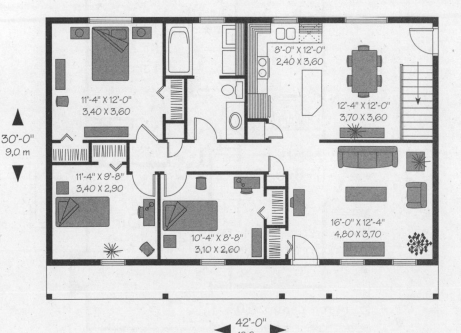

11'-4" X 12'-0"
3,40 X 3,60

8'-0" X 12'-0"
2,40 X 3,60

12'-4" X 12'-0"
3,70 X 3,60

11'-4" X 9'-8"
3,40 X 2,90

10'-4" X 8'-8"
3,10 X 2,60

16'-0" X 12'-4"
4,80 X 3,70

30'-0"
9,0 m

42'-0"
12,6 m

Special features

- Sunken family room adds interest
- Nice-sized bedrooms all are convenient to bath
- Handy work island in kitchen
- 3 bedrooms, 1 bath
- Basement foundation

Stylish Retreat For A Narrow Lot

1,084 total square feet of living area

Price Code AA

Special features

- Delightful country porch for quiet evenings
- Living room has a front feature window which invites the sun and includes a fireplace and dining area with private patio
- The U-shaped kitchen features lots of cabinets and bayed breakfast room with built-in pantry
- Both bedrooms have walk-in closets and access to their own bath
- 2 bedrooms, 2 baths
- Basement foundation

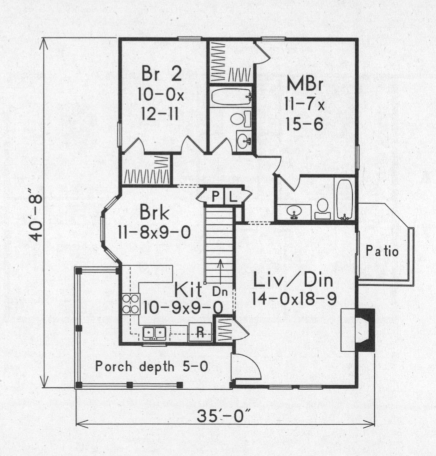

Br 2
10-0x
12-11

MBr
11-7 x
15-6

Brk
11-8x9-0

P L

Kit
10-9x9-0
Dn

Liv/Din
14-0x18-9

Patio

R

40'-8"

Porch depth 5-0

35'-0"

TO ORDER BLUEPRINTS USE THE FORM ON PAGE 15 OR CALL TOLL FREE 1-877-671-6036

View thousands more home plans online at www.familyhandyman.com/homeplans

Lovely Ranch Living

© 2003, Garrell Associates, Inc.

Christine 2/02

1,277 total square feet of living area

Price Code E

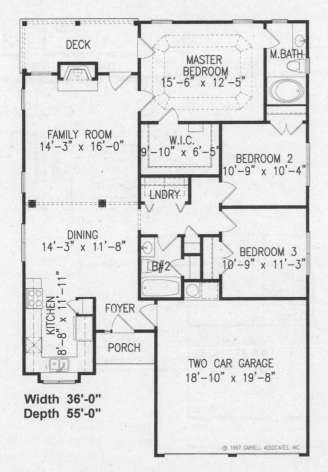

DECK

MASTER BEDROOM
15'-6" x 12'-5"

M. BATH

FAMILY ROOM
14'-3" x 16'-0"

W.I.C.
9'-10" x 6'-5"

BEDROOM 2
10'-9" x 10'-4"

LNDRY.

DINING
14'-3" x 11'-8"

B#2

BEDROOM 3
10'-9" x 11'-3"

KITCHEN
8'-8" x 11'-11"

FOYER

PORCH

TWO CAR GARAGE
18'-10" x 19'-8"

Width 36'-0"
Depth 55'-0"

© 1997 CARRELL ASSOCIATES, INC.

Special features

- Both the family room and master bedroom have direct access to an outdoor deck
- Compact, yet efficient kitchen
- Columns add distinction between dining and family rooms
- 3 bedrooms, 2 baths, 2-car garage
- Slab foundation

Traditional Farmhouse Feeling With This Home

2,582 total square feet of living area

Price Code D

Special features

- Both the family and living rooms are warmed by hearths

- The master suite on the second floor has a bayed sitting room and a private bath with whirl-pool tub

- Old-fashioned window seat in second floor landing is a charming touch

- 4 bedrooms, 3 baths, 2-car side entry garage

- Basement or crawl space foundation, please specify when ordering

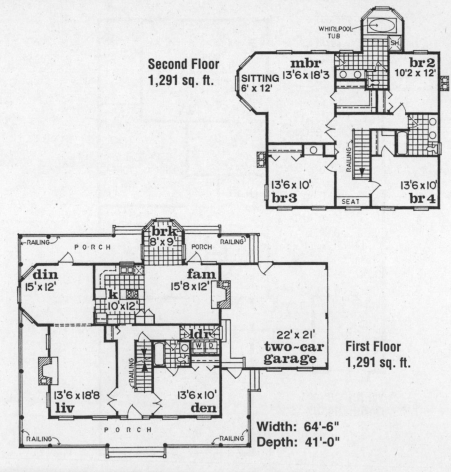

Second Floor 1,291 sq. ft.

WHIRLPOOL TUB

mbr 13'6 x 18'3

SITTING 6' x 12'

br 2 10'2 x 12'

RAILING

13'6 x 10' **br 3**

SEAT

13'6 x 10' **br 4**

First Floor 1,291 sq. ft.

RAILING · PORCH

brk 8' x 9'

PORCH · RAILING

din 15' x 12'

fam 15'8 x 12'

k 10' x 12'

ldr

W D

22' x 21' **two-car garage**

RAILING

13'6 x 18'8 **liv**

13'6 x 10' **den**

PORCH

RAILING · RAILING

Width: 64'-6"
Depth: 41'-0"

204

TO ORDER BLUEPRINTS USE THE FORM ON PAGE 15 OR CALL TOLL-FREE 1-877-671-6036
View thousands more home plans online at www.familyhandyman.com/homeplans

Attractive Entry Created By Full-Length Porch

2,357 total square feet of living area

Price Code D

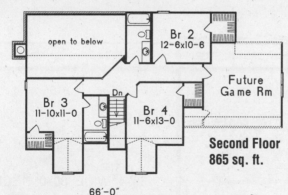

open to below

Br 2
12-6x10-6

Future Game Rm

Br 3
11-10x11-0

Dn

Br 4
11-6x13-0

Second Floor
865 sq. ft.

Special features

- 9' ceilings on first floor
- Secluded master bedroom includes private bath with double walk-in closets and vanity
- Balcony overlooks living room with large fireplace
- Second floor has three bed-rooms and an expansive game room
- 4 bedrooms, 3 1/2 baths, 2-car side entry garage
- Slab foundation, drawings also include crawl space foundation

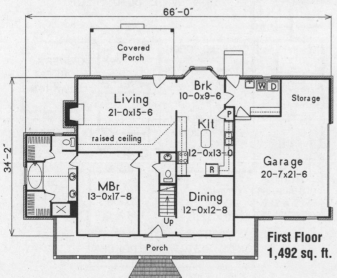

66'-0"

Covered Porch

Living
21-0x15-6

raised ceiling

Brk
10-0x9-6

W D

Storage

Kit
12-0x13-0

P

Garage
20-7x21-6

34'-2"

MBr
13-0x17-8

R

Dining
12-0x12-8

Up

Porch

First Floor
1,492 sq. ft.

Traditional Southern Design With Modern Floor Plan

2,214 total square feet of living area

Price Code D

Special features

- Great room has built-in cabinets for entertainment system, fireplace and French doors leading to private rear covered porch

- Dining room has an arched opening from foyer

- Breakfast room has lots of windows for a sunny open feel

- 3 bedrooms, 2 baths, 2-car side entry garage

- Crawl space or slab foundation, please specify when ordering

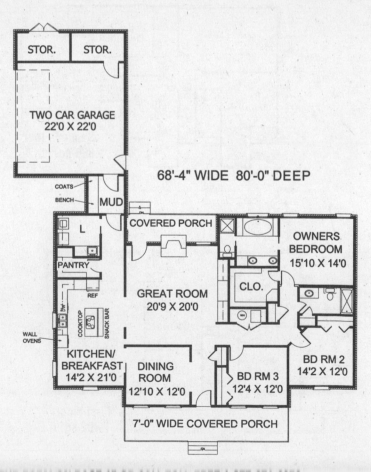

STOR.　STOR.

TWO CAR GARAGE
22'0 X 22'0

68'-4" WIDE　80'-0" DEEP

COATS
BENCH
MUD

COVERED PORCH

OWNERS BEDROOM
15'10 X 14'0

L

PANTRY

CLO.

GREAT ROOM
20'9 X 20'0

REF

COOKTOP

SNACK BAR

WALL OVENS

KITCHEN/ BREAKFAST
14'2 X 21'0

DINING ROOM
12'10 X 12'0

BD RM 3
12'4 X 12'0

BD RM 2
14'2 X 12'0

7'-0" WIDE COVERED PORCH

206

TO ORDER BLUEPRINTS USE THE FORM ON PAGE 15 OR CALL TOLL-FREE 1-877-671-6036
View thousands more home plans online at www.familyhandyman.com/homeplans

Handsome, Compact Ranch

1,296 total square feet of living area

Price Code B

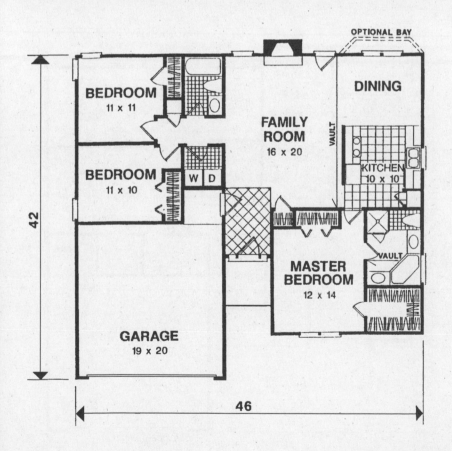

BEDROOM 11 x 11

BEDROOM 11 x 10

W D

FAMILY ROOM 16 x 20

VAULT

DINING

KITCHEN 10 x 10

MASTER BEDROOM 12 x 14

VAULT

GARAGE 19 x 20

OPTIONAL BAY

42

46

Special features

- Two secondary bedrooms share a bath and have convenient access to the laundry room
- Family room has a large fireplace flanked by sunny windows
- Master bedroom includes privacy as well as an amenity-full bath
- 3 bedrooms, 2 baths, 2-car garage
- Basement, crawl space or slab foundation, please specify when ordering

Plan #705-NDG-150

Unique Grilling Porch

1,353 total square feet of living area

Price Code A

Special features

- All bedrooms located together and away from living areas
- Dining room overlooks great room with fireplace
- Kitchen has counterspace for eating as well as plenty of storage
- 3 bedrooms, 2 baths, 2-car garage
- Slab or crawl space foundation, please specify when ordering

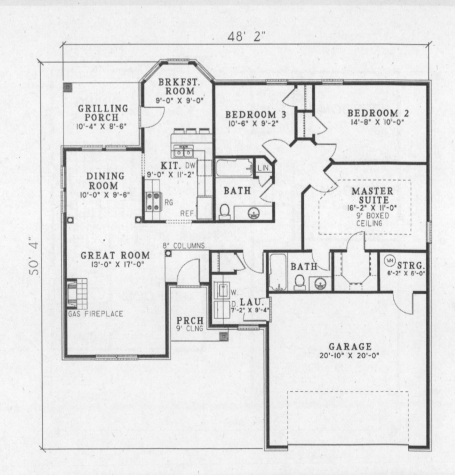

Wrap-Around Porch Adds Outdoor Living

1,814 total square feet of living area

Price Code C

Second Floor
890 sq. ft.

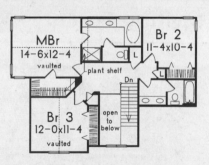

MBr
14-6x12-4
vaulted

Br 2
11-4x10-4

plant shelf

Dn

Br 3
12-0x11-4
vaulted

open to below

Special features

- Vaulted master bedroom features a walk-in closet and a private bath

- Exciting two-story entry with views into the dining room

- Family room, dining room and kitchen combine to make a great entertaining space with lots of windows

- 3 bedrooms, 2 1/2 baths, 2-car garage

- Basement foundation

50'-0"

Deck

42'-0"

Family
16-0x12-5

Dining
10-0x
12-5

Kit
13-2x
12-5

Living
12-0x12-4

Dn

Up

First Floor
924 sq. ft.

Porch Depth 6-0

Garage
22-5x22-9

Cottage-Style, Appealing And Cozy — Plan #705-0461

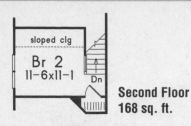

**Second Floor
168 sq. ft.**

Br 2
11-6x11-1

sloped clg

Dn

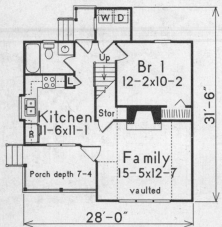

W D

Up

Br 1
12-2x10-2

Kitchen
11-6x11-1

Stor

Family
15-5x12-7
vaulted

Porch depth 7-4

31'-6"

28'-0"

**First Floor
660 sq. ft.**

828 total square feet of living area   Price Code AAA

Special features

- Vaulted ceiling in living area enhances space
- Convenient laundry room
- Sloped ceiling creates unique style in bedroom #2
- Covered entry porch provides cozy sitting area and plenty of shade
- 2 bedrooms, 1 bath
- Crawl space foundation

Quaint Cottage Has Inviting Porch — Plan #705-0650

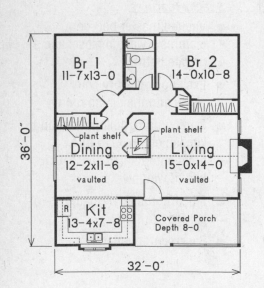

Br 1
11-7x13-0

Br 2
14-0x10-8

plant shelf

plant shelf

Dining
12-2x11-6
vaulted

Living
15-0x14-0
vaulted

Kit
13-4x7-8

Covered Porch
Depth 8-0

36'-0"

32'-0"

1,020 total square feet of living area   Price Code AA

Special features

- Living room is warmed by a fireplace
- Dining and living rooms are enhanced by vaulted ceilings and plant shelves
- U-shaped kitchen has a large window over the sink
- 2 bedrooms, 1 bath
- Slab foundation

Ideal For A Starter Home

800 total square feet of living area   **Price Code AAA**

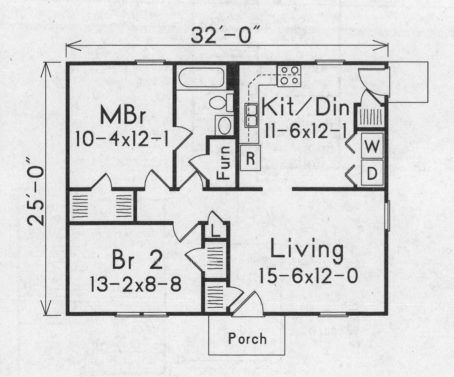

32'-0"

25'-0"

MBr
10-4x12-1

Kit/Din
11-6x12-1

Furn

R

W

D

Br 2
13-2x8-8

Living
15-6x12-0

L

Porch

Special features

- Master bedroom has walk-in closet and private access to bath
- Large living room features handy coat closet
- Kitchen includes side entrance, closet and convenient laundry area
- 2 bedrooms, 1 bath
- Crawl space foundation, drawings also include basement and slab foundations

Second Floor Study Area

1,751 total square feet of living area

Price Code B

Special features

- Charming covered front porch
- Elegant two-story entry
- Beautifully designed great room with fireplace opens to kitchen
- Large eating counter and walk-in pantry
- Second floor study area is perfect for a growing family
- 3 bedrooms, 2 1/2 baths, 2-car garage
- Crawl space foundation

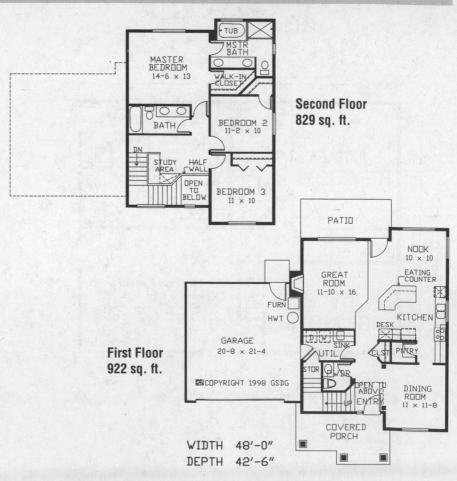

Second Floor
829 sq. ft.

MASTER BEDROOM 14-6 x 13
MSTR BATH
TUB
WALK-IN CLOSET
BATH
BEDROOM 2 11-2 x 10
DN
STUDY AREA
HALF WALL
OPEN TO BELOW
BEDROOM 3 11 x 10

First Floor
922 sq. ft.

PATIO
GREAT ROOM 11-10 x 16
NOOK 10 x 10
EATING COUNTER
FURN
HWT
GARAGE 20-8 x 21-4
KITCHEN
DESK
SINK
UTIL
CLST
PANTRY
STOR
PWDR
OPEN TO ABOVE
ENTRY
UP
DINING ROOM 11 x 11-8
COVERED PORCH
COPYRIGHT 1998 GSDG

WIDTH 48'-0"
DEPTH 42'-6"

Cottage With Atrium

969 total square feet of living area

Price Code AA

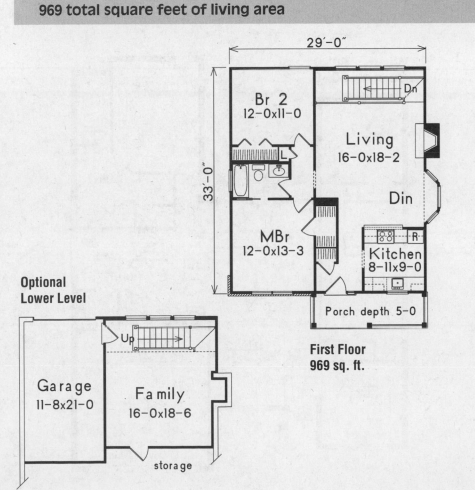

29'-0"

33'-0"

Br 2
12-0x11-0

Living
16-0x18-2

Din

MBr
12-0x13-3

Kitchen
8-11x9-0

Porch depth 5-0

**First Floor
969 sq. ft.**

**Optional
Lower Level**

Up

Garage
11-8x21-0

Family
16-0x18-6

storage

Special features

- Eye-pleasing facade enjoys stone accents with country porch for quiet evenings
- A bayed dining area, cozy fireplace and atrium with sunny two-story windows are the many features of the living room
- Step-saver kitchen includes a pass-through snack bar
- 325 square feet of optional living area available on the lower level
- 2 bedrooms, 1 bath, 1-car rear entry garage
- Walk-out basement foundation

Beautiful Brickwork Adds Elegance

1,960 total square feet of living area

Price Code C

Special features

- Open floor plan suitable for an active family
- Desk space in bedroom #3 ideal for a young student
- Effective design creates enclosed courtyard in rear of home
- 3 bedrooms, 2 baths, 2-car garage
- Slab foundation

Width: 50'-0"
Depth: 60'-8"

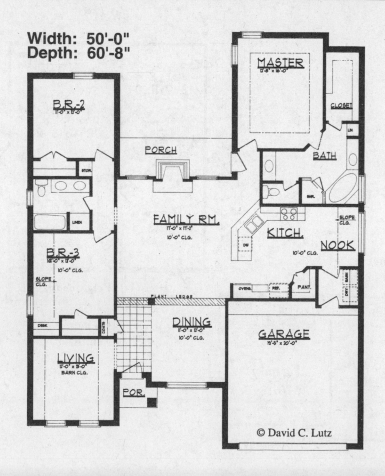

© David C. Lutz

TO ORDER BLUEPRINTS USE THE FORM ON PAGE 15 OR CALL TOLL-FREE 1-877-671-6036
View thousands more home plans online at www.familyhandyman.com/homeplans

THE Family Handyman

Massive Ranch With Classy Features

2,874 total square feet of living area

Price Code E

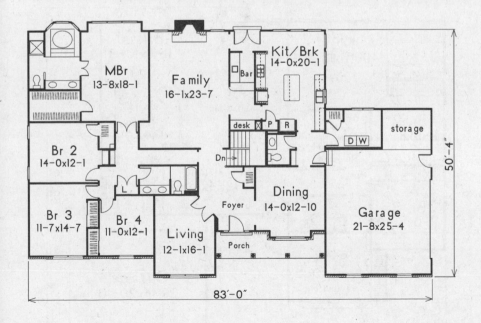

Special features

- Large family room with sloped ceiling and wood beams adjoins the kitchen and breakfast area with windows on two walls

- Large foyer opens to family room with massive stone fireplace and open stairs to the basement

- Private master bedroom with raised tub under the bay window, dramatic dressing area and a huge walk-in closet

- 4 bedrooms, 2 1/2 baths, 2-car side entry garage

- Basement foundation

Small Ranch For A Perfect Country Haven

1,761 total square feet of living area

Price Code B

Special features

- Exterior window dressing, roof dormers and planter boxes provide visual warmth and charm

- Great room boasts a vaulted ceiling, fireplace and opens to a pass-through kitchen

- Master bedroom is vaulted with luxury bath and walk-in closet

- Home features eight separate closets with an abundance of storage

- 4 bedrooms, 2 baths, 2-car side entry garage

- Basement foundation

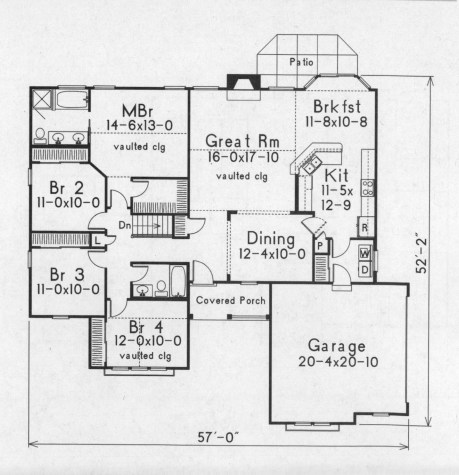

Covered Deck Off Breakfast Room   Plan #705-HDG-99004

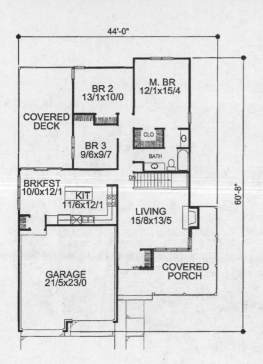

1,231 total square feet of living area   **Price Code A**

Special features

- Covered front porch
- Master bedroom has separate sink area
- Large island in kitchen for eat-in dining or preparation area
- 3 bedrooms, 1 bath, 2-car garage
- Basement foundation

Country Charm For A Narrow Lot   Plan #705-VL-1372

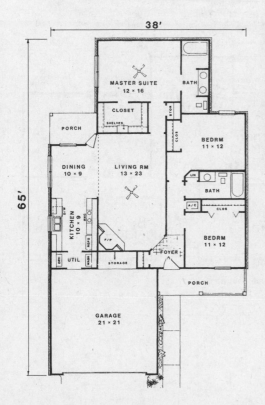

1,372 total square feet of living area   **Price Code A**

Special features

- Cozy living room with large corner fireplace
- Master suite has a very spacious closet and a private bath
- The secondary bedrooms are located in their own hall and away from other living areas
- 3 bedrooms, 2 baths, 2-car garage
- Slab or crawl space foundation, please specify when ordering

Classic Ranch, Pleasant Covered Front Porch

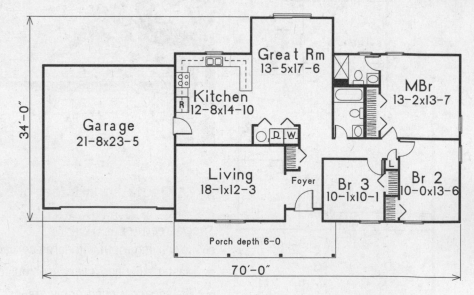

1,416 total square feet of living area

Price Code A

Special features

- Excellent floor plan eases traffic
- Master bedroom features private bath
- Foyer opens to both formal living room and informal family room
- Great room has access to the outdoors through sliding doors
- 3 bedrooms, 2 baths, 2-car garage
- Crawl space foundation, drawings also include basement foundation

Garage 21-8x23-5

Great Rm 13-5x17-6

Kitchen 12-8x14-10

MBr 13-2x13-7

Living 18-1x12-3

Foyer

Br 3 10-1x10-1

Br 2 10-0x13-6

34'-0"

70'-0"

Porch depth 6-0

TO ORDER BLUEPRINTS USE THE FORM ON PAGE 15 OR CALL TOLL-FREE 1-877-671-6036
View thousands more home plans online at www.familyhandyman.com/homeplans

Great Room Forms Core Of This Home

2,076 total square feet of living area

Price Code C

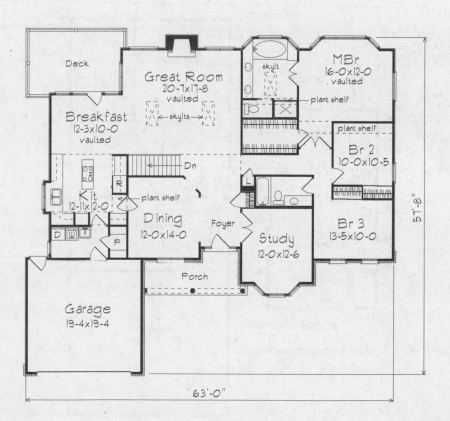

Special features

- Vaulted great room has fireplace flanked by windows and skylights that welcome the sun
- Kitchen leads to vaulted breakfast room and rear deck
- Study located off foyer provides great location for home office
- Large bay windows grace master bedroom and bath
- 3 bedrooms, 2 baths, 2-car garage
- Basement foundation

Arched Entry Adds Appeal

1,263 total square feet of living area

Price Code A

Special features

- 9' ceilings throughout most of this home

- Kitchen features large island eating bar ideal for extra seating when entertaining

- 3 bedrooms, 2 baths, 2-car side entry garage

- Basement foundation

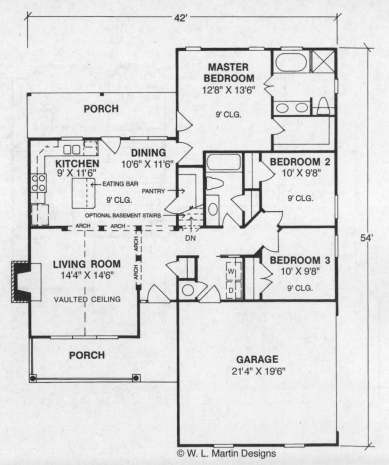

42'

MASTER BEDROOM
12'8" X 13'6"
9' CLG.

PORCH

DINING
10'6" X 11'6"

KITCHEN
9' X 11'6"

EATING BAR
9' CLG.

PANTRY

BEDROOM 2
10' X 9'8"
9' CLG.

OPTIONAL BASEMENT STAIRS

ARCH   ARCH

DN

54'

LIVING ROOM
14'4" X 14'6"

ARCH

ARCH

BEDROOM 3
10' X 9'8"
9' CLG.

W
D

VAULTED CEILING

PORCH

GARAGE
21'4" X 19'6"

© W. L. Martin Designs

Cottage-Style Adds Charm

1,496 total square feet of living area

Price Code A

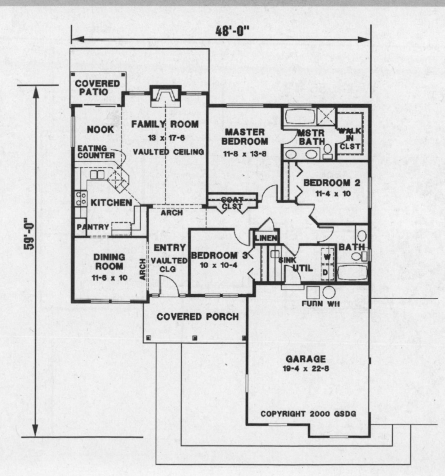

Special features

- Large utility room with sink and extra counterspace
- Covered patio off breakfast nook extends dining to the outdoors
- Eating counter in kitchen overlooks vaulted family room
- 3 bedrooms, 2 baths, 2-car side entry garage
- Crawl space foundation

Stone Facade Creates A Charming Feel

COPYRIGHTED 1997
GREG MARQUIS

1,842 total square feet of living area

Price Code C

Special features

■ Vaulted family room features fireplace and elegant bookcase

■ Island countertop in kitchen makes cooking convenient

■ Rear facade has intimate porch area ideal for relaxing

■ 3 bedrooms, 2 baths, 2-car garage

■ Slab or crawl space foundation, please specify when ordering

Width: 56'-4"
Depth: 68'-6"

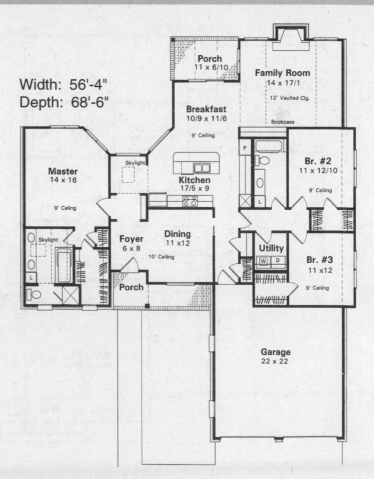

Porch
11 x 6/10

Family Room
14 x 17/1
12' Vaulted Clg.

Bookcase

Breakfast
10/9 x 11/6

9' Ceiling

Skylight

P

Br. #2
11 x 12/10

9' Ceiling

Master
14 x 16

9' Ceiling

Kitchen
17/5 x 9

L

Skylight

Foyer
6 x 8

Dining
11 x12

Utility

W D

Br. #3
11 x12

9' Ceiling

10' Ceiling

Porch

Garage
22 x 22

Prominent Central Living Room

2,177 total square feet of living area

Price Code C

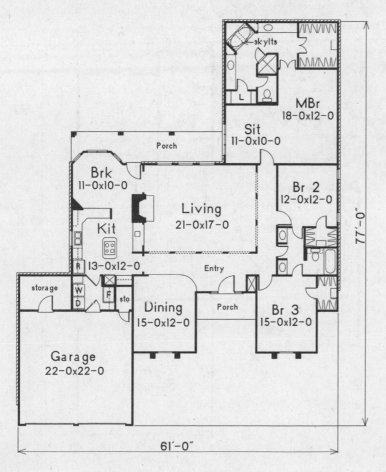

Special features

- Master suite features sitting area and double-door entry to elegant master bath
- Secondary bedrooms are spacious with walk-in closets and a shared bath
- Breakfast room with full windows open to the rear porch
- Exterior window treatments create a unique style
- Kitchen features an island cooktop, eating bar and wet bar that ls accessible to the living room
- 3 bedrooms, 2 baths, 2-car garage
- Slab foundation, drawings also include basement and crawl space foundations

Vaulted Living Area Adds Appeal

1,689 total square feet of living area

Price Code B

Special features

- Distinct covered entrance
- Large, open living and dining areas including vaulted ceiling, corner fireplace and access to the rear deck
- Stylish angled kitchen offers large counter work space and nook
- Master bedroom boasts spacious bath with step-up tub, separate shower and large walk-in closet
- 3 bedrooms, 2 baths, 2-car garage
- Basement foundation, drawings also include slab and crawl space foundations

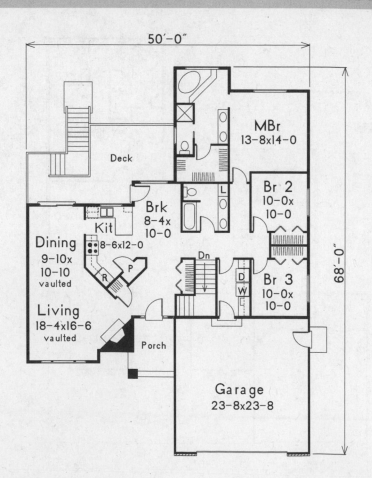

50'-0"

68'-0"

Deck

MBr
13-8x14-0

Br 2
10-0x
10-0

Brk
8-4x
10-0

Kit

Dining
9-10x
10-10
vaulted

8-6x12-0

Dn

Br 3
10-0x
10-0

Living
18-4x16-6
vaulted

Porch

Garage
23-8x23-8

TO ORDER BLUEPRINTS USE THE FORM ON PAGE 13 OR CALL TOLL FREE 1 877 671 6270
View thousands more home plans online at www.familyhandyman.com/HOMEPLANS

Open Breakfast/Family Room Combination

2,135 total square feet of living area

Price Code D

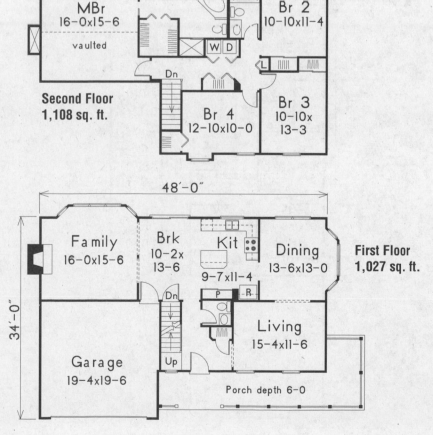

MBr
16-0x15-6
vaulted

Br 2
10-10x11-4

W D

Second Floor
1,108 sq. ft.

Dn

Br 4
12-10x10-0

Br 3
10-10x
13-3

48'-0"

Family
16-0x15-6

Brk
10-2x
13-6

Kit
9-7x11-4

Dining
13-6x13-0

First Floor
1,027 sq. ft.

34'-0"

Dn

P R

Living
15-4x11-6

Garage
19-4x19-6

Up

Porch depth 6-0

Special features

- Family room features extra space, impressive fireplace and full wall of windows that joins breakfast room creating a spacious entertainment area

- Washer and dryer conveniently located on the second floor

- Kitchen features island counter and pantry

- 4 bedrooms, 2 1/2 baths, 2-car garage

- Basement foundation

Ideal Ranch For A Narrow Lot

1,624 total square feet of living area   **Price Code B**

Special features

- Complete master bedroom suite with private entry from the outdoors

- Garage adjacent to utility room has a convenient storage closet

- Large family room and dining area with fireplace and porch access

- Pass-through kitchen opens directly to cozy breakfast area

- 3 bedrooms, 2 baths, 2-car side entry garage

- Basement foundation, drawings also include crawl space and slab foundations

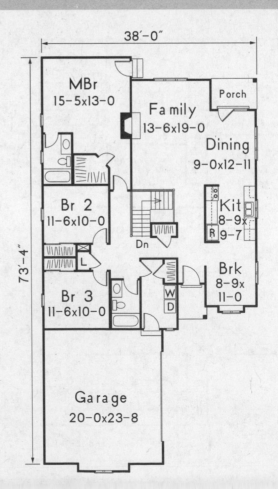

38'-0"

MBr
15-5x13-0

Family
13-6x19-0

Porch

Dining
9-0x12-11

73'-4"

Br 2
11-6x10-0

Kit
8-9x
9-7

Dn

L

Brk
8-9x
11-0

Br 3
11-6x10-0

W D

Garage
20-0x23-8

TO ORDER BLUEPRINTS USE THE FORM ON PAGE 15 OR CALL TOLL-FREE 1-877-671-6036
View thousands more home plans online at www.familyhandyman.com/homeplans

Built-In Media Center Focal Point In Living Room

1,539 total square feet of living area

Price Code B

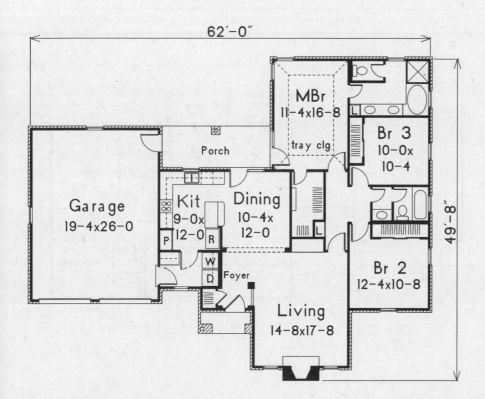

62'-0"

MBr
11-4x16-8

tray clg

Porch

Br 3
10-0x
10-4

Garage
19-4x26-0

Kit
9-0x
12-0

Dining
10-4x
12-0

49'-8"

P

R

W
D Foyer

Br 2
12-4x10-8

Living
14-8x17-8

Special features

- Standard 9' ceilings
- Master bedroom features 10' tray ceiling, access to porch, ample closet space and full bath
- Serving counter separates kitchen and dining room
- Foyer with handy coat closet opens to living area with fireplace
- Handy utility room near kitchen
- 3 bedrooms, 2 baths, 2-car garage
- Slab foundation

Lovely Arched Touches On The Covered Porch

1,594 total square feet of living area

Price Code B

Special features

- Corner fireplace in the great room creates a cozy feel
- Spacious kitchen combines with the dining room creating a terrific gathering place
- A handy family and guest entrance is a casual and convenient way to enter the home
- 3 bedrooms, 2 baths, 2-car garage
- Slab or crawl space foundation, please specify when ordering

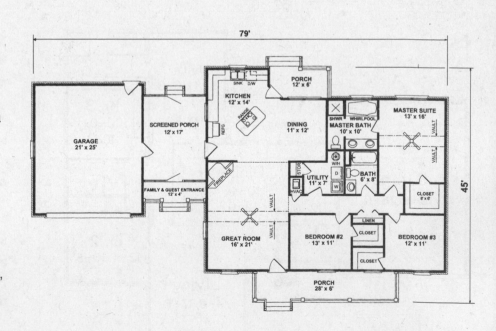

228

TO ORDER BLUEPRINTS USE THE FORM ON PAGE 15 OR CALL TOLL-FREE 1-877-671-6036
View thousands more home plans online at www.familyhandyman.com/homeplans

Front Porch Adds Style To This Ranch

1,496 total square feet of living area

Price Code A

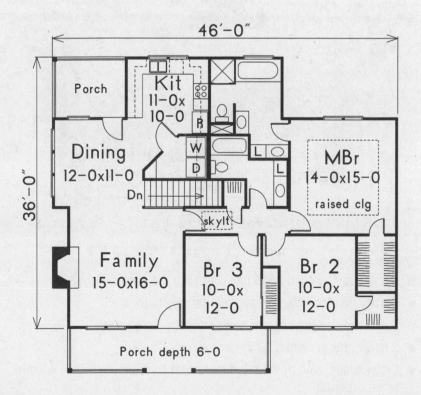

46'-0"

36'-0"

Porch

Kit
11-0x
10-0

Dining
12-0x11-0

Dn

sky lt

MBr
14-0x15-0

raised clg

Family
15-0x16-0

Br 3
10-0x
12-0

Br 2
10-0x
12-0

Porch depth 6-0

Special features

- Master bedroom features coffered ceiling, walk-in closet and spacious bath

- Vaulted ceiling and fireplace grace family room

- Dining room is adjacent to kitchen and features access to rear porch

- Convenient access to utility room from kitchen

- 3 bedrooms, 2 baths, 2-car drive under garage

- Basement foundation

Country Colonial Feel To This Home — Plan #705-DH-1377

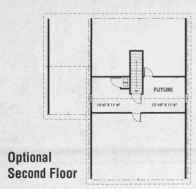

Optional Second Floor

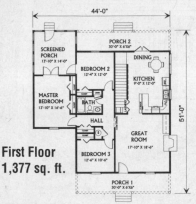

First Floor 1,377 sq. ft.

1,377 total square feet of living area — Price Code A

Special features

- Master bedroom has double-door access into screened porch
- Cozy dining area is adjacent to kitchen for convenience
- Great room includes fireplace
- Optional second floor has an additional 349 square feet of living area
- 3 bedrooms, 1 bath
- Crawl space or slab foundation, please specify when ordering

Traditional Ranch With Extras — Plan #705-FB-282

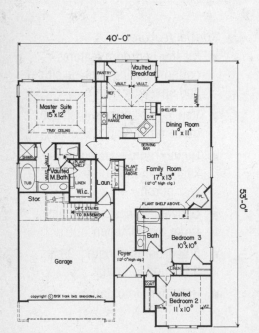

1,425 total square feet of living area — Price Code A

Special features

- Kitchen and vaulted breakfast room are the center of activity
- Corner fireplace warms spacious family room
- Oversized serving bar extends seating in dining room
- 3 bedrooms, 2 baths, 2-car garage
- Crawl space, slab or walk-out basement foundation, please specify when ordering

230

TO ORDER BLUEPRINTS USE THE FORM ON PAGE 15 OR CALL TOLL-FREE 1-877-671-6036
View thousands more home plans online at www.familyhandyman.com/homeplans

The Family **Handyman**

See-Through Fireplace Joins Gathering Rooms

1,684 total square feet of living area

Price Code B

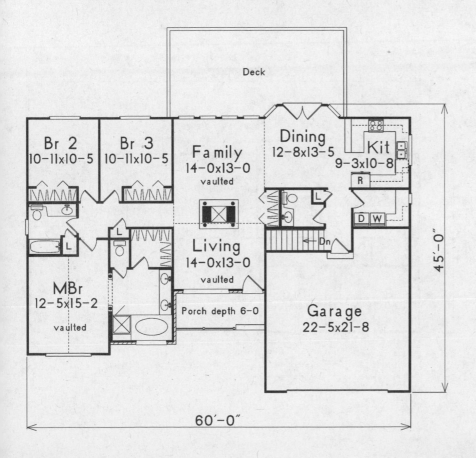

Deck

Br 2
10-11x10-5

Br 3
10-11x10-5

Family
14-0x13-0
vaulted

Dining
12-8x13-5

Kit
9-3x10-8

R

MBr
12-5x15-2
vaulted

Living
14-0x13-0
vaulted

D W

Dn

Porch depth 6-0

Garage
22-5x21-8

45'-0"

60'-0"

Special features

- Convenient double-doors in dining area provide access to large deck
- Family room features several large windows for brightness
- Bedrooms separate from living areas for privacy
- Master bedroom suite offers bath with walk-in closet, double-bowl vanity and both a shower and whirlpool tub
- 3 bedrooms, 2 1/2 baths, 2-car garage
- Basement foundation

Simplicity With Livability

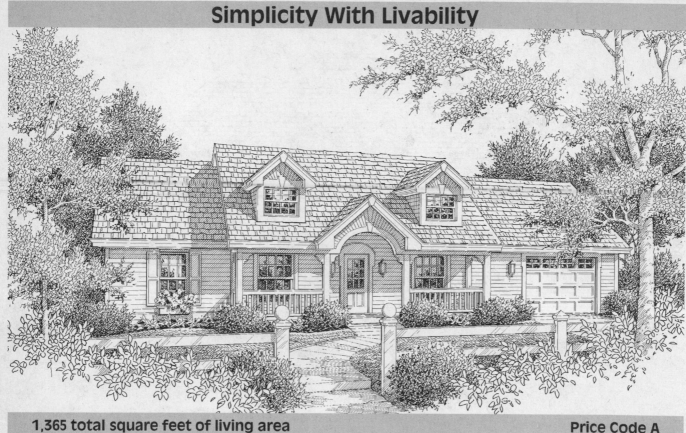

1,365 total square feet of living area

Price Code A

Special features

- Home is easily adaptable to physical accessibility featuring no stairs and extra wide hallways, baths laundry and garage

- Living room has separate entry and opens to a spacious dining room with views of rear patio

- L-shaped kitchen is well-equipped and includes a built-in pantry

- Both bedrooms are spaciously sized and offer generous closet storage

- 3 bedrooms, 2 baths, 1-car garage

- Slab foundation

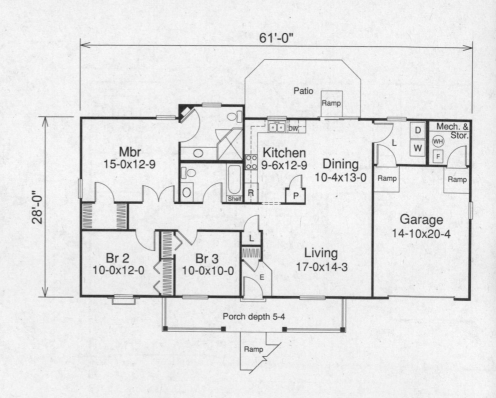

Distinctive Interior Design Elements

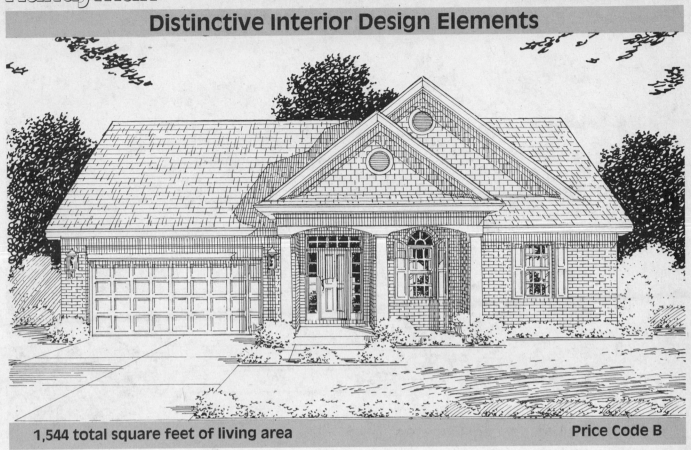

1,544 total square feet of living area

Price Code B

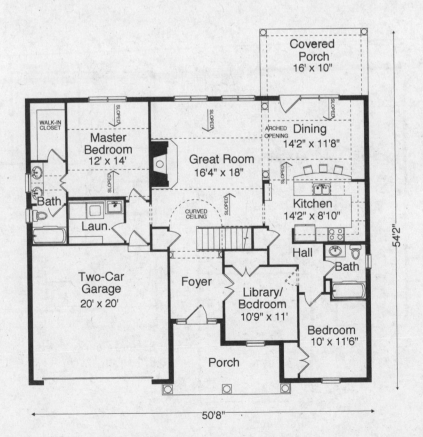

Special features

- A curved counter top with seating creates a delightful bar for quick meals
- Double-doors off the foyer enable one bedroom to function as a library offering flexibility
- Arched openings and sloped ceilings are nice additions to the design
- 3 bedrooms, 2 baths, 2-car garage
- Basement foundation

Great Room's Symmetry Steals The Show

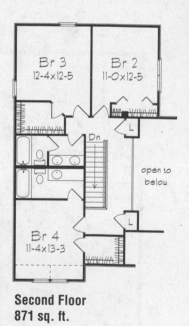

1,985 total square feet of living area

Price Code C

Special features

- Charming design for narrow lot
- Dramatic sunken great room features vaulted ceiling, large double-hung windows and transomed patio doors
- Grand master suite includes double entry doors, large closet, elegant bath and patio access
- 4 bedrooms, 3 1/2 baths, 2-car garage
- Basement foundation

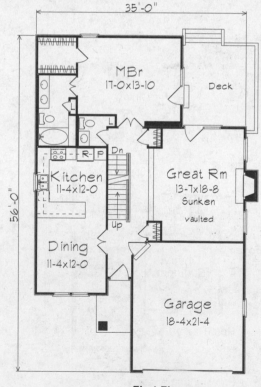

35'-0"

MBr
17-0x13-10

Deck

Br 3
12-4x12-5

Br 2
11-0x12-5

56'-0"

Kitchen
11-4x12-0

Great Rm
13-7x18-8
Sunken
vaulted

open to below

Dining
11-4x12-0

Br 4
11-4x13-3

Garage
18-4x21-4

Second Floor
871 sq. ft.

First Floor
1,114 sq. ft.

234

TO ORDER BLUEPRINTS USE THE FORM ON PAGE 15 OR CALL TOLL-FREE 1-877-671-6036
View thousands more home plans online at www.familyhandyman.com/homeplans

Popular Energy Efficient Design

1,536 total square feet of living area

Price Code B

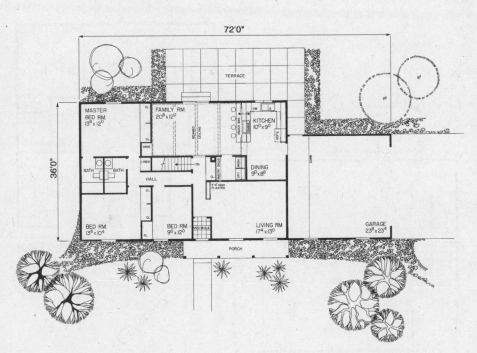

Special features

- Energy efficient design with 2" x 6" exterior walls
- Entry opens to a spacious living room
- Kitchen includes snack bar to make meal times easy and a nook ideal as a breakfast area
- 3 bedrooms, 2 baths, 2-car side entry garage
- Basement foundation

Plan #705-0734

Three-Car Apartment Garage With Country Flair

929 total square feet of living area

Price Code AA

Special features

- Spacious living room with dining area has access to 8' x 12' deck through glass sliding doors

- Splendid U-shaped kitchen features a breakfast bar, oval window above sink and impressive cabinet storage

- Master bedroom enjoys a walk-in closet and large elliptical feature window

- Laundry, storage closet and mechanical space are located off first floor garage

- 2 bedrooms, 1 bath, 3-car side entry garage

- Slab foundation

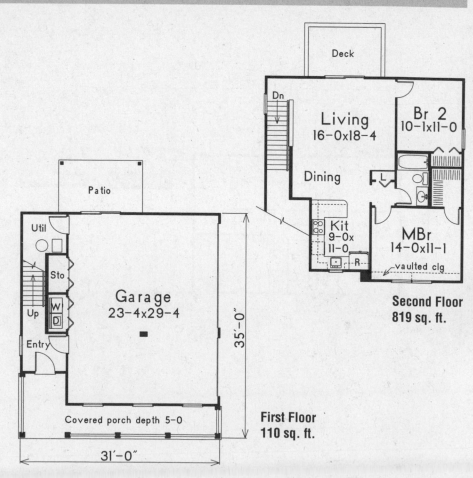

Second Floor
819 sq. ft.

First Floor
110 sq. ft.

TO ORDER BLUEPRINTS USE THE FORM ON PAGE 15 OR CALL TOLL-FREE 1-877-671-6036
View thousands more home plans online at www.familyhandyman.com/homeplans

Octagon-Shaped Dining Area

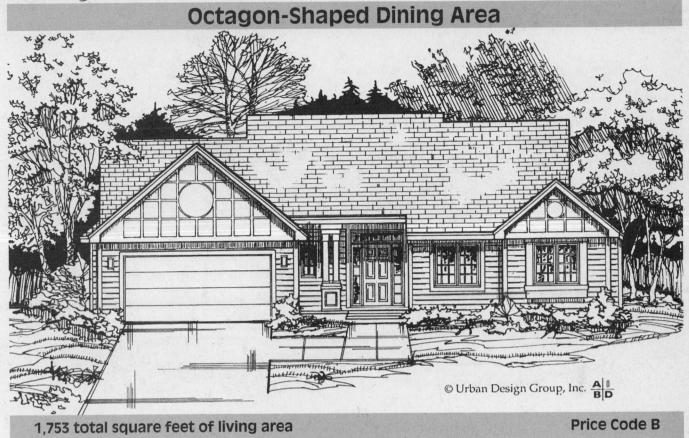

© Urban Design Group, Inc.

1,753 total square feet of living area

Price Code B

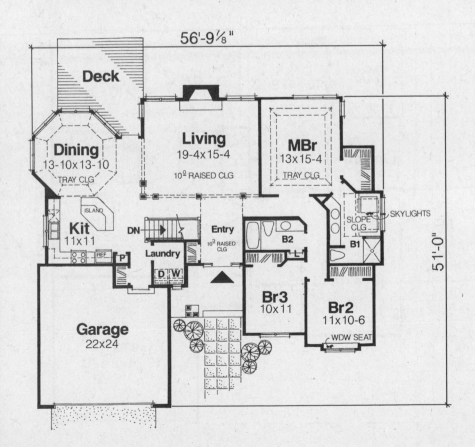

56'-9 1/8"

Deck

Dining
13-10 x 13-10
TRAY CLG

Living
19-4 x 15-4
10° RAISED CLG

MBr
13 x 15-4
TRAY CLG

ISLAND

Kit
11 x 11

REF

P

DN

Laundry

D W

Entry
10° RAISED CLG

B2

SLOPE CLG

SKYLIGHTS

B1

Garage
22 x 24

Br3
10 x 11

Br2
11 x 10-6
WDW SEAT

51'-0"

Special features

- Sloped ceiling and skylights brighten master bath
- Living room flooded with sunlight from windows flanking fireplace
- Kitchen has large island ideal for workspace or dining
- 3 bedrooms, 2 baths, 2-car garage
- Basement foundation

Designed For Handicap Access

1,578 total square feet of living area

Price Code B

Special features

- Plenty of closet, linen and storage space
- Covered porches in the front and rear of the home add charm to this design
- Open floor plan has unique angled layout
- 3 bedrooms, 2 baths, 2-car garage
- Basement foundation

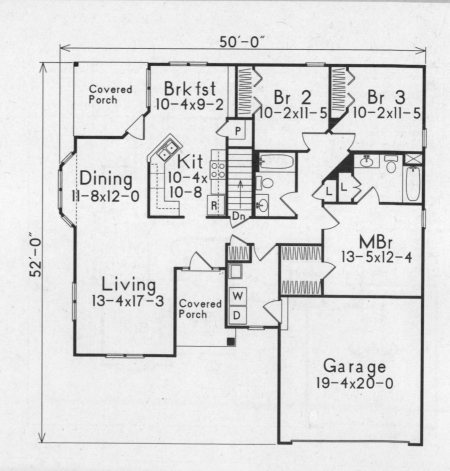

50'-0"

52'-0"

Covered Porch

Brkfst 10-4x9-2

Br 2 10-2x11-5

Br 3 10-2x11-5

Dining 11-8x12-0

Kit 10-4x 10-8

MBr 13-5x12-4

Living 13-4x17-3

Covered Porch

Garage 19-4x20-0

238

TO ORDER BLUEPRINTS USE THE FORM ON PAGE 15 OR CALL TOLL-FREE 1-877-671-6036
View thousands more home plans online at www.familyhandyman.com/homeplans

Distinctive Home For Sloping Terrain

1,340 total square feet of living area

Price Code A

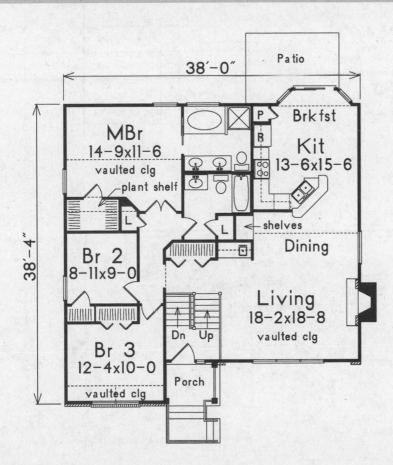

Special features

- Grand-sized vaulted living and dining rooms offer fireplace, wet bar and breakfast counter open to spacious kitchen
- Vaulted master suite features double entry doors, walk-in closet and elegant bath
- Basement includes a huge two-car garage and space for a bedroom/bath expansion
- 3 bedrooms, 2 baths, 2-car drive under garage with storage area
- Basement foundation

Charming Home Arranged For Open Living

1,609 total square feet of living area

Price Code B

Special features

- Kitchen captures full use of space with pantry, ample cabinets and workspace
- Master bedroom is well-secluded with walk-in closet and private bath
- Large utility room includes sink and extra storage
- Attractive bay window in dining area provides light
- 3 bedrooms, 2 1/2 baths, 2-car garage
- Slab foundation

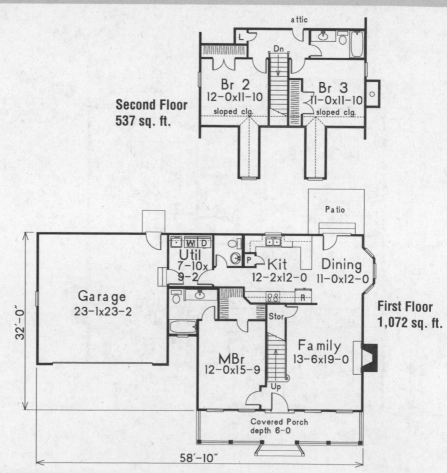

Second Floor
537 sq. ft.

First Floor
1,072 sq. ft.

Traditional-Style Two-Story

2,400 total square feet of living area

Price Code D

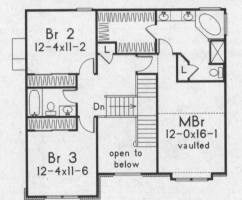

Second Floor
1,013 sq. ft.

- Br 2
  12-4x11-2
- Br 3
  12-4x11-6
- MBr
  12-0x16-1
  vaulted
- Dn
- open to below

Special features

- Use of T-stair makes efficient room travel
- Large kitchen/breakfast area has planning desk, center island and a walk-in pantry
- Generous closets are found in every bedroom
- 3 bedrooms, 2 1/2 baths, 3-car side entry garage
- Basement foundation

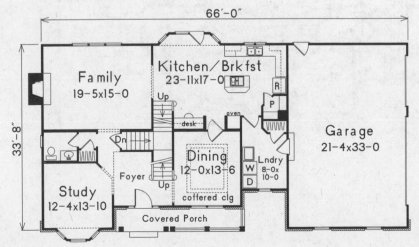

66'-0"

33'-8"

- Family
  19-5x15-0
- Kitchen/Brkfst
  23-11x17-0
- Garage
  21-4x33-0
- Dining
  12-0x13-6
  coffered clg
- Study
  12-4x13-10
- Lndry
  8-0x10-0
- Foyer
- Covered Porch
- Up
- Dn
- desk
- oven
- R
- P
- W D

First Floor
1,387 sq. ft.

TO ORDER BLUEPRINTS USE THE FORM ON PAGE 15 OR CALL TOLL-FREE 1-877-671-6036
View thousands more home plans online at www.familyhandyman.com/homeplans

Covered Patio For Outdoor Dining

2,061 total square feet of living area

Price Code C

Special features

- Charming stone facade entry
- Centrally located great room
- Private study in the front of the home is ideal as a home office
- Varied ceiling heights throughout this home
- 3 bedrooms, 2 1/2 baths, 2-car garage
- Crawl space or slab foundation, please specify when ordering

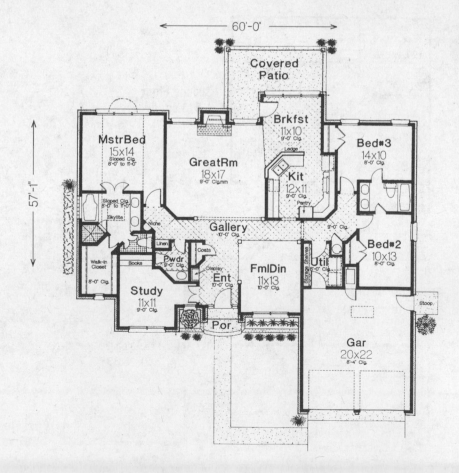

Open Layout Ensures Easy Living   Plan #705-0493

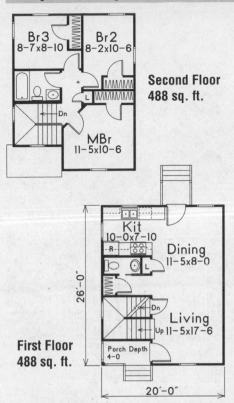

Second Floor
488 sq. ft.

First Floor
488 sq. ft.

976 total square feet of living area   Price Code AA

Special features

- Cozy front porch opens into large living room
- Convenient half bath is located on first floor
- All bedrooms are located on second floor for privacy
- Dining room has access to the outdoors
- 3 bedrooms, 1 1/2 baths
- Basement foundation

Perfect Fit For Narrow Lot   Plan #705-0494

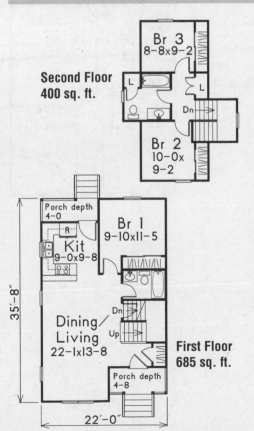

Second Floor
400 sq. ft.

First Floor
685 sq. ft.

1,085 total square feet of living area   Price Code AA

Special features

- Rear porch is a handy access through the kitchen
- Convenient hall linen closet located on the second floor
- Breakfast bar in kitchen offers additional counterspace
- Living and dining rooms combine for an open living atmosphere
- 3 bedrooms, 2 baths
- Basement foundation

TO ORDER BLUEPRINTS USE THE FORM ON PAGE 15 OR CALL TOLL-FREE 1-877-671-6036
View thousands more home plans online at www.familyhandyman.com/homeplans

243

Enhanced By Columned Porch

1,887 total square feet of living area

Price Code C

Special features

- Enormous great room is the heart of this home with an overlooking kitchen and dining room
- Formal dining room has a lovely bay window
- Master bedroom has spacious bath with corner step-up tub, double vanity and walk-in closet
- 3 bedrooms, 2 1/2 baths, 2-car garage
- Basement foundation

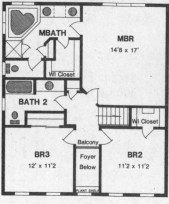

Second Floor
926 sq. ft.

MBATH

MBR
14'8 x 17'

WI Closet

BATH 2

WI Closet

Balcony

BR3
12' x 11'2

Foyer
Below

BR2
11'2 x 11'2

PLANT SHELF

PANTRY

DESK

DIN
10'6 x 11'8

GREAT RM
15'8 x 17'

Width: 52'-2"
Depth: 40'-0"

STOVE

KIT
12'3 x 11'

REF

Entry

DIN RM
11'10 x 12'

Two-Story
FOYER

Lav

Laun

W
D

GARAGE
23'4 x 23'4

Covered Entry

First Floor
961 sq. ft.

Modest Farmhouse Ranch

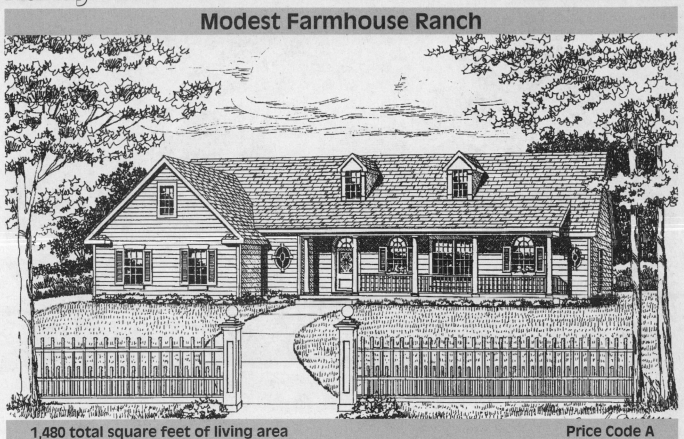

1,480 total square feet of living area　　　　**Price Code A**

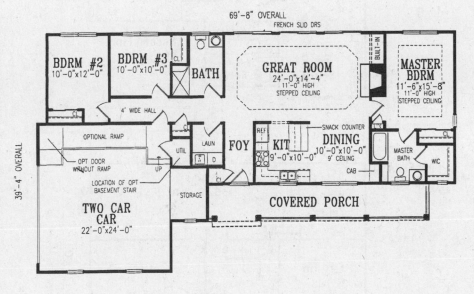

Special features

- Split bedroom floor plan with private master suite includes large bath and walk-in closet

- Fabulous great room features 11' high step ceiling, fireplace and media center

- Floor plan designed to be fully accessible for handicapped

- 3 bedrooms, 2 baths, 2-car side entry garage

- Basement, crawl space or slab foundation, please specify when ordering

Practical Two-Story, Full Of Features

2,058 total square feet of living area

Price Code C

Special features

- Handsome two-story foyer with balcony creates a spacious entrance area

- Vaulted ceiling in the master bedroom with private dressing area and large walk-in closet

- Skylights furnish natural lighting in the hall and master bath

- Conveniently located second floor laundry near bedrooms

- 3 bedrooms, 2 1/2 baths, 2-car garage

- Basement foundation, drawings also include slab and crawl space foundations

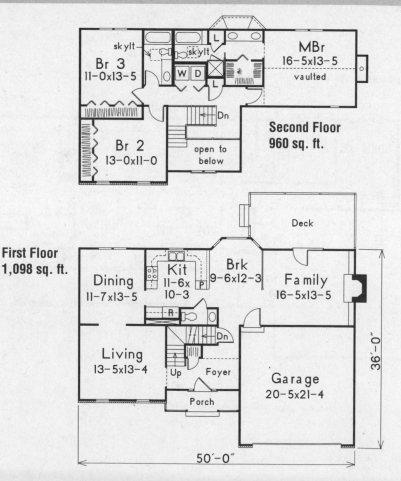

Second Floor 960 sq. ft.

Br 3 11-0x13-5
MBr 16-5x13-5 vaulted
W D
Br 2 13-0x11-0
open to below
Dn

First Floor 1,098 sq. ft.

Dining 11-7x13-5
Kit 11-6x 10-3
Brk 9-6x12-3
Family 16-5x13-5
Deck
Living 13-5x13-4
Foyer
Garage 20-5x21-4
Porch
Up
Dn
36'-0"
50'-0"

Old-Fashioned Porch Gives Welcoming Appeal

1,664 total square feet of living area

Price Code B

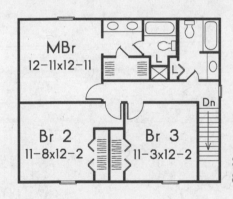

MBr
12-11x12-11

Br 2
11-8x12-2

Br 3
11-3x12-2

Dn

Second Floor
832 sq. ft.

Special features

- L-shaped country kitchen includes pantry and cozy breakfast area
- Bedrooms located on second floor for privacy
- Master bedroom includes walk-in closet, dressing area and bath
- 3 bedrooms, 2 1/2 baths, 2-car garage
- Crawl space foundation, drawings also include basement and slab foundations

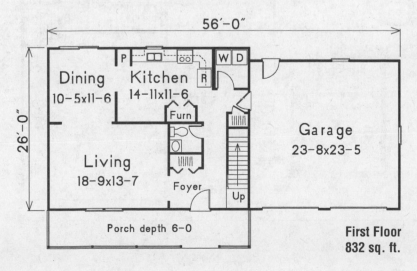

56'-0"

26'-0"

Dining
10-5x11-6

Kitchen
14-11x11-6

P

W D

R

Furn

Garage
23-8x23-5

Living
18-9x13-7

Foyer

Up

Porch depth 6-0

First Floor
832 sq. ft.

TO ORDER BLUEPRINTS USE THE FORM ON PAGE 15 OR CALL TOLL-FREE 1-877-671-6036
View thousands more home plans online at www.familyhandyman.com/homeplans

Country Flair In A Flexible Ranch

1,461 total square feet of living area

Price Code A

Special features

- Casual dining room
- Cathedral ceilings in great room and dining room give home a spacious feel
- Two bedroom home has option to become three bedroom
- 3 bedrooms, 2 baths, 2-car garage
- Basement foundation

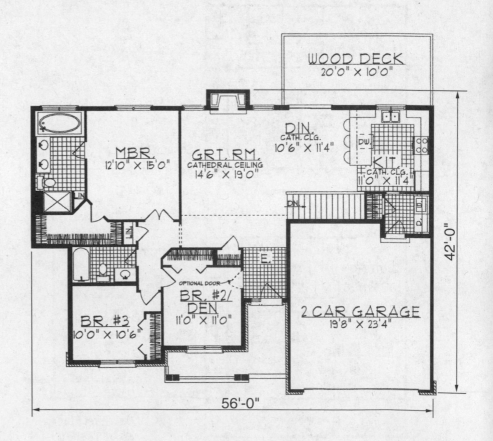

Compact, Convenient And Charming

1,266 total square feet of living area

Price Code A

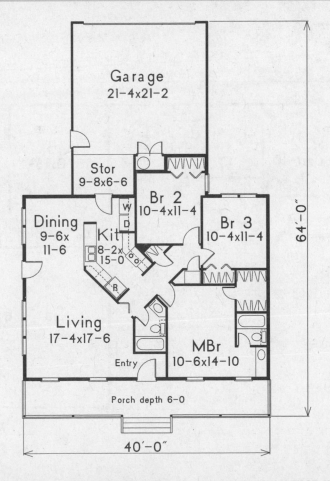

Special features

- Narrow frontage is perfect for small lots
- Energy efficient home with 2" x 6" exterior walls
- Prominent central hall provides a convenient connection for all main rooms
- Design incorporates full-size master bedroom complete with dressing room, bath and walk-in closet
- Angled kitchen includes handy laundry facilities and is adjacent to an oversized storage area
- 3 bedrooms, 2 baths, 2-car rear entry garage
- Crawl space foundation, drawings also include slab foundation

TO ORDER BLUEPRINTS USE THE FORM ON PAGE 15 OR CALL TOLL-FREE 1-877-671-6036

View thousands more home plans online at www.familyhandyman.com/homeplans

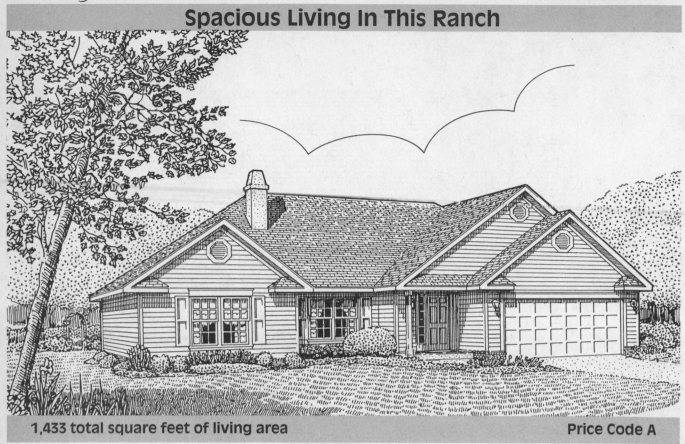

Spacious Living In This Ranch

1,433 total square feet of living area

Price Code A

Special features

- Vaulted living room includes cozy fireplace and an oversized entertainment center

- Bedrooms #2 and #3 share a full bath

- Master bedroom has a full bath and large walk-in closet

- 3 bedrooms, 2 baths, 2-car garage

- Basement foundation, drawings also include crawl space and slab foundations

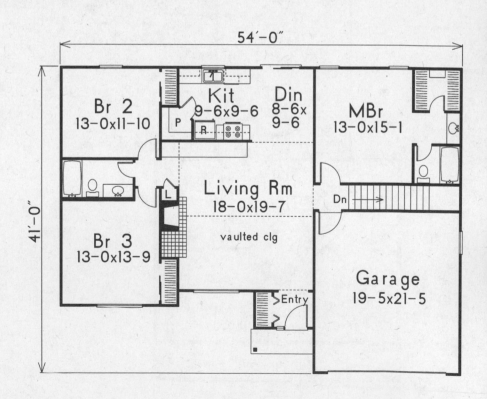

54'-0"

41'-0"

Br 2
13-0x11-10

Kit
9-6x9-6

Din
8-6x
9-6

MBr
13-0x15-1

P

R

Living Rm
18-0x19-7

vaulted clg

Dn

Br 3
13-0x13-9

L

Entry

Garage
19-5x21-5

Island Work Space

1,464 total square feet of living area

Price Code C

Second Floor
809 sq. ft.

MASTER
12/0 X 13/0

LINEN

BR. 3
10/8 X 10/0

W.D.

DN

FOYER BELOW

BR. 2
11/0 X 11/8

Special features

- Contemporary styled home has breathtaking two-story foyer and lovely open staircase
- Efficiently designed U-shaped kitchen
- Elegant great room has a cozy fireplace
- 3 bedrooms, 2 1/2 baths, 2-car garage
- Crawl space foundation

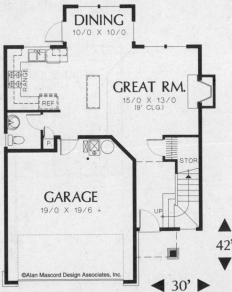

DINING
10/0 X 10/0

RANGE

REF

GREAT RM.
15/0 X 13/0
(9' CLG.)

P.

STOR

GARAGE
19/0 X 19/6 +

UP

42'

30'

First Floor
655 sq. ft.

©Alan Mascord Design Associates, Inc.

Narrow Lot Design

1,093 total square feet of living area

Price Code AA

Special features

- Family room with fireplace overlooks large covered porch
- Vaulted family and dining rooms are adjacent to kitchen
- Bedroom #2 has its own entrance into bath
- Plant shelf accents vaulted foyer
- Centrally located laundry area
- 2 bedrooms, 2 baths, 2-car garage
- Slab foundation

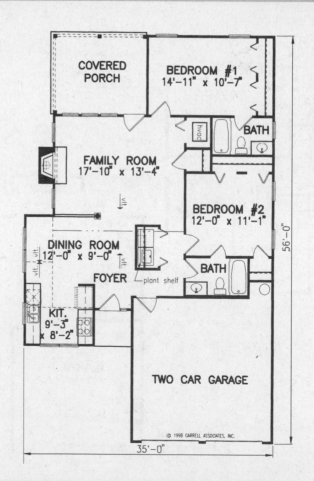

1,429 total square feet of living area

Price Code A

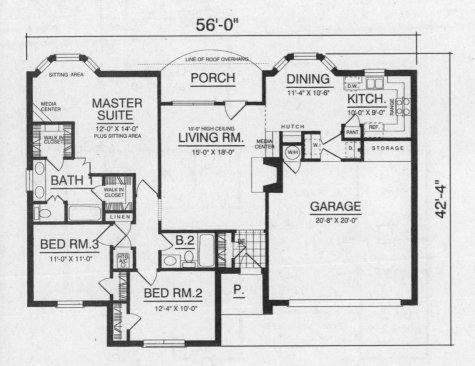

56'-0"

LINE OF ROOF OVERHANG

SITTING AREA

MEDIA CENTER

MASTER SUITE
12'-0" X 14'-0"
PLUS SITTING AREA

WALK IN CLOSET

PORCH

DINING
11'-4" X 10'-6"

KITCH.
10'-0" X 9'-0"

D.W.

RANGE

HUTCH

10'-0" HIGH CEILING
LIVING RM.
15'-0" X 18'-0"

MEDIA CENTER

PANT

REF.

W/H

W.

D.

STORAGE

BATH 1

WALK IN CLOSET

LINEN

BED RM.3
11'-0" X 11'-0"

HTG A/C

B.2

GARAGE
20'-8" X 20'-0"

42'-4"

BED RM.2
12'-4" X 10'-0"

P.

Special features

- Master suite with sitting area and private bath includes double walk-in closets
- Kitchen and dining area overlook living room
- Living room has fireplace, media center and access to covered porch
- 3 bedrooms, 2 baths, 2-car garage
- Slab or crawl space foundation, please specify when ordering

Isolated Master Suite Has Grand Master Bath

1,856 total square feet of living area

Price Code C

Special features

- Living room features include fireplace, 12' ceiling and skylights

- Energy efficient home with 2" x 6" exterior walls

- Common vaulted ceiling creates open atmosphere in kitchen and breakfast room

- Garage with storage areas conveniently accesses home through handy utility room

- Private hall separates secondary bedrooms from living areas

- 3 bedrooms, 2 baths, 2-car side entry garage

- Slab foundation, drawings also include crawl space foundation

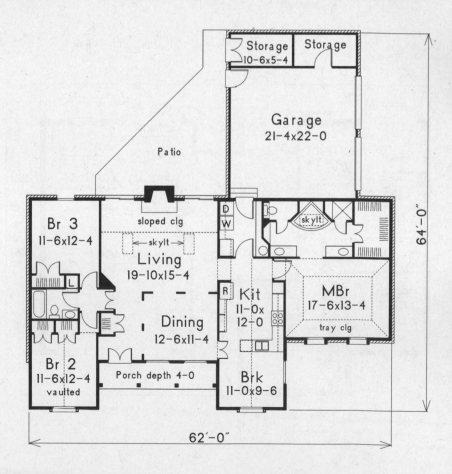

Gables Accent This Home

1,239 total square feet of living area

Price Code A

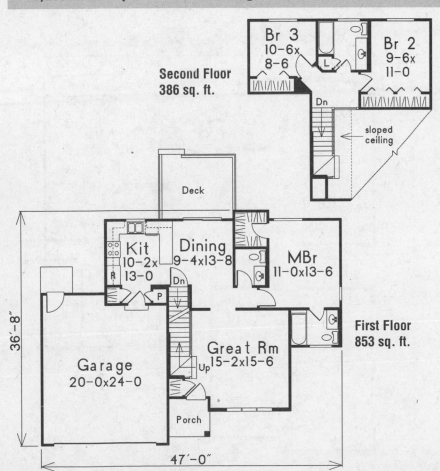

Second Floor
386 sq. ft.

Br 3
10-6x
8-6

Br 2
9-6x
11-0

Dn

sloped ceiling

Deck

Kit
10-2x
13-0

Dining
9-4x13-8

MBr
11-0x13-6

Dn

P

First Floor
853 sq. ft.

Garage
20-0x24-0

Great Rm
15-2x15-6

Up

Porch

36'-8"

47'-0"

Special features

- Master suite has private bath and walk-in closet
- Convenient coat closet and pantry located near the garage entrance
- Kitchen and dining area open onto deck
- Open stairway with sloped ceiling creates an open atmosphere in the great room
- 3 bedrooms, 2 1/2 baths, 2-car garage
- Basement foundation

TO ORDER BLUEPRINTS USE THE FORM ON PAGE 15 OR CALL TOLL-FREE 1-877-671-6036
View thousands more home plans online at www.familyhandyman.com/homeplans

255

Flexible Design Is Popular

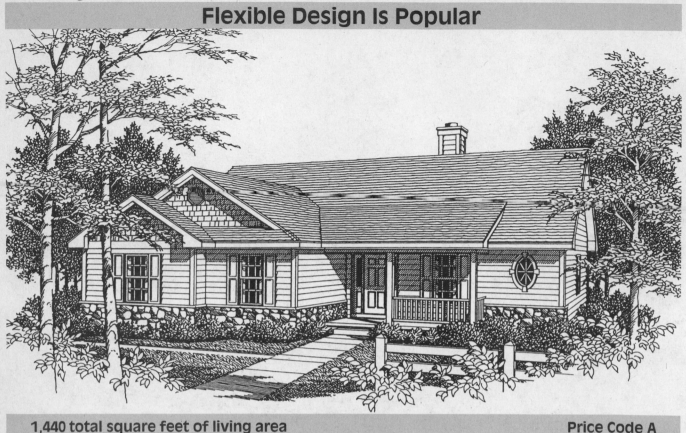

1,440 total square feet of living area

Price Code A

Special features

- Open floor plan with access to covered porches in front and back
- Lots of linen, pantry and closet space throughout
- Laundry/mud room between kitchen and garage is a convenient feature
- 2 bedrooms, 2 baths, 2-car side entry garage
- Basement foundation

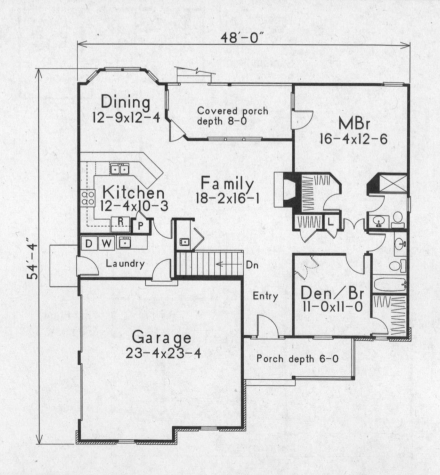

Gable Facade Adds Appeal To This Ranch

1,304 total square feet of living area

Price Code A

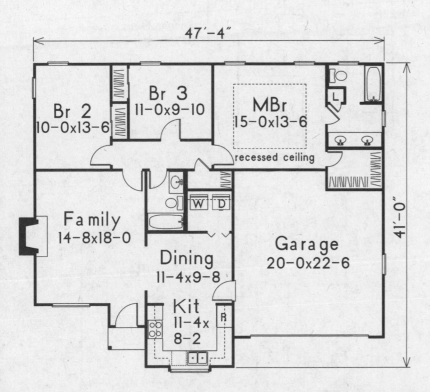

47'-4"

Br 2
10-0x13-6

Br 3
11-0x9-10

MBr
15-0x13-6
recessed ceiling

Family
14-8x18-0

Dining
11-4x9-8

Garage
20-0x22-6

Kit
11-4x
8-2

W D

41'-0"

Special features

- Covered entrance leads into family room with 10' ceiling and fireplace

- 10' ceilings in kitchen, dining and family rooms

- Master bedroom features coffered ceiling, walk-in closet and private bath

- Efficient kitchen includes large window over the sink

- 3 bedrooms, 2 baths, 2-car garage

- Slab foundation

TO ORDER BLUEPRINTS USE THE FORM ON PAGE 15 OR CALL TOLL-FREE 1-877-671-6036
View thousands more home plans online at www.familyhandyman.com/homeplans

257

Spacious Family Room For Growing Families

2,147 total square feet of living area

Price Code C

Special features

- Living and dining rooms adjacent to entry foyer for easy access
- Kitchen conveniently located to sunny breakfast nook
- Master suite includes large walk-in closet and luxurious bath
- Breakfast area offers easy access to deck
- 4 bedrooms, 2 1/2 baths, 2-car garage
- Basement foundation

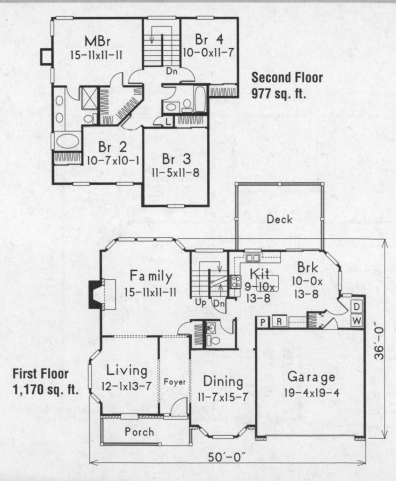

MBr 15-11x11-11

Br 4 10-0x11-7

Second Floor 977 sq. ft.

Br 2 10-7x10-1

Br 3 11-5x11-8

Deck

Family 15-11x11-11

Kit 9-10x 13-8

Brk 10-0x 13-8

First Floor 1,170 sq. ft.

Living 12-1x13-7

Foyer

Dining 11-7x15-7

Garage 19-4x19-4

Porch

36'-0"

50'-0"

Spacious And Open Family Living Area

1,416 total square feet of living area

Price Code A

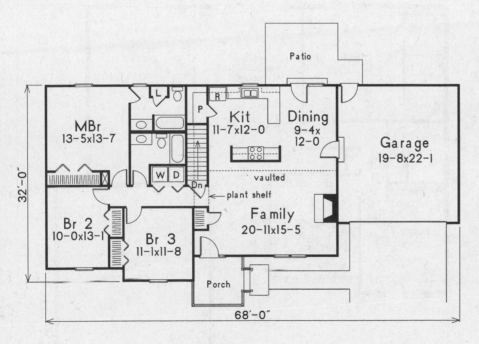

Special features

- Family room includes fireplace, elevated plant shelf and vaulted ceiling
- Patio is accessible from dining area and garage
- Centrally located laundry area
- Oversized walk-in pantry
- 3 bedrooms, 2 baths, 2-car garage
- Basement foundation, drawings also include crawl space and slab foundations

A Vaulted Ceiling And Lots Of Windows In Living Room

1,508 total square feet of living area

Price Code B

Special features

- A spacious kitchen layout makes food preparation easy
- A vaulted entry is inviting
- Varied ceiling heights throughout
- 3 bedrooms, 2 baths, 2-car garage
- Basement foundation

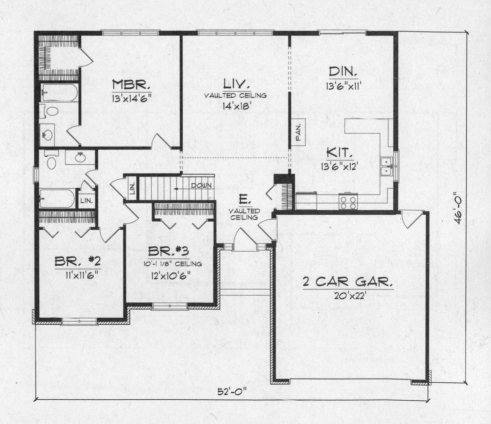

260

TO ORDER BLUEPRINTS USE THE FORM ON PAGE 15 OR CALL TOLL-FREE 1-877-671-6036
View thousands more home plans online at www.familyhandyman.com/homeplans

Bold Windows Enhance Front Entry

2,252 total square feet of living area

Price Code D

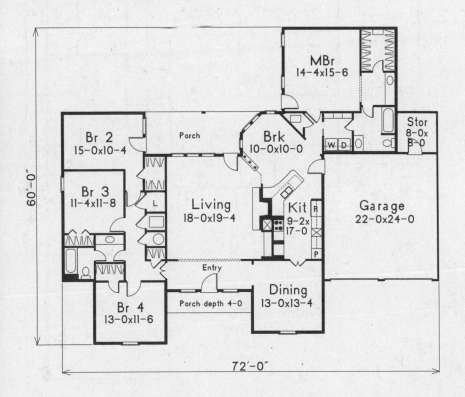

MBr
14-4x15-6

Stor
8-0x
8-0

Br 2
15-0x10-4

Porch

Brk
10-0x10-0

W D

Br 3
11-4x11-8

L

Living
18-0x19-4

Kit
9-2x
17-0

R
P

Garage
22-0x24-0

Entry

Br 4
13-0x11-6

Porch depth 4-0

Dining
13-0x13-4

60'-0"

72'-0"

Special features

- Energy efficient home with 2" x 6" exterior walls
- Central living area
- Private master bedroom with large walk-in closet, dressing area and bath
- Secondary bedrooms are in a suite arrangement with plenty of closet space
- Sunny breakfast room looks out over the porch and patio
- Large entry area highlighted by circle-top transoms
- 4 bedrooms, 2 baths, 2-car garage
- Slab foundation, drawings also include basement and crawl space foundations

Office/Game Room With Separate Entrance

2,361 total square feet of living area

Price Code D

Special features

- Enormous breakfast area and kitchen area create a perfect gathering place
- Family room enhanced with wall of windows and a large fireplace
- Office/gameroom easily accessible through separate side entrance
- 4 bedrooms, 3 baths, 2-car side entry garage
- Basement foundation

Master
14 x 17
9' Clg.

Family Room
17/2 x 18/4
14' Clg.
Sloped Clg.

Porch
16 x 8

Br.#3
12 x 11
9' Clg.

Breakfast
12 x 13
9' Clg.

Br.#2
13/8 x 11
9' Clg.

8 x 13

Dining
11 x 12
9' Clg.

Foyer
5/10 x 9

Kitchen
12 x 13/6

Desk

Shelves

Snack Bar

Stairs Down

Pan

D W

Porch
23/10 x 6

Office / Gameroom
17/5 x 14
9' Clg.

Garage
22 x 22

Width: 66'-10"
Depth: 69'-5"

1,230 total square feet of living area

Price Code A

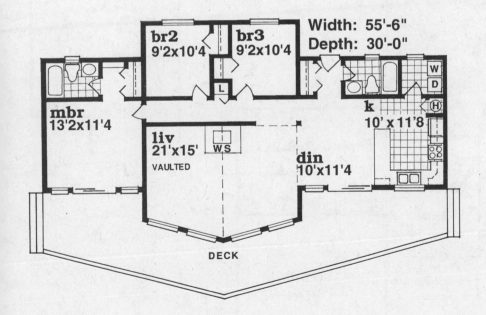

Width: 55'-6"
Depth: 30'-0"

br2
9'2x10'4

br3
9'2x10'4

mbr
13'2x11'4

liv
21'x15'
W S
VAULTED

din
10'x11'4

k
10' x 11'8

W
D

H

L

DECK

Special features

- Full-width deck creates plenty of outdoor living area

- The master bedroom accesses the deck through sliding glass doors and features a private bath

- Vaulted living room has a woodstove

- 3 bedrooms, 2 baths

- Crawl space or basement foundation, please specify when ordering

TO ORDER BLUEPRINTS USE THE FORM ON PAGE 15 OR CALL TOLL-FREE 1-877-671-6036
View thousands more home plans online at www.familyhandyman.com/homeplans

263

Spacious Vaulted Great Room

1,189 total square feet of living area

Price Code AA

Special features

- All bedrooms are located on the second floor

- Dining room and kitchen both have views of the patio

- Convenient half bath located near the kitchen

- Master bedroom has private bath

- 3 bedrooms, 2 1/2 baths, 2-car garage

- Basement foundation

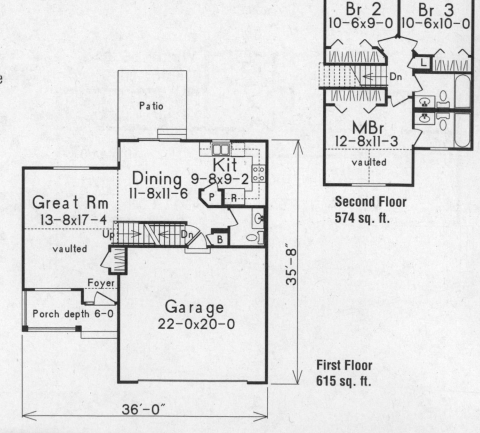

Second Floor
574 sq. ft.

First Floor
615 sq. ft.

Spacious Dining And Living Areas

1,104 total square feet of living area

Price Code AA

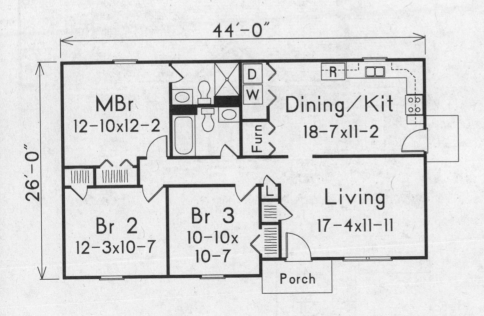

44'-0"

26'-0"

MBr
12-10x12-2

Dining/Kit
18-7x11-2

D
W

Furn

Br 2
12-3x10-7

Br 3
10-10x
10-7

L

Living
17-4x11-11

Porch

R

Special features
- Master bedroom includes private bath
- Convenient side entrance to dining area/kitchen
- Laundry area located near kitchen
- Large living area creates a comfortable atmosphere
- 3 bedrooms, 2 baths
- Crawl space foundation, drawings also include basement and slab foundations

Arched Window Is A Focal Point   Plan #705-RJ-A1079

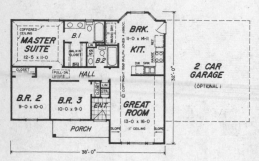

1,021 total square feet of living area   Price Code AA

Special features

- 11' ceiling in great room expands living area
- Combination kitchen/breakfast room allows for easy preparation and cleanup
- Master suite features private bath and an oversized walk-in closet
- 3 bedrooms, 2 baths, optional 2-car garage
- Slab or crawl space foundation, please specify when ordering

Inviting Victorian Details   Plan #705-VL947

Special features

- Efficiently designed kitchen/dining area accesses the outdoors onto a rear porch
- Future expansion plans included which allow the home to become 392 square feet larger with 3 bedrooms and 2 baths
- 2 bedrooms, 1 bath
- Crawl space or slab foundation, please specify when ordering

947 total square feet of living area   Price Code AA

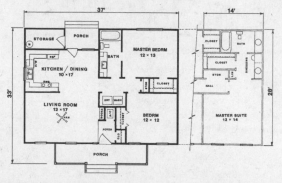

TO ORDER BLUEPRINTS USE THE FORM ON PAGE 15 OR CALL TOLL-FREE 1-877-671-6036
View thousands more home plans online at www.familyhandyman.com/homeplans

Open Living Area Adds Drama To Home

1,340 total square feet of living area

Price Code A

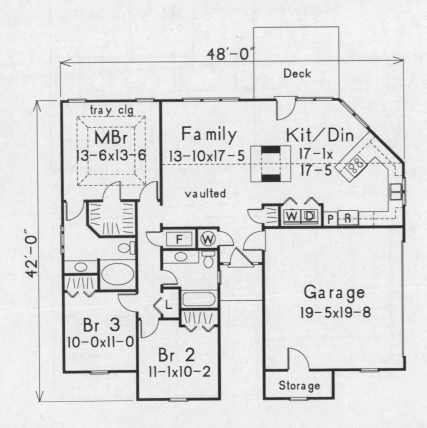

Special features

- Master bedroom has private bath and walk-in closet

- Recessed entry leads to vaulted family room with see-through fireplace to dining area

- Garage includes handy storage area

- Convenient laundry closet in the kitchen

- 3 bedrooms, 2 baths, 2-car side entry garage

- Slab foundation, drawings also include crawl space foundation

Plan #705-0222

Traditional Styling At Its Best

2,358 total square feet of living area

Price Code D

Special features

- U-shaped kitchen provides an ideal layout while adjoining breakfast room allows for casual dining

- Formal dining and living rooms have attractive floor-to-ceiling windows

- Master bedroom includes deluxe bath

- 4 bedrooms, 2 1/2 baths, 2-car garage

- Basement foundation, drawings also include crawl space and slab foundations

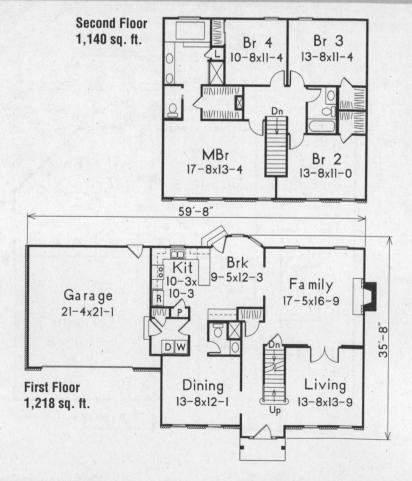

Second Floor 1,140 sq. ft.

Br 4
10-8x11-4

Br 3
13-8x11-4

Dn

MBr
17-8x13-4

Br 2
13-8x11-0

59'-8"

First Floor 1,218 sq. ft.

Garage
21-4x21-1

Kit
10-3x
10-3

P

R

D W

Brk
9-5x12-3

Family
17-5x16-9

Dn

Dining
13-8x12-1

Living
13-8x13-9

Up

35'-8"

Corner Windows Grace Library

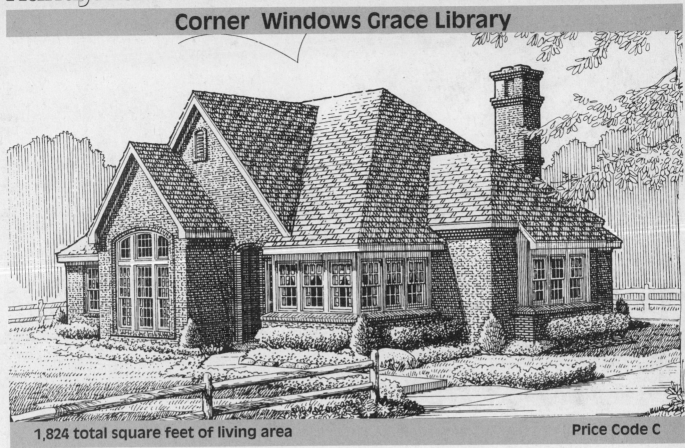

1,824 total square feet of living area

Price Code C

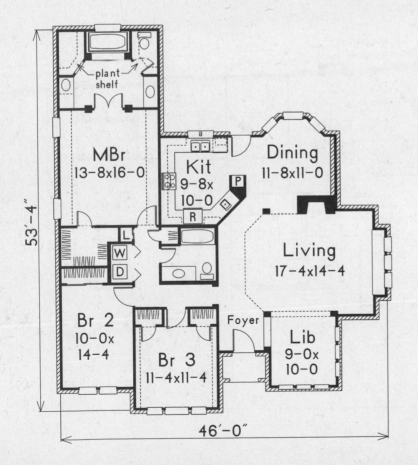

53'-4"

46'-0"

plant shelf

MBr
13-8x16-0

Kit
9-8x
10-0

Dining
11-8x11-0

Living
17-4x14-4

Br 2
10-0x
14-4

Br 3
11-4x11-4

Foyer

Lib
9-0x
10-0

Special features

- Living room features 10' ceiling, fireplace and media center
- Dining room includes bay window and convenient kitchen access
- Master bedroom features large walk-in closet and double-doors leading into master bath
- Modified U-shaped kitchen features pantry and bar
- 3 bedrooms, 2 baths, 2-car detached garage
- Slab foundation

Upscale Ranch Boasts Both Formal And Casual Areas

1,950 total square feet of living area

Price Code C

Special features

- Large corner kitchen with island cooktop opens to family room
- Master suite features double-door entry, raised ceiling, double-bowl vanity and walk-in closet
- Plant shelf accents hall
- 4 bedrooms, 2 baths, 3-car garage
- Crawl space foundation

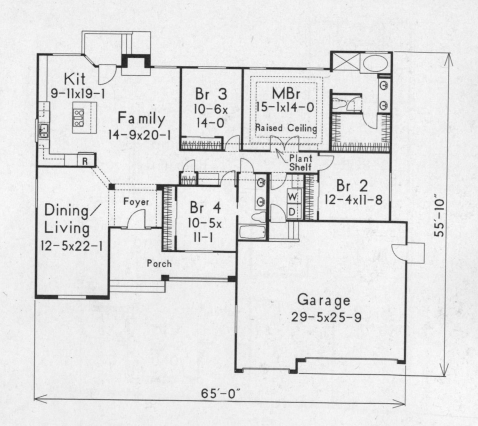

Kit
9-11x19-1

Family
14-9x20-1

Br 3
10-6x
14-0

MBr
15-1x14-0
Raised Ceiling

Plant Shelf

Br 2
12-4x11-8

Dining/
Living
12-5x22-1

Foyer

Br 4
10-5x
11-1

W
D

Porch

Garage
29-5x25-9

55'-10"

65'-0"

Charming Exterior And Cozy Interior

1,127 total square feet of living area

Price Code AA

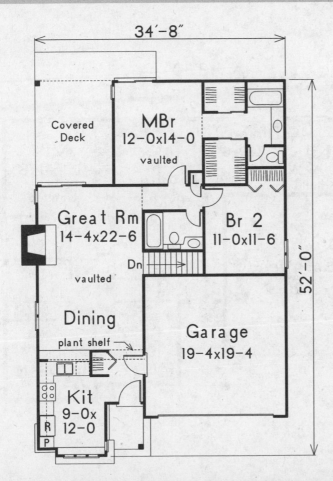

34'-8"

Covered Deck

MBr
12-0x14-0
vaulted

Great Rm
14-4x22-6

vaulted

Br 2
11-0x11-6

Dn

52'-0"

Dining

plant shelf

Garage
19-4x19-4

Kit
9-0x
12-0

R
P

Special features

- Plant shelf joins kitchen and dining room
- Vaulted master suite has double walk-in closets, deck access and private bath
- Great room features vaulted ceiling, fireplace and sliding doors to covered deck
- Ideal home for a narrow lot
- 2 bedrooms, 2 baths, 2-car garage
- Basement foundation

Vaulted Ceilings Show Off This Ranch

1,135 total square feet of living area

Price Code AA

Special features

- Living and dining rooms feature vaulted ceilings and a corner fireplace

- Energy efficient home with 2" x 6" exterior walls

- Master bedroom offers vaulted ceilings, private bath and generous closet space

- Compact but functional kitchen complete with pantry and adjacent utility room

- 3 bedrooms, 2 baths, 2-car garage

- Basement foundation, drawings also include crawl space foundation

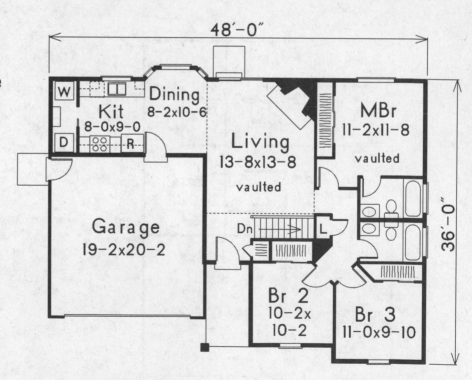

TO ORDER BLUEPRINTS USE THE FORM ON PAGE 15 OR CALL TOLL-FREE 1-877-671-6036
View thousands more home plans online at www.familyhandyman.com/homeplans

Full Windows Grace Elegant Family Room

2,558 total square feet of living area

Price Code D

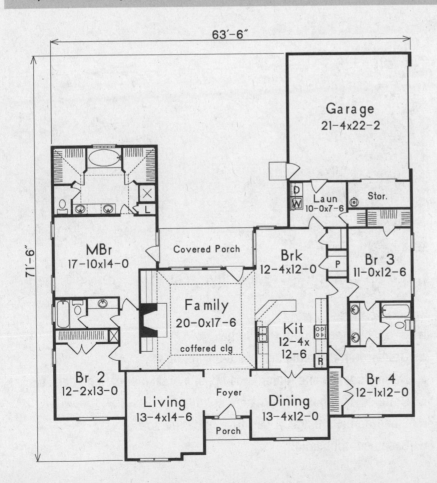

Special features

- 9' ceilings throughout home
- Angled counter in kitchen serves breakfast and family rooms
- Entry foyer flanked by formal living and dining rooms
- Garage includes storage space
- 4 bedrooms, 3 baths, 2-car side entry garage
- Slab foundation, drawings also include crawl space foundation

TO ORDER BLUEPRINTS USE THE FORM ON PAGE 15 OR CALL TOLL-FREE 1-877-671-6036
View thousands more home plans online at www.familyhandyman.com/homeplans

273

Divided Bedroom Areas Lend Privacy   Plan #705-0119

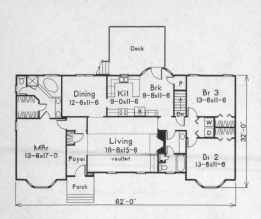

1,833 total square feet of living area   Price Code C

Special features

- Master bedroom suite comes with a garden tub, walk-in closet and bay window
- Walk-through kitchen and breakfast room
- Front bay windows offer a deluxe touch
- Foyer with convenient coat closet opens into large vaulted living room with attractive fireplace
- 3 bedrooms, 2 baths, 2-car drive under garage
- Basement foundation

Family Room Perfect For Gathering   Plan #705-0237

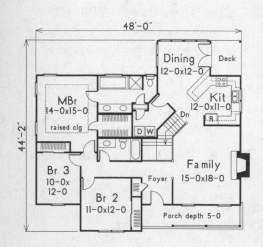

1,631 total square feet of living area   Price Code B

Special features

- 9' ceilings throughout this home
- Utility room conveniently located near kitchen
- Roomy kitchen and dining area boast a breakfast bar and deck access
- Coffered ceiling accents master suite
- 3 bedrooms, 2 baths, 2-car drive under garage
- Basement foundation

A Ranch Home With Flair

© COPYRIGHT 1990 RALPH JONES & ASSOC.

1,656 total square feet of living area

Price Code B

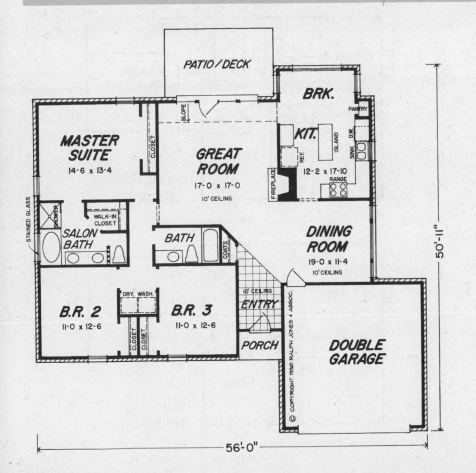

PATIO / DECK

SLOPE

CLOSET

MASTER SUITE
14-6 x 13-4

STAINED GLASS

SHOWER

WALK-IN CLOSET

SALON BATH

B.R. 2
11-0 x 12-6

CLOSET

DRY. WASH.

CLOSET

B.R. 3
11-0 x 12-6

BATH

COATS

ENTRY
10' CEILING

PORCH

GREAT ROOM
17-0 x 17-0
10' CEILING

FIREPLACE

BRK.

PANTRY

KIT.
12-2 x 17-10

REF.

ISLAND

SINK

D.W.

RANGE

DINING ROOM
19-0 x 11-4
10' CEILING

DOUBLE GARAGE

© COPYRIGHT 1990 RALPH JONES & ASSOC.

50'-11"

56'-0"

Special features

- Well-designed kitchen area has center island adding extra work space and a sunny breakfast area nearby

- Master suite has a luxurious bath with walk-in closet

- Washer and dryer closet located in terrific area near all bedrooms

- 3 bedrooms, 2 baths, 2-car garage

- Slab foundation

Flexible Yet Traditional Two-Story Home

2,458 total square feet of living area

Price Code D

Special features

- Study in the front of the home makes an ideal home office

- Second floor has four bedrooms centered around a bonus room that could easily convert to a family room or fifth bedroom

- Private second floor master bedroom is situated above garage

- 4 bedrooms, 2 1/2 baths, 2-car garage

- Basement foundation

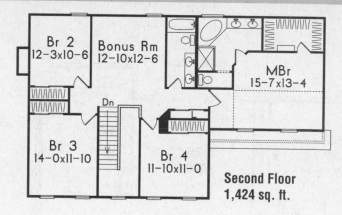

Br 2
12-3x10-6

Bonus Rm
12-10x12-6

MBr
15-7x13-4

Dn

Br 3
14-0x11-10

Br 4
11-10x11-0

**Second Floor
1,424 sq. ft.**

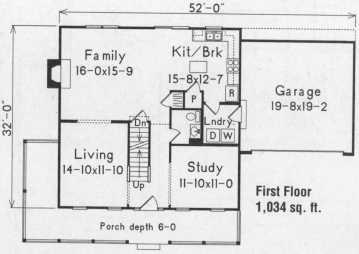

52'-0"

Family
16-0x15-9

Kit/Brk
15-8x12-7

Garage
19-8x19-2

32'-0"

P

R

Dn

Lndry.
D   W

Living
14-10x11-10

Up

Study
11-10x11-0

**First Floor
1,034 sq. ft.**

Porch depth 6-0

276

TO ORDER BLUEPRINTS USE THE FORM ON PAGE 15 OR CALL TOLL-FREE 1 877 671-6036
View thousands more home plans online at www.familyhandyman.com/homeplans

Stonework Entry Adds Character To This Home

1,358 total square feet of living area

Price Code A

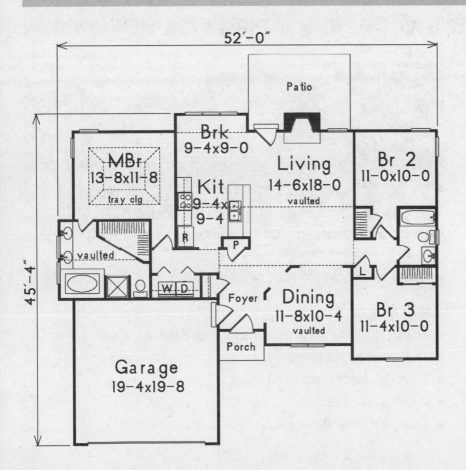

52'-0"

Patio

Brk
9-4x9-0

MBr
13-8x11-8
tray clg.

Living
14-6x18-0
vaulted

Br 2
11-0x10-0

Kit
9-4x
9-4

vaulted

R

P

45'-4"

W D

Foyer

Dining
11-8x10-4
vaulted

L

Br 3
11-4x10-0

Porch

Garage
19-4x19-8

Special features

- Vaulted master bath has walk-in closet, double-bowl vanity, large tub, shower and toilet area
- Galley kitchen opens to both the living room and the breakfast area
- Vaulted ceiling joins dining and living rooms
- Breakfast room with full wall of windows
- 3 bedrooms, 2 baths, 2-car garage
- Slab foundation

Traditional Style With Extras   Plan #705-UDG-99003

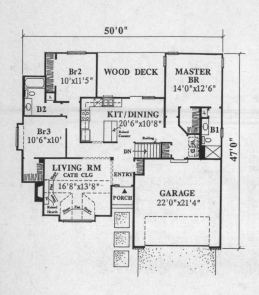

1,425 total square feet of living area   Price Code A

Special features

- Living room has a very interesting cathedral ceiling
- Secondary bedrooms have plenty of closet space
- Raised eating counter separates kitchen and dining area
- Bedroom #3 has seated window overlooking landscape
- 3 bedrooms, 2 baths, 2-car garage
- Basement foundation

Perfect For A Narrow Lot   Plan #705-HDG-97006

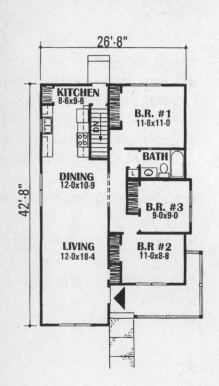

1,042 total square feet of living area   Price Code AA

Special features

- Dining and living areas combine for added space
- Cozy covered front porch
- Plenty of closet space throughout
- 3 bedrooms, 1 bath
- Basement foundation

Cozy Traditional

1,310 total square feet of living area

Price Code A

WIDTH 49–10

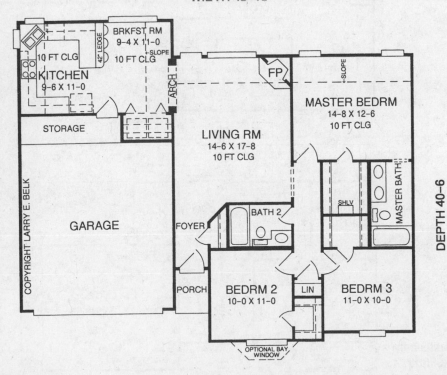

Special features

- Family room features corner fireplace adding warmth
- Efficiently designed kitchen has a corner sink with windows
- Master bedroom includes large walk-in closet and private bath
- 3 bedrooms, 2 baths, 2-car garage
- Crawl space or slab foundation, please specify when ordering

Two-Story Country Home Features Large Living Areas

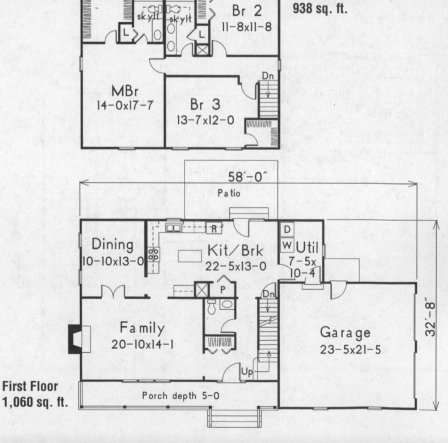

1,998 total square feet of living area

Price Code D

Special features

- Large family room features fireplace and access to kitchen and dining area

- Skylights add daylight to second floor baths

- Utility room conveniently located near garage and kitchen

- Kitchen/breakfast area includes pantry, island work space and easy access to the patio

- 3 bedrooms, 2 1/2 baths, 2-car side entry garage

- Basement foundation, drawings also include crawl space and slab foundations

Second Floor
938 sq. ft.

Br 2
11-8x11-8

MBr
14-0x17-7

Br 3
13-7x12-0

Dn

First Floor
1,060 sq. ft.

58'-0"

Patio

Dining
10-10x13-0

Kit/Brk
22-5x13-0

Util
7-5x
10-4

Family
20-10x14-1

Garage
23-5x21-5

32'-8"

Porch depth 5-0

Country-Style With Spacious Rooms

1,197 total square feet of living area

Price Code AA

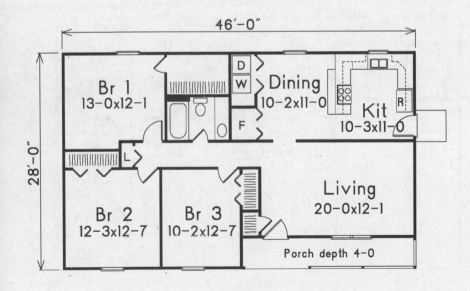

Special features

- U-shaped kitchen includes ample work space, breakfast bar, laundry area and direct access to the outdoors

- Large living room with convenient coat closet

- Master bedroom features large walk-in closet

- 3 bedrooms, 1 bath

- Crawl space foundation, drawings also include basement and slab foundations

Private Master Suite

1,458 total square feet of living area

Price Code A

Special features

- Divider wall allows for some privacy in the formal dining area
- Two secondary bedrooms share a full bath
- Covered front and rear porches create enjoyable outdoor living spaces
- 3 bedrooms, 2 baths, 2-car garage
- Slab or crawl space foundation, please specify when ordering

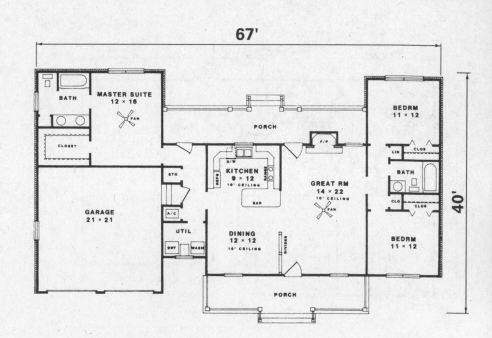

TO ORDER BLUEPRINTS USE THE FORM ON PAGE 13 OR CALL TOLL FREE 1 877 671-6036
View thousands more home plans online at www.familyhandyman.com/homeplans

Great Family Plan

© COPYRIGHT 1991
RALPH JONES

1,382 total square feet of living area

Price Code A

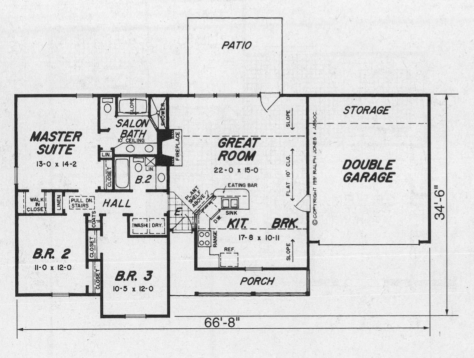

Special features

- An appealing open feel with kitchen, breakfast room and great room combining for the ultimate use of space

- All bedrooms separate from living areas for privacy

- Extra storage in garage

- 3 bedrooms, 2 baths, 2-car garage

- Slab or crawl space foundation, please specify when ordering

Brick Accents Front Facade

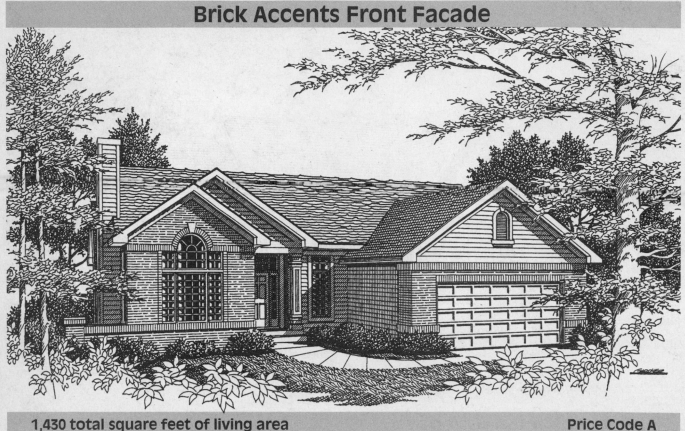

1,430 total square feet of living area

Price Code A

Special features

- Master suite features a private master bath and wall of windows
- U-shaped kitchen makes organization easy
- Great room has several windows making this a bright and cheerful place
- 2 bedrooms, 2 baths, 2-car garage
- Basement foundation

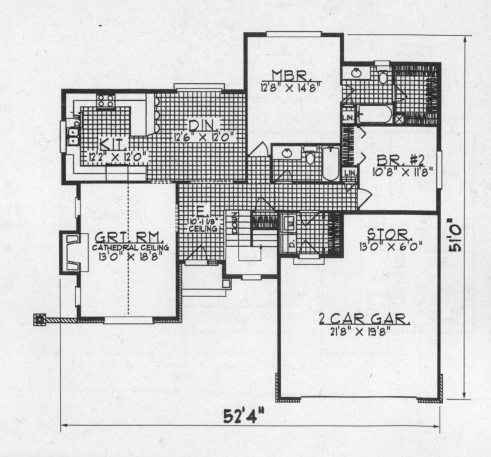

Kitchen Overlooks Living Area

1,815 total square feet of living area

Price Code C

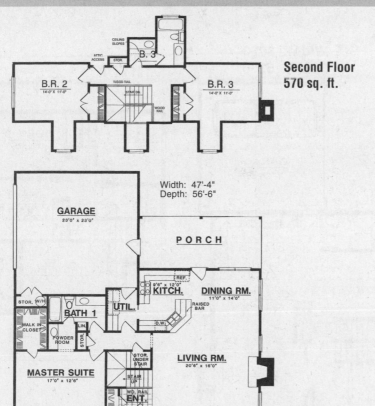

Second Floor
570 sq. ft.

B.R. 2
14'-0" X 11'-0"

B.3

B.R. 3
14'-0" X 11'-0"

ATTIC
ACCESS

STOR.

CEILING
SLOPES

WOOD RAIL

STAIR DN.

WOOD
RAIL

GARAGE
23'0" x 23'0"

Width: 47'-4"
Depth: 56'-6"

PORCH

REF.

KITCH.
9'6" x 12'0"

DINING RM.
11'0" x 14'0"

STOR. W/H

BATH 1

UTIL.

RAISED
BAR

WALK IN
CLOSET

POWDER
ROOM

LIN.

STOR.

D.W

MASTER SUITE
17'0" x 12'8"

STOR.
UNDER
STAIR

STAIR
UP

LIVING RM.
20'8" x 16'0"

WD. RAIL

ENT.

First Floor
1,245 sq. ft.

P O R C H

Special features

- Well-designed kitchen opens to dining room and features raised breakfast bar

- First floor master suite has walk-in closet

- Front and back porches unite this home with the outdoors

- 3 bedrooms, 2 baths, 2-car side entry garage

- Basement, crawl space or slab foundation, please specify when ordering

Craftsman Cottage

1,649 total square feet of living area

Price Code B

Special features

- Energy efficient home with 2" x 6" exterior walls
- Ideal design for a narrow lot
- Country kitchen includes an island and eating bar
- Master bedroom has 12' vaulted ceiling and a charming arched window
- 4 bedrooms, 2 1/2 baths, 2-car side entry garage
- Basement or crawl space foundation, please specify when ordering

Width: 30'-0"
Depth: 52'-0"

Second Floor
791 sq. ft.

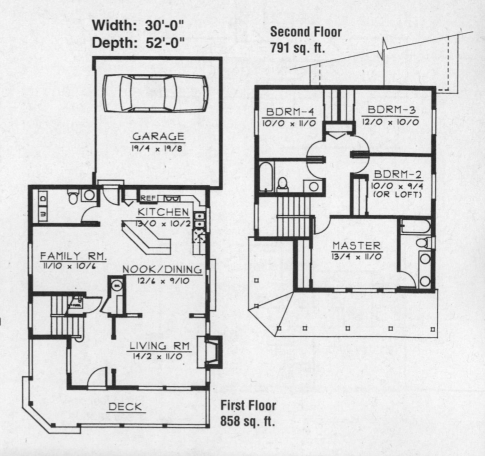

GARAGE
19/4 x 19/8

KITCHEN
13/0 x 10/2

FAMILY RM.
11/10 x 10/6

NOOK/DINING
12/6 x 9/10

REF

LIVING RM
14/2 x 11/0

DECK

First Floor
858 sq. ft.

BDRM-4
10/0 x 11/0

BDRM-3
12/0 x 10/0

BDRM-2
10/0 x 9/4
(OR LOFT)

MASTER
13/4 x 11/0

Bay Window In Dining Room

1,225 total square feet of living area

Price Code A

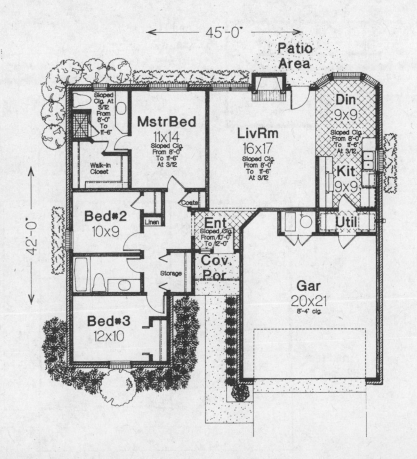

← 45'-0" →

Patio Area

42'-0"

Sloped Clg. At 3/12 From 8'-0" To 11'-6"

MstrBed
11x14
Sloped Clg. From 8'-0" To 11'-6" At 3/12

Walk-In Closet

LivRm
16x17
Sloped Clg. From 8'-0" To 11'-6" At 3/12

Din
9x9
Sloped Clg. From 8'-0" To 11'-6" At 3/12

Kit
9x9

Coats

Bed#2
10x9

Linen

Ent
Sloped Clg. From 10'-0" To 12'-0"

Util

Cov. Por.

Storage

Bed#3
12x10

Gar
20x21
8'-4" clg.

Special features

- Utility room accesses kitchen and garage for convenience
- Extra closets and storage space throughout
- All bedrooms located on one side of the home for privacy
- 3 bedrooms, 2 baths, 2-car garage
- Slab foundation

Family Room Has Cozy Fireplace

1,505 total square feet of living area

Price Code B

Special features

- Spacious living room opens into the dining area which flows into an efficient kitchen

- All bedrooms located on the second floor for privacy

- Master suite has a large walk-in closet and a private bath with step-in shower

- 4 bedrooms, 2 1/2 baths, 2-car garage

- Basement, crawl space or slab foundation, please specify when ordering

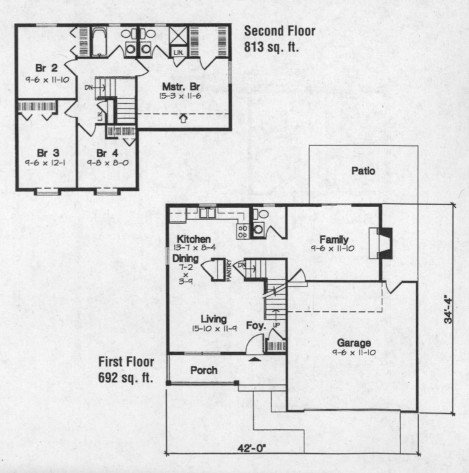

Second Floor
813 sq. ft.

Br 2
9-6 x 11-10

Mstr. Br
15-3 x 11-6

Br 3
9-6 x 12-1

Br 4
9-8 x 8-0

Patio

Kitchen
13-7 x 8-4

Family
9-6 x 11-10

Dining
7-2 x 3-9

PANTRY

Living
15-10 x 11-9

Foy.

Garage
9-6 x 11-10

Porch

First Floor
692 sq. ft.

34'-4"

42'-0"

Great-Looking Gables Add Style

© 2003, Garrell Associates, Inc.

Christine Canova 9/02

1,821 total square feet of living area

Price Code E

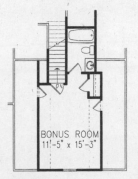

Optional Second Floor

BONUS ROOM
11'-5" x 15'-3"

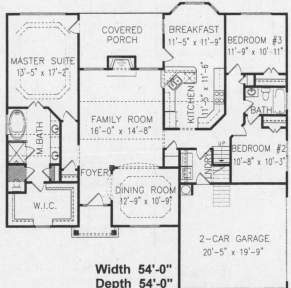

First Floor 1,821 sq. ft.

MASTER SUITE
13'-5" x 17'-2"

COVERED PORCH

BREAKFAST
11'-5" x 11'-9"

BEDROOM #3
11'-9" x 10'-11"

M. BATH

FAMILY ROOM
16'-0" x 14'-8"

KITCHEN
11'-5" x 11'-6"

BATH

FOYER

DINING ROOM
12'-9" x 10'-9"

W.I.C.

LNDRY.

UP

BEDROOM #2
10'-8" x 10'-3"

2-CAR GARAGE
20'-5" x 19'-9"

Width 54'-0"
Depth 54'-0"

Special features

- 9' ceilings throughout first floor
- Master suite is secluded for privacy and has a spacious bath
- Sunny breakfast room features bay window
- Bonus room on the second floor has an additional 191 square feet of living area
- 3 bedrooms, 2 baths, 2-car side entry garage
- Basement or slab foundation, please specify when ordering

TO ORDER BLUEPRINTS USE THE FORM ON PAGE 15 OR CALL TOLL-FREE 1-877-671-6036
View thousands more home plans online at www.familyhandyman.com/homeplans

289

Affordable Home With Farmhouse Appeal

2,092 total square feet of living area

Price Code D

Special features

- Dining room can used as an office or den

- Living room can be converted to a guest room

- Expansion loft is ideal for a playroom or a fourth bedroom

- Bonus room on the second floor has an additional 300 square feet of living area

- 3 bedrooms, 2 1/2 baths, 2-car garage

- Basement, crawl space or slab foundation, please specify when ordering

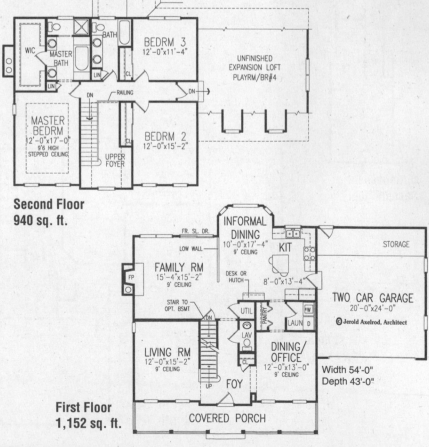

Second Floor
940 sq. ft.

First Floor
1,152 sq. ft.

Width 54'-0"
Depth 43'-0"

Private Breakfast Room Provides Casual Dining

1,708 total square feet of living area

Price Code B

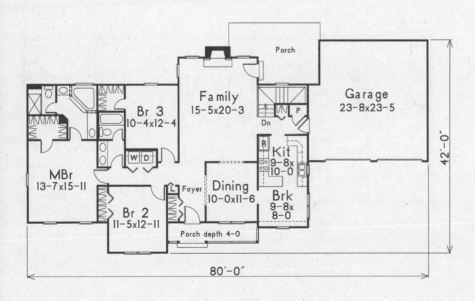

Special features

- Massive family room enhanced with several windows, fireplace and access to porch
- Deluxe master bath accented by step-up corner tub flanked by double vanities
- Closets throughout maintain organized living
- Bedrooms isolated from living areas
- 3 bedrooms, 2 baths, 2-car garage
- Basement foundation, drawings also include crawl space foundation

Charming Country Styling In This Ranch

1,600 total square feet of living area

Price Code C

Special features

- Energy efficient home with 2" x 6" exterior walls

- Impressive sunken living room has massive stone fireplace and 16' vaulted ceilings

- Dining room conveniently located next to kitchen and divided for privacy

- Special amenities include sewing room, glass shelves in kitchen and master bath and a large utility area

- Sunken master bedroom features a distinctive sitting room

- 3 bedrooms, 2 baths, 2-car side entry garage

- Slab foundation, drawings also include crawl space and basement foundations

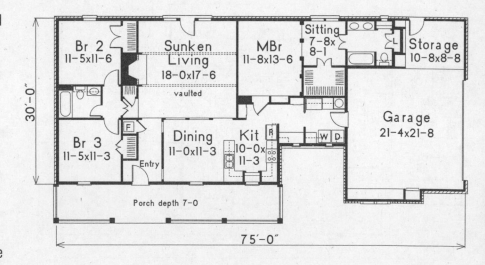

Picture Perfect For A Country Setting

2,967 total square feet of living area

Price Code E

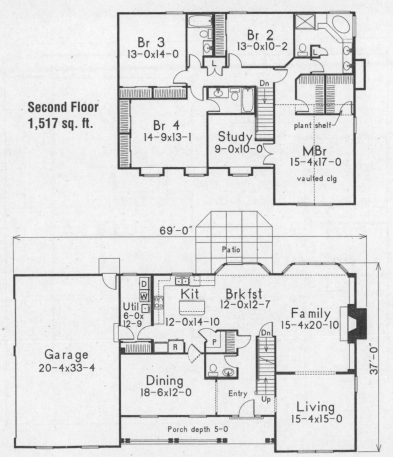

Second Floor 1,517 sq. ft.

Br 3
13-0x14-0

Br 2
13-0x10-2

Br 4
14-9x13-1

Study
9-0x10-0

plant shelf

MBr
15-4x17-0

vaulted clg

Dn

First Floor 1,450 sq. ft.

69'-0"

Patio

37'-0"

Garage
20-4x33-4

Util
6-0x
12-9

D
W

Kit
12-0x14-10

Brkfst
12-0x12-7

Family
15-4x20-10

R

P

Dn

Dining
18-6x12-0

Entry

Up

Living
15-4x15-0

Porch depth 5-0

Special features

- An exterior with charm graced with country porch and multiple arched projected box windows
- Dining area is oversized and adjoins a fully equipped kitchen with walk-in pantry
- Two bay windows light up the enormous informal living area to the rear
- 4 bedrooms, 3 1/2 baths, 3-car side entry garage
- Basement foundation

Master Suite Has Access Outdoors

1,680 total square feet of living area

Price Code B

Special features

- Enormous and luxurious master suite
- Kitchen and dining room have vaulted ceiling creating an open feeling
- Double sinks grace second bath
- 3 bedrooms, 2 baths, 2-car garage
- Walk-out basement, basement, crawl space or slab foundation, please specify when ordering

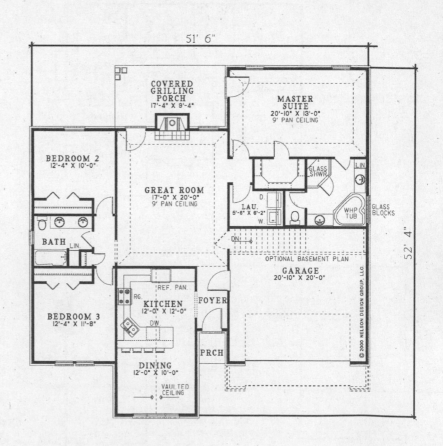

TO ORDER BLUEPRINTS USE THE FORM ON PAGE 15 OR CALL TOLL FREE 1-877-671-6036

View thousands more home plans online at www.familyhandyman.com/homeplans

Two-Story Solarium Welcomes The Sun

3,850 total square feet of living area

Price Code F

Second Floor
1,544 sq. ft.

Br 5
12-1x14-3

Sunken Solarium Below

Br 2
13-11x15-9

Loft

Dn

Br 4
12-1x12-0

Library
15-8x9-8

Br 3
15-5x12-0

open to below

Interior View

Special features

- Entry, with balcony above, leads into a splendid great room with sunken solarium

- Kitchen layout boasts a half-circle bar and cooktop island with banquet-sized dining nearby

- Solarium features U-shaped stairs with balcony and arched window

- Master suite includes luxurious bath and large study with bay window

- 5 bedrooms, 3 1/2 baths, 3-car garage

- Basement foundation

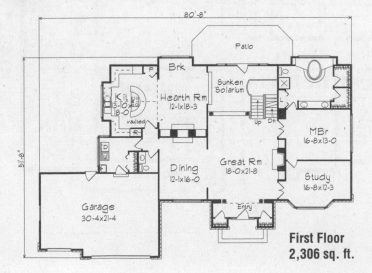

80'-8"

Patio

Brk

Sunken Solarium

Kit.
5-10x
18-0

Hearth Rm
12-1x18-3

vaulted

MBr
16-8x13-0

51'-8"

Up Dn

Dining
12-1x16-0

Great Rm
18-0x21-8

Study
16-8x12-3

Garage
30-4x21-4

Entry

First Floor
2,306 sq. ft.

Inviting Ranch Home

1,397 total square feet of living area

Price Code A

Special features

- Decorative ceiling in formal dining room adds excitement to the exterior
- Bedroom #3 is highlighted by a charming window seat
- Eating bar in breakfast provides additional space
- 3 bedrooms, 2 baths
- Slab foundation

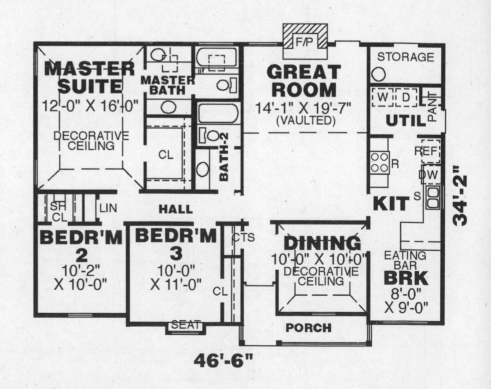

MASTER SUITE
12'-0" X 16'-0"
DECORATIVE CEILING

MASTER BATH

GREAT ROOM
14'-1" X 19'-7"
(VAULTED)

STORAGE

W D

UTIL

CL

BATH-2

KIT

REF

R

DW

S

HALL

SH CL

LIN

BEDR'M 2
10'-2" X 10'-0"

BEDR'M 3
10'-0" X 11'-0"

CTS

CL

DINING
10'-0" X 10'-0"
DECORATIVE CEILING

EATING BAR

BRK
8'-0" X 9'-0"

SEAT

PORCH

34'-2"

46'-6"

Stylish Living For A Narrow Lot

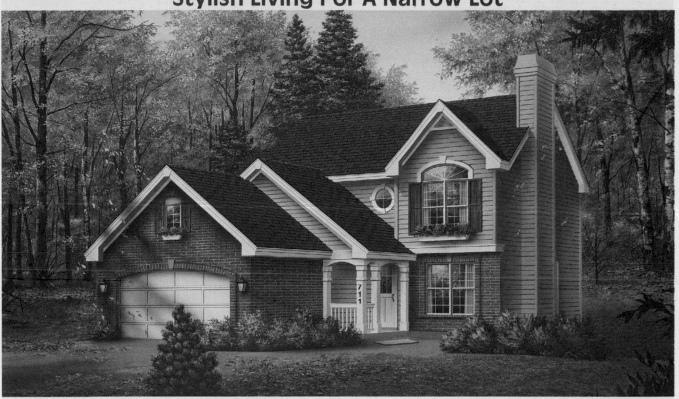

1,575 total square feet of living area

Price Code B

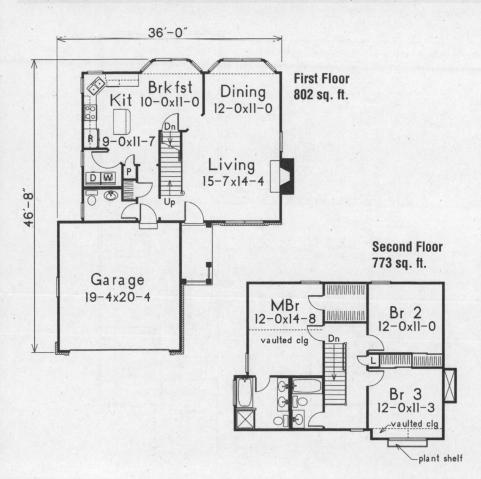

36'-0"

46'-8"

Kit 9-0x11-7

Brkfst 10-0x11-0

Dining 12-0x11-0

Living 15-7x14-4

Dn

Up

P

D W

R

First Floor 802 sq. ft.

Garage 19-4x20-4

Second Floor 773 sq. ft.

MBr 12-0x14-8

vaulted clg

Dn

Br 2 12-0x11-0

L

Br 3 12-0x11-3

vaulted clg

plant shelf

Special features

- Inviting porch leads to spacious living and dining rooms
- Kitchen with corner windows features an island snack bar, attractive breakfast room bay, convenient laundry and built-in pantry
- A luxury bath and walk-in closet adorn master bedroom suite
- 3 bedrooms, 2 1/2 baths, 2-car garage
- Basement foundation

Master Bedroom Opens Onto Covered Porch

2,481 total square feet of living area

Price Code D

Special features

- All bedrooms separate from main living areas for privacy
- Enormous master bath with double walk-in closets
- Unique covered porch off living area and breakfast room
- Cozy fireplace with built-in bookshelves in living area
- 4 bedrooms, 2 1/2 baths, 2-car side entry garage
- Crawl space or slab foundation, please specify when ordering

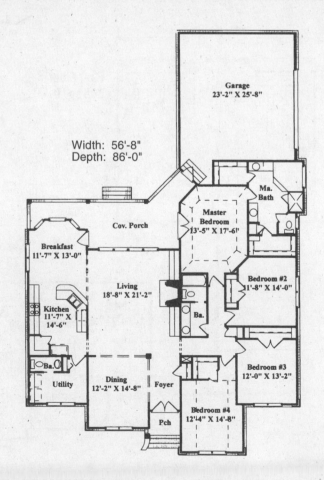

Width: 56'-8"
Depth: 86'-0"

Garage 23'-2" X 25'-8"

Ma. Bath

Master Bedroom 13'-5" X 17'-6"

Cov. Porch

Breakfast 11'-7" X 13'-0"

Bedroom #2 11'-8" X 14'-0"

Living 18'-8" X 21'-2"

Kitchen 11'-7" X 14'-6"

Ba.

Bedroom #3 12'-0" X 13'-2"

Ba.

Dining 12'-2" X 14'-8"

Foyer

Utility

Pch

Bedroom #4 12'4" X 14'-8"

Plan #705-0417

Five Bedroom Home Embraces Large Family

2,828 total square feet of living area

Price Code E

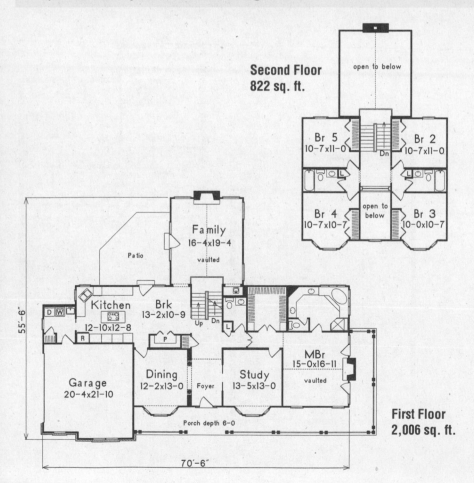

Second Floor 822 sq. ft.

open to below

Br 5
10-7x11-0

Br 2
10-7x11-0

Dn

Br 4
10-7x10-7

open to below

Br 3
10-0x10-7

First Floor 2,006 sq. ft.

Patio

Family
16-4x19-4
vaulted

Kitchen
12-10x12-8

Brk
13-2x10-9

Up Dn

Garage
20-4x21-10

Dining
12-2x13-0

Foyer

Study
13-5x13-0

MBr
15-0x16-11
vaulted

Porch depth 6-0

55'-6"

70'-6"

Special features

- Popular wrap-around porch gives home country charm
- Secluded, oversized family room with vaulted ceiling and wet bar features many windows
- Any chef would be delighted to cook in this smartly designed kitchen with island and corner windows
- Spectacular master suite
- 5 bedrooms, 3 1/2 baths, 2-car side entry garage
- Basement foundation, drawings also include crawl space and slab foundations

TO ORDER BLUEPRINTS USE THE FORM ON PAGE 15 OR CALL TOLL-FREE 1-877-671-6036
View thousands more home plans online at www.familyhandyman.com/homeplans

297

Traditional Farmhouse Appeal

1,245 total square feet of living area

Price Code A

Special features

- Energy efficient home with 2" x 6" exterior walls
- Master bedroom has a reading area and private balcony
- Bay window brightens living area
- Combined laundry area and half bath
- 3 bedrooms, 1 1/2 baths
- Basement foundation

**First Floor
626 sq. ft.**

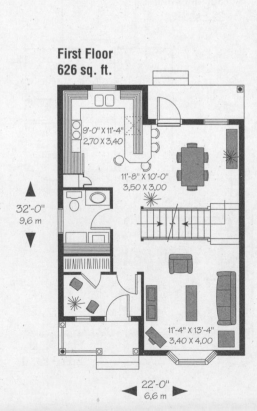

9'-0" X 11'-4"
2,70 X 3,40

11'-8" X 10'-0"
3,50 X 3,00

32'-0"
9,6 m

11'-4" X 13'-4"
3,40 X 4,00

22'-0"
6,6 m

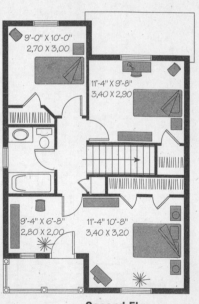

9'-0" X 10'-0"
2,70 X 3,00

11'-4" X 9'-8"
3,40 X 2,90

9'-4" X 6'-8"
2,80 X 2,00

11'-4" 10'-8"
3,40 X 3,20

**Second Floor
619 sq. ft.**

300

TO ORDER BLUEPRINTS USE THE FORM ON PAGE 15 OR CALL TOLL-FREE 1-877-671-6036
View thousands more home plans online at www.familyhandyman.com/homeplans

Vaulted Ceilings And Light Add Dimension

1,676 total square feet of living area

Price Code B

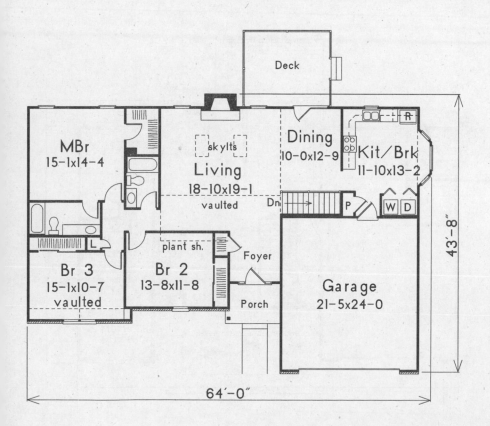

Special features

- The living area skylights and large breakfast room with bay window provide plenty of sunlight
- The master bedroom has a walk-in closet and both the secondary bedrooms have large closets
- Vaulted ceilings, plant shelving and a fireplace provide a quality living area
- 3 bedrooms, 2 baths, 2-car garage
- Basement foundation, drawings also include crawl space and slab foundations

TO ORDER BLUEPRINTS USE THE FORM ON PAGE 15 OR CALL TOLL-FREE 1-877-671-6036
View thousands more home plans online at www.familyhandyman.com/homeplans

301

A Traditional Feel To This Ranch

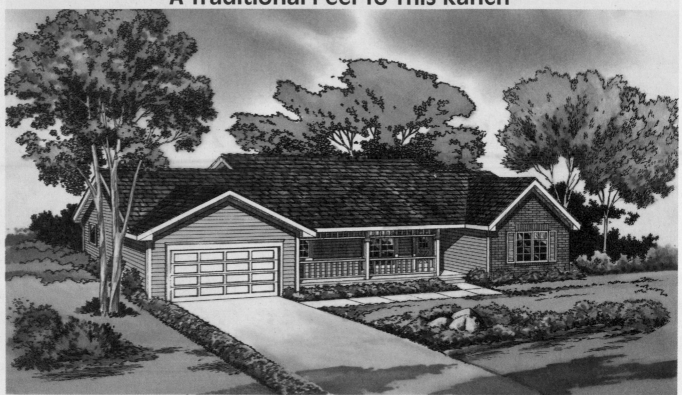

1,575 total square feet of living area

Price Code B

Special features

- Two secondary bedrooms share a full bath
- Formal dining room features column accents
- Breakfast room has sliding glass doors leading to an outdoor deck
- 3 bedrooms, 2 baths, 2-car garage
- Basement foundation

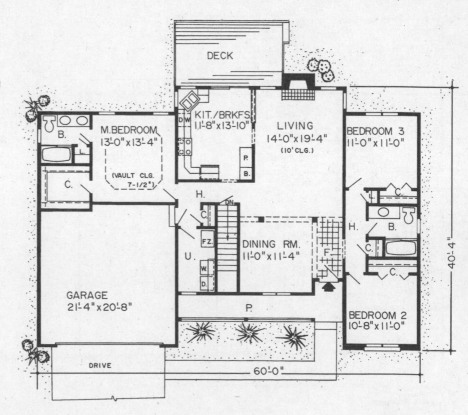

DECK

KIT./BRKFS.
11'-8"x13'-10"

LIVING
14'-0"x19'-4"
(10' CLG.)

BEDROOM 3
11'-0"x11'-0"

M.BEDROOM
13'-0"x13'-4"

(VAULT CLG. 7-1/2")

B.

C.

H.

DINING RM.
11'-0"x11'-4"

GARAGE
21'-4"x20'-8"

BEDROOM 2
10'-8"x11'-0"

P.

DRIVE

60'-0"

40'-4"

Impressive Victorian Blends Charm And Efficiency

2,286 total square feet of living area

Price Code E

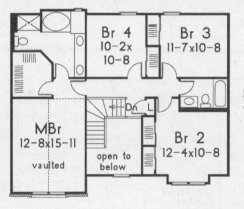

Br 4
10-2x 10-8

Br 3
11-7x10-8

**Second Floor
1,003 sq. ft.**

MBr
12-8x15-11
vaulted

open to below

Br 2
12-4x10-8

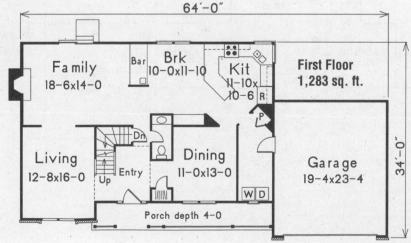

64'-0"

Family
18-6x14-0

Bar

Brk
10-0x11-10

Kit
11-10x
10-6

**First Floor
1,283 sq. ft.**

Living
12-8x16-0

Entry
Up

Dn

Dining
11-0x13-0

P

Garage
19-4x23-4

34'-0"

W D

Porch depth 4-0

Special features

- Fine architectural detail makes this home a showplace with its large windows, intricate brick-work and fine woodwork and trim
- Stunning two-story entry with attractive wood railing and balustrades in foyer
- Convenient wrap-around kitchen with window view, planning center and pantry
- Oversized master suite with walk-in closet and master bath
- 4 bedrooms, 2 1/2 baths, 2-car garage
- Basement foundation, drawings also include crawl space and slab foundations

Brick and Stucco Exterior

2,187 total square feet of living area

Price Code C

Special features

- Lots of windows create a sunny atmosphere in the breakfast room

- Exceptional master suite with an enormous bath and unique morning porch

- Vaulted and raised ceilings adorn many rooms throughout this home

- The roomy deck may be accessed from the family room and master suite

- 4 bedrooms, 2 1/2 baths, 2-car side entry garage

- Basement, crawl space or slab foundation, please specify when ordering

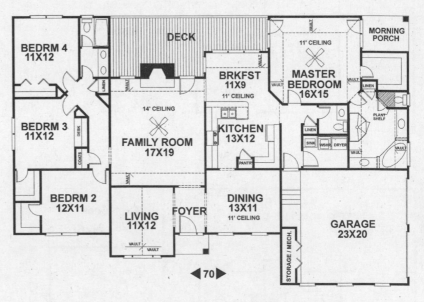

10' Ceilings

1,862 total square feet of living area

Price Code C

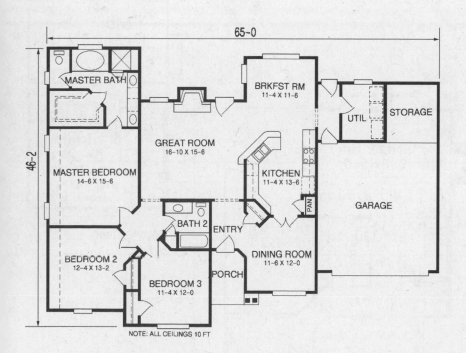

65~0

MASTER BATH

46-2

GREAT ROOM
16-10 X 15-6

MASTER BEDROOM
14-6 X 15-6

BRKFST RM
11-4 X 11-6

UTIL   STORAGE

KITCHEN
11-4 X 13-6

PAN

GARAGE

BATH 2

ENTRY

BEDROOM 2
12-4 X 13-2

DINING ROOM
11-6 X 12-0

PORCH

BEDROOM 3
11-4 X 12-0

NOTE: ALL CEILINGS 10 FT

Special features

- Comfortable traditional has all the amenities of a larger plan in a compact layout
- Angled eating bar separates kitchen and great room while leaving these areas open to one another for entertaining
- 3 bedrooms, 2 baths, 2-car garage
- Crawl space or slab foundation, please specify when ordering

TO ORDER BLUEPRINTS USE THE FORM ON PAGE 15 OR CALL TOLL-FREE 1-877-671-6036
View thousands more home plans online at www.familyhandyman.com/homeplans

305

Trendsetting Appeal For A Narrow Lot

1,294 total square feet of living area

Price Code A

Special features

- Great room features fireplace and large bay with windows and patio doors

- Enjoy a laundry room immersed in light with large windows, arched transom and attractive planter box

- Vaulted master bedroom with bay window and walk-in closets

- Bedroom #2 boasts a vaulted ceiling, plant shelf and half bath, perfect for a studio

- 2 bedrooms, 1 full bath, 2 half baths, 1-car rear entry garage

- Basement foundation

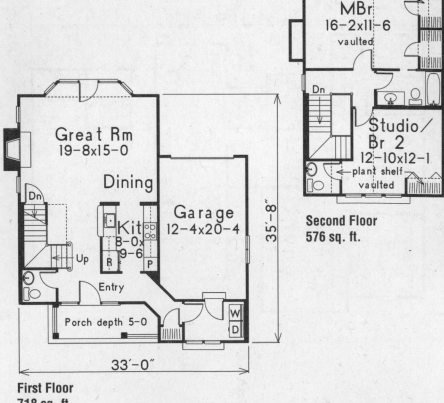

Great Rm
19-8x15-0

Dining

Garage
12-4x20-4

Kit
8-0x
9-6

Up

Dn

Entry

Porch depth 5-0

W
D

35'-8"

33'-0"

First Floor
718 sq. ft.

plant
shelf

MBr
16-2x11-6
vaulted

Dn

**Studio/
Br 2**
12-10x12-1
plant shelf
vaulted

Second Floor
576 sq. ft.

306

TO ORDER BLUEPRINTS USE THE FORM ON PAGE 15 OR CALL TOLL-FREE 1-877-671-6036
View thousands more home plans online at www.familyhandyman.com/homeplans

Comfortable Family Living In This Ranch

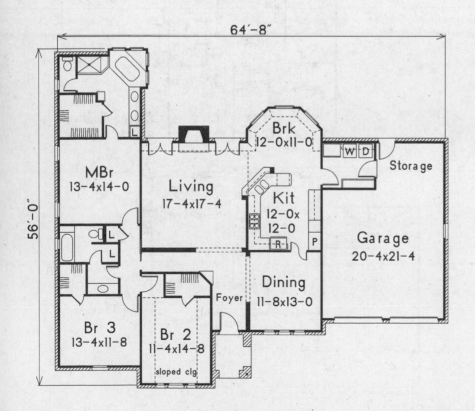

1,994 total square feet of living area

Price Code D

Special features

- Convenient entrance from the garage into the main living area through the utility room

- Standard 9' ceilings, bedroom #2 features a 12' vaulted ceiling and a 10' ceiling in the dining room

- Master bedroom offers a full bath with oversized tub, separate shower and walk-in closet

- Entry leads to formal dining room and attractive living room with double French doors and fireplace

- 3 bedrooms, 2 baths, 2-car garage

- Slab foundation

Large Utility Room

1,998 total square feet of living area

Price Code C

Special features

■ Lovely designed family room offers double-door entrance into living area

■ Roomy kitchen with breakfast area is a natural gathering place

■ 10' ceiling in master bedroom

■ 3 bedrooms, 2 1/2 baths, 2-car garage

■ Basement foundation

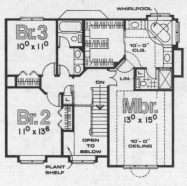

Second Floor
905 sq. ft.

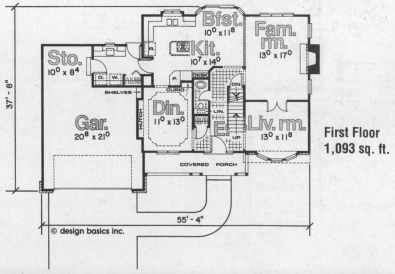

First Floor
1,093 sq. ft.

© design basics inc.

Great Views At Rear Of Home

2,050 total square feet of living area

Price Code C

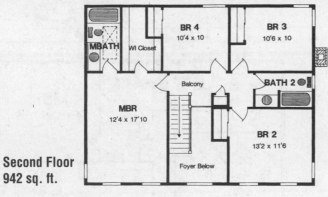

Second Floor
942 sq. ft.

BR 4
10'4 x 10

BR 3
10'6 x 10

MBATH

WI Closet

Balcony

BATH 2

MBR
12'4 x 17'10

BR 2
13'2 x 11'6

Foyer Below

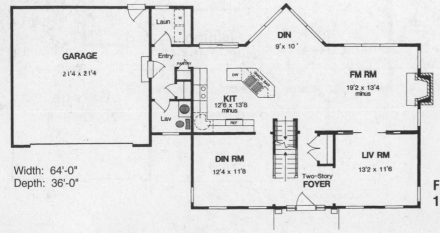

GARAGE
2 1'4 x 21'4

Laun

W
D

Entry

DIN
9' x 10'

PANTRY

KIT
12'6 x 13'8
minus

DW

SNACK BAR

FM RM
19'2 x 13'4
minus

Lav

REF

DIN RM
12'4 x 11'8

LIV RM
13'2 x 11'6

Two-Story
FOYER

Width: 64'-0"
Depth: 36'-0"

First Floor
1,108 sq. ft.

Special features

- Angled dining area has lots of windows and opens into family room and kitchen
- All bedrooms located on second floor for privacy from living areas
- Master suite has private bath and a walk-in closet
- 4 bedrooms, 2 1/2 baths, 2-car garage
- Basement foundation

Rustic Stone Exterior

1,466 total square feet of living area

Price Code A

Special features

- Energy efficient home with 2" x 6" exterior walls

- Foyer separates the living room from the dining room and contains a generous coat closet

- Large living room with corner fireplace, bay window and pass-through to the kitchen

- Informal breakfast area opens to a large terrace through sliding glass doors which brightens area

- Master bedroom has a large walk-in closet and private bath

- 3 bedrooms, 2 baths, 2-car garage

- Basement foundation, drawings also include slab foundation

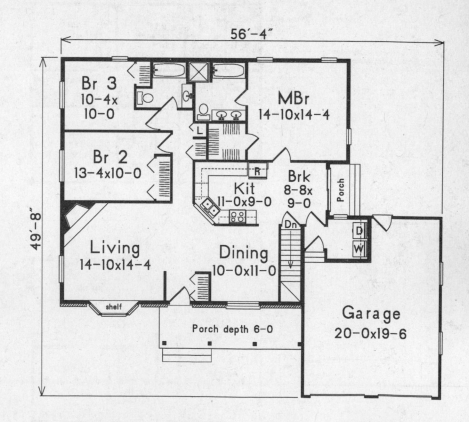

Generous Closets In All The Bedrooms

2,240 total square feet of living area

Price Code D

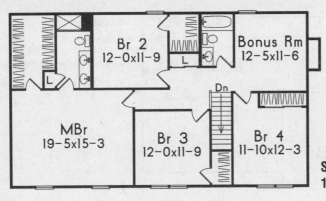

Br 2
12-0x11-9

Bonus Rm
12-5x11-6

MBr
19-5x15-3

Br 3
12-0x11-9

Br 4
11-10x12-3

Dn

Second Floor
1,344 sq. ft.

Special features

- Floor plan makes good use of space above garage allowing for four bedrooms and a bonus room on the second floor

- Formal dining room easily accessible to kitchen

- Cozy family room with fireplace and sunny bay window

- 4 bedrooms, 2 1/2 baths, 2-car garage

- Basement foundation

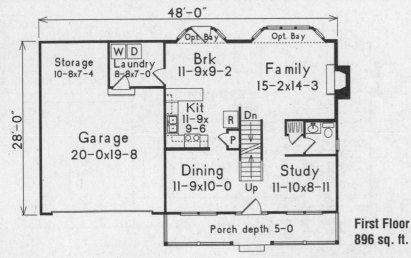

48'-0"

Storage
10-8x7-4

W D

Laundry
8-8x7-0

Opt. Bay

Opt. Bay

Brk
11-9x9-2

Family
15-2x14-3

28'-0"

Garage
20-0x19-8

Kit
11-9x
9-6

R
P

Dn

Up

Dining
11-9x10-0

Study
11-10x8-11

Porch depth 5-0

First Floor
896 sq. ft.

Charming Victorian Has Unexpected Pleasures

2,935 total square feet of living area

Price Code E

Special features

- Gracious entry foyer with handsome stairway opens to separate living and dining rooms

- Kitchen has vaulted ceiling and skylight, island worktop, breakfast area with bay window and two separate pantries

- Large second floor master bedroom suite with fireplace, raised tub, dressing area with vaulted ceiling and skylight

- 4 bedrooms, 2 1/2 baths, 2-car side entry garage

- Basement foundation

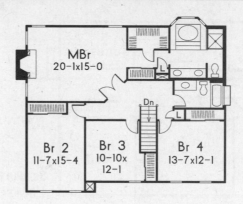

Second Floor 1,320 sq. ft.

MBr 20-1x15-0

Br 2 11-7x15-4

Br 3 10-10x12-1

Br 4 13-7x12-1

Dn

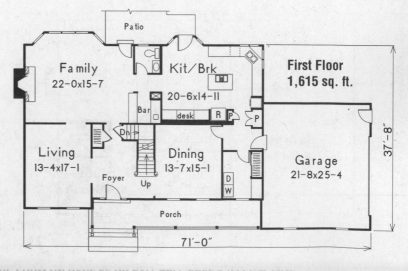

First Floor 1,615 sq. ft.

Patio

Family 22-0x15-7

Kit/Brk 20-6x14-11

Living 13-4x17-1

Bar

desk

Dining 13-7x15-1

Foyer

Up

Dn

Garage 21-8x25-4

Porch

37'-8"

71'-0"

Vaulted Ceiling Frames Circle-Top Window

1,195 total square feet of living area

Price Code AA

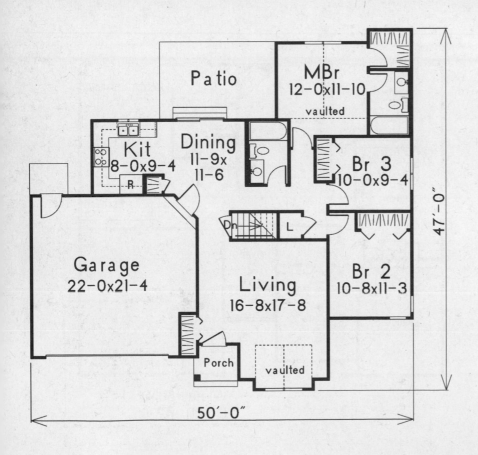

Special features

- Dining room opens onto the patio
- Master bedroom features vaulted ceiling, private bath and walk-in closet
- Coat closets located by both the entrances
- Convenient secondary entrance at the back of the garage
- 3 bedrooms, 2 baths, 2-car garage
- Basement foundation

Corner Fireplace In Grand Room

1,606 total square feet of living area   Price Code B

Special features

- Kitchen has snack bar which overlooks dining area for convenience

- Master bedroom has lots of windows with a private bath and large walk-in closet

- Cathedral vault in great room adds spaciousness

- 3 bedrooms, 2 baths, 2-car garage

- Slab foundation

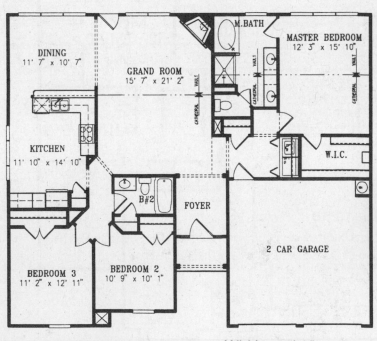

DINING
11' 7" x 10' 7"

GRAND ROOM
15' 7" x 21' 2"

M.BATH

MASTER BEDROOM
12' 3" x 15' 10"

KITCHEN
11' 10" x 14' 10"

W.I.C.

B#2

FOYER

BEDROOM 3
11' 2" x 12' 11"

BEDROOM 2
10' 9" x 10' 1"

2 CAR GARAGE

Width: 50'-0"
Depth: 42'-0"

Traditional Brick Ranch

2,697 total square feet of living area

Price Code E

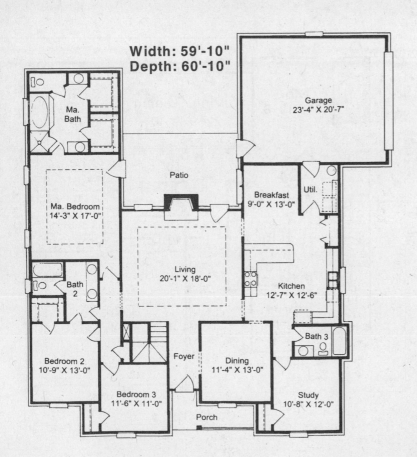

Width: 59'-10"
Depth: 60'-10"

Garage
23'-4" X 20'-7"

Ma. Bath

Patio

Breakfast
9'-0" X 13'-0"

Util.

Ma. Bedroom
14'-3" X 17'-0"

Living
20'-1" X 18'-0"

Kitchen
12'-7" X 12'-6"

Bath 2

Bath 3

Bedroom 2
10'-9" X 13'-0"

Foyer

Dining
11'-4" X 13'-0"

Bedroom 3
11'-6" X 11'-0"

Study
10'-8" X 12'-0"

Porch

Special features

- Secluded study with full bath nearby is an ideal guest room or office
- Master bedroom has access to outdoor patio
- 351 square feet of unfinished living space available in the attic
- 3 bedrooms, 3 baths, 2-car side entry garage
- Slab foundation

High-Styled Master Bedroom Suite

2,255 total square feet of living area

Price Code D

Special features

- Walk-in closets in all bedrooms
- Plant shelf graces hallway
- Large functional kitchen adjoins family room with fireplace and access outdoors
- Master bath comes complete with double vanity, enclosed toilet, separate tub and shower and cozy fireplace
- Living/dining room combine for a large formal gathering room
- 4 bedrooms, 2 1/2 baths, 3-car garage
- Slab foundation

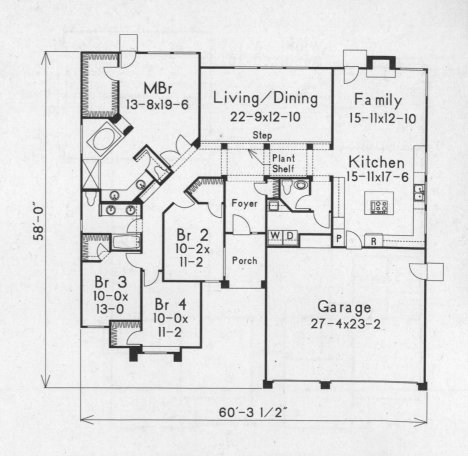

MBr
13-8x19-6

Living/Dining
22-9x12-10

Family
15-11x12-10

Step

Plant
Shelf

Kitchen
15-11x17-6

Foyer

Br 2
10-2x
11-2

W D

P

R

Porch

Br 3
10-0x
13-0

Br 4
10-0x
11-2

Garage
27-4x23-2

58'-0"

60'-3 1/2"

High Ceilings Create A Feeling Of Luxury

1,707 total square feet of living area

Price Code C

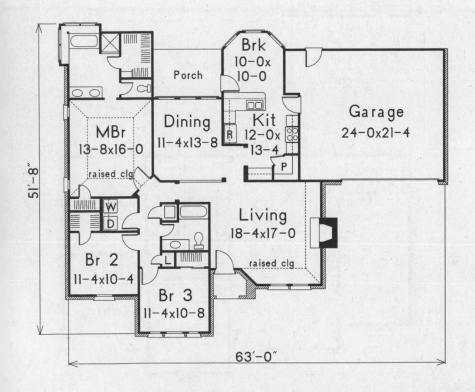

Porch

Brk
10-0x
10-0

Garage
24-0x21-4

Dining
11-4x13-8

Kit
12-0x
13-4

R

P

MBr
13-8x16-0

raised clg

W
D

Living
18-4x17-0

raised clg

L

Br 2
11-4x10-4

Br 3
11-4x10-8

51'-8"

63'-0"

Special features

- The formal living room off the entry hall has a high sloping ceiling and a prominent fireplace

- Kitchen and breakfast area allow access to garage and rear porch

- Oversized garage provides direct access to the kitchen

- Master bedroom has impressive vaulted ceiling, luxurious master bath, large walk-in closet and separate tub and shower

- Utility room conveniently located near bedrooms

- 3 bedrooms, 2 baths, 2-car garage

- Slab foundation

Central Living Areas Away From Bedrooms

2,424 total square feet of living area   **Price Code D**

Special features

- Utility room off kitchen for convenience

- Large closets in all bedrooms

- Open living area for added spaciousness

- 3 bedrooms, 2 baths, 2-car side entry carport

- Slab or crawl space foundation, please specify when ordering

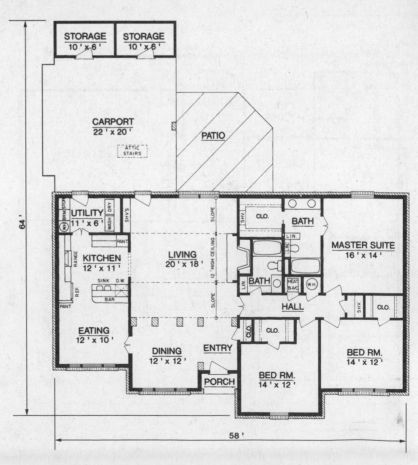

TO ORDER BLUEPRINTS USE THE FORM ON PAGE 15 OR CALL TOLL-FREE 1-877-671-6036
View thousands more home plans online at www.familyhandyman.com/homeplans

Quaint Box Window Seat

1,665 total square feet of living area

Price Code B

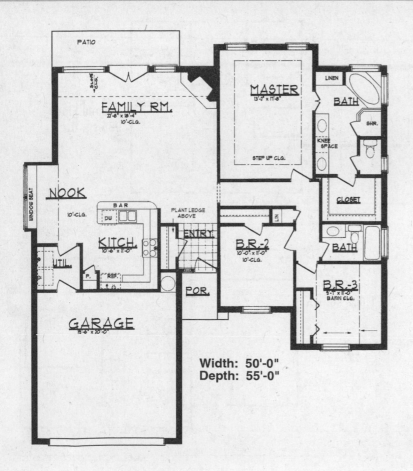

Width: 50'-0"
Depth: 55'-0"

Special features

- Oversized family room has a corner fireplace and double-doors leading to the patio
- Bedroom locations give privacy from gathering areas
- 3 bedrooms, 2 baths, 2-car garage
- Slab foundation

Perfect Two-Story Traditional

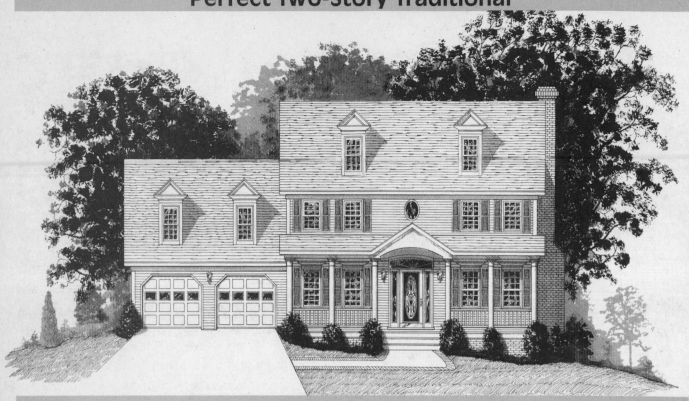

1,998 total square feet of living area　　　　**Price Code C**

Special features

- Large open living areas have enough space for gathering
- All bedrooms on the second floor for peace and quiet from living areas
- Formal dining space has direct access to the kitchen
- Bonus room on the second floor has an additional 320 square feet of living area
- 4 bedrooms, 2 1/2 baths, 2-car garage
- Crawl space foundation

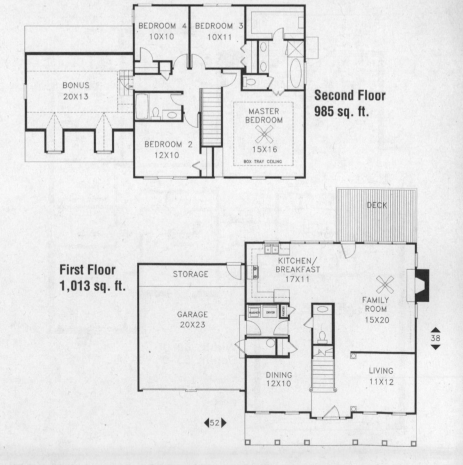

Second Floor 985 sq. ft.

First Floor 1,013 sq. ft.